CORRECTIONS

CORRECTIONS

GENERAL EDITOR
William J. Chambliss
George Washington University

KEY ISSUES IN *Crime* AND PUNISHMENT

Los Angeles | London | New Delhi
Singapore | Washington DC

Los Angeles | London | New Delhi
Singapore | Washington DC

FOR INFORMATION:

SAGE Publications, Inc.
2455 Teller Road
Thousand Oaks, California 91320
E-mail: order@sagepub.com

SAGE Publications India Pvt. Ltd.
B 1/I 1 Mohan Cooperative Industrial Area
Mathura Road, New Delhi 110 044
India

SAGE Publications Ltd.
1 Oliver's Yard
55 City Road
London EC1Y 1SP
United Kingdom

SAGE Publications Asia-Pacific Pte. Ltd.
33 Pekin Street #02-01
Far East Square
Singapore 048763

Vice President and Publisher: Rolf A. Janke
Senior Editor: Jim Brace-Thompson
Project Editor: Tracy Buyan
Cover Designer: Candice Harman
Editorial Assistant: Michele Thompson
Reference Systems Manager: Leticia Gutierrez
Reference Systems Coordinator: Laura Notton

Golson Media
President and Editor: J. Geoffrey Golson
Author Manager: Lisbeth Rogers
Layout and Copy Editor: Stephanie Larson
Proofreader: Mary Le Rouge
Indexer: J S Editorial

Printed in the United States of America.

Library of Congress Cataloging-in-Publication Data

Key issues in crime and punishment / William Chambliss, general editor.

    v. cm.

    Contents: v. 1. Crime and criminal behavior — v. 2. Police and law enforcement — v. 3. Courts, law, and justice — v. 4. Corrections — 5. Juvenile crime and justice.

    Includes bibliographical references and index.

    ISBN 978-1-4129-7855-2 (v. 1 : cloth) — ISBN 978-1-4129-7859-0 (v. 2 : cloth) — ISBN 978-1-4129-7857-6 (v. 3 : cloth) — ISBN 978-1-4129-7856-9 (v. 4 : cloth) — ISBN 978-1-4129-7858-3 (v. 5 : cloth)

    1. Crime. 2. Law enforcement. 3. Criminal justice, Administration of. 4. Corrections. 5. Juvenile delinquency. I. Chambliss, William J.

    HV6025.K38 2011

    364—dc22   2010054579

11 12 13 14 15 10 9 8 7 6 5 4 3 2 1

Contents

Introduction

Corrections

Not long ago, the field now known as corrections was called *penology*. Literally, penology meant the scientific study of punishment. Then, as now, the word *scientific* was something of a misnomer, since any attempt to analyze or discuss punishment is fraught with social policy implications that do not lend themselves readily to scientific conclusions. Nonetheless, as the chapters in this volume demonstrate, social scientists attempt to rest their policy recommendations on the best available scientific evidence. Unfortunately, science rarely produces policy conclusions on which there is consensus. Even the most highly developed sciences like quantum mechanics are fraught with conflicting theories and therefore different implications of what social policies should follow. Some physical and mathematical scientists applied the knowledge of the field to the production of nuclear weapons, while others, like Albert Einstein, steadfastly rejected the morality of using his theories for the purpose of constructing such devastating weapons.

What used to be known as penology is conventionally referred to as *corrections*, which is also in some ways a misleading term. The word *corrections* implies that the goal of prisons, parole, probation, and other forms of sanctioning behavior defined as illegal is to correct people's behavior. As the chapters in this volume point out, however, there are many reasons why illegal behavior is sanctioned: revenge; incapacitation of the offender so they cannot reoffend; and rehabilitation, which is closest to the notion that criminal justice sanctions are correction oriented.

Whatever the goal of the legal institutions subsumed under the name *corrections*, the fact is that only a small fraction of the crimes committed result in the offender entering the correctional branch of the criminal justice system. The chapters in this volume look at the correctional system and then offer arguments for and against the practice of the laws and policies that make up the correctional system from parole and probation to imprisonment, to the application of the death penalty. The chapters look at what the goals of the correctional system should be, how these goals should be achieved, and who should decide; current conditions within the correctional system that impact the environment; and how offenders should be treated while under the correctional system in order to maintain a balance between the system's ability to meet its goals and the inmates' civil rights.

First, it is necessary to address the purpose of the correctional system. Throughout this volume, a number of chapters will address what the goals of the correctional system have been historically, what they are today, and how changes have taken place over time. In their chapter *Rehabilitation vs. Punishment,* Faye Taxman and Danielle Rudes provide an overview of the intended purposes of corrections: deterrence, incapacitation, retribution, rehabilitation, or expiation.

The purpose of corrections greatly relates to and affects how prisoners and those on supervised release are treated. The intended goal of corrections also affects the type of sentence that inmates will receive. If the goal is deterrence or incapacitation, should early release or work furloughs be given to prisoners? Rudes and Taxman help answer this question in their chapter *Early Release,* as does Brenda Vose in *Furloughs and Work Release Programs.*

If the goal is rehabilitation, should shaming techniques, life sentences, or the death penalty be used? Leonard Steverson's chapter *Shaming Penalties* gives a historical overview of many types of punishments that have been used in order to shame offenders and discusses the pros and cons of using these methods. If the goal is expiation, is it acceptable to use preventive detention? Should the executive branch be allowed to award clemency? Margaret Leigey's chapter *Life Sentences* looks at the pros and cons of life sentences; the impact these sentences have on the inmate, prisons, and society; and the differences between life sentences with parole and life sentences without parole. William Wood's chapter on capital punishment gives an overview of the death penalty across time and space and weighs the debatable negative and positive effects of putting offenders to death for their crimes.

Next, a number of the chapters give an inside view of the current state of the correctional system so that its environment can be better understood.

Gang violence, as discussed by Kristine M. Levan, is a huge problem faced by jails and prisons. Levan's chapter gives an overview of the types of gangs in the correctional system, who is involved, and how they are operated. She also discusses the activities that gangs are frequently involved in—including the inmate economy and violence—and possible ways to reduce gang related violence in jails and prisons.

Many of the problems in the correctional system are due to overcrowding and understaffing, which is related to budgetary restrictions, particularly as incarceration rates soar while states' economies are suffering. One method of trying to reduce costs has been to privatize the prison system. Antje Deckert and William Wood discuss the reasons why some prisons have been privatized, as well as the pros and cons of housing and supervising inmates in the private sector instead of government facilities. Although initial savings may be beneficial, legal, safety, and ethical issues bring into question the long-term benefits of privatization.

Finally, while incarcerated or on supervised release, offenders posses a very unique status as they are the responsibility of the state and are under the state's control, yet they also maintain certain constitutional and human rights. They do not, however, maintain all of the rights traditionally given by the U.S. Constitution. There is a great deal of controversy about what rights prisoners and those on supervised release should maintain, and what rights they should be forced to give up as part of their punishment so that the correctional facility can safely and effectively maintain control and meet its intended goals. It is generally accepted that some rights must be relinquished, but which ones, to what degree, and for how long they should be relinquished is debatable.

In particular, the chapters *Religious Rights* (Kamesha Spates and Michael Royster), *Free Speech Rights of Prisoners* (Julie Beck), *Due Process Rights of Prisoners* (Kenneth Haas), and *Legal Assistance for Prisoners* (Christopher Smith) discuss prisoner rights issues and the ongoing struggle between prisoners and the state. Additionally, *Cruel and Unusual Punishment* by Smith discusses prison conditions and treatment of prisoners, including different types of punishment such as capital punishment and isolation, and how over time the definition of *cruel and unusual* has changed.

William J. Chambliss
General Editor

1

Capital Punishment/ Death Penalty

William R. Wood
University of Auckland

There are many lively debates surrounding the ethics, efficacy, and policy implications of capital punishment as they pertain to its use within the United States. Globally, the United States is one of about 60 nations that regularly employ this type of punishment.

However, within the group of Western industrialized nations, it remains the only country that routinely puts people to death. To the extent that the United States shares similar legal and political systems with other Western industrialized countries, it has not followed the trend of most European and Western-hemisphere states that have abolished the use of capital punishment within the last four decades.

Historically, what has been called the *exceptionalism* of the United States is a relatively new phenomenon. While the abolition of capital punishment was first argued by the Italian criminologist Cesare Beccaria in the late 18th century, by the beginning of the 20th century, only a few nations had banned this type of punishment, and it was not until the 1960s that the trend toward abolition in European and Western Hemisphere countries began in earnest. Thus, while the United States is unique among Western industrial states in terms of the continued use of this punishment, in the long history of punishment in the Western world, it is the abolition of capital punishment, rather than its ubiquity, that stands as an anomaly.

The history of the use of capital punishment begins in pre-modern times, and continues its journey through Beccaria's opposition to the practice, its use within the United States, the growth of abolition in Western industrial and Western Hemisphere states, and the current global distribution and frequency of capital punishment in the early 21st century.

There are compelling arguments for and against the use of capital punishment, particularly as they pertain to its use within the United States. Both public and political positions, as well as academic research, surround these debates, which center primarily on the following questions:

1. Do some people "deserve" to die?
2. Is the state justified in taking a life?
3. Does capital punishment deter violent crime and save lives?
4. Does capital punishment disproportionally effect and/or harm minorities?

History of Capital Punishment

Capital punishment has been used for thousands of years. The earliest codified forms of law such as Mosaic Law and the Codex Hammurabi detailed numerous crimes for which a person could be executed. The Greeks, Romans, and other empires employed it frequently, both as punishment for a host of criminal offenses, as well as a tool of political, economic, and cultural domination. Prior to the 18th century, the use of capital punishment was both common and unremarkable, and there was little controversy surrounding the idea that some people deserved to be put to death.

Cesare Beccaria

The first widely influential opposition to the use of capital punishment did not occur until 1764, when the Italian criminologist Cesare Beccaria published his treatise *On Crimes and Punishments*. The work was immediate popular; six editions were published within the first 18 months of its release, and it was translated into French by Voltaire as well as into numerous other languages throughout Europe, and later, in the United States. The root of Beccaria's work was vested in the concept of the social contract, and like many of his intellectual peers, Beccaria believed that the most just form of government for the largest number of people was one in which individual members freely gave up a small amount freedom in exchange for the benefits of social order. Beccaria's main interest, however, lay in the question of what should happen when people violated this "social contract." Beccaria recognized that crime could be controlled through the brute force of absolutist rule, yet such approaches negated any possibility of a freely chosen social contract between individuals and their governors. He equally saw that the lack of any restraint on individuals would lead to a system of social relations where the strong perennially preyed on the weak—a state of affairs characterized in Hobbes's *Leviathan* as a "war of all against all."

Beccaria's solution to this problem was an elegantly simple, if ultimately flawed, proposition based in the utilitarian philosophy of social action, which argued that people naturally seek to maximize pleasure and minimize pain. Beccaria argued that as rational actors, individuals should be free to act within a system of governance that upholds the requisite conditions of the social contract, yet limits their ability to maximize pleasure at the expense of others' pain. The only legitimate power of the state in cases where the social contract was violated, he argued, was then in its representative authority to deter violators through a system of gradated punishments that mitigated the potential pleasure one might gain by violating the social contract. To this end, Beccaria imagined the development of a correlate system of punishments administered by the state—punishments that would ideally represent only the amount of pain necessary to encourage individuals to adhere to the social contact, and to deter those who had violated the contract from further crimes.

In the case of capital punishment, however, Beccaria argued against its use for two reasons. First, he argued that life itself was a right that could not be justly deprived by the state. Second, Beccaria argued that capital punishment was a less effective form of deterrence than prolonged depravation of liberty, insofar as he viewed the former as ultimately less concrete and more transient than the latter. Violators and spectators, he argued, would be more deterred by a more easily imagined threat of prolonged or "perpetual slavery" than by the more abstract and unknowable experience of death. In terms of his classical approach to crime control, Beccaria found many supporters in his day. The implementation of the French Penal Code in 1791 and Napoleonic Penal Code of 1810 were based on his principles of rational deterrence. Influenced by Beccaria's work, Leopold II banned the use of capital punishment in Tuscany in 1786, and a small number of other countries followed suit in the 19th century, including the Roman Republic (1849),

Venezuela (1863), San Marino (1965), and Portugal (1867). However, it would be another century before the roots of Beccaria's opposition began to seriously flourish in the rapid movement toward abolition in Europe and other areas of the world that began in the 1960s.

The Rationality of Capital Punishment

Perhaps ironically, Beccaria died in 1794, in the middle of the Reign of Terror in France that had introduced the guillotine as an enlightened alternative to the humiliating and barbaric execution practices of the *ancien régime*. The introduction of the electric chair some 100 years later in the United States was similarly proposed as a humane and technological improvement over the use of hangings and firing squads. These two forms of capital punishment stand in many ways as bookends for the shift that occurred in Europe and the northern United States in the 19th and early 20th centuries away from the spectacle of public corporal punishments, toward an increasing bureaucratic administration of punishment via the depravation of liberty.

This movement was most evident in the rise of modern prisons in western Europe and the northern United States as a means of correcting socially deviant and criminal behaviors. For several reasons, punishment became increasingly wedded to the modern penitentiary: the profitable use of prison labor, the rise of modern biological and psychological theories of crime, and social reform movements that viewed corporeal punishment as antithetical to values and principles of Christian charity and reformation. However, in the case of capital punishment, while some reformers opposed it, public executions remained common throughout the 19th and early 20th centuries. Rather, what changed during this period was the means by which people were put to death. In line with what were considered the progressive values of the penitentiary was the belief that even the most violent offenders should be shown mercy, and that even the most extreme of punishments should acquiesce to humane means. The guillotine (1792), electric chair (1890), gas chamber (1924), and lethal injection (1982) thus represent a historical, if discursive, gradient toward the rationalization of punishment under the auspices of the modern state.

This rationalization included increasingly humane forms of execution in the 19th century, but it also included the eventual eclipse of the public execution itself. Social historians of death have noted that, beginning in the 20th century in the United States and western Europe, death became increasingly shielded from public view—occurring with more and more frequency behind the closed doors of the hospital. Executions similarly moved behind the walls of the penitentiary, with the last formal public execution in Britain in 1868, in the United States in 1936, and in France in 1939. Yet the idea that public executions were ceased as result of changing social attitudes toward death is only partially borne out in the research; executions in the latter 19th and early 20th centuries regularly drew huge crowds. The last U.S. public execution in Kentucky in 1936 witnessed a crowd of 20,000. The last beheading in France in 1939 was a similarly public spectacle, and was evidently such a drunken and rancorous affair that the "hysterical behavior" of the crowd prompted the French government to ban any further public executions. In this sense, contrary to their long history as a tool of social control and deterrence, public executions had become rather an increasing threat to social order, and in particular, a threat to the growing rationalization of punishment as a bureaucratic instrument of state power.

The Movement Toward Abolition

The 20th century began with only a small number of nations having barred or abolished the use of capital punishment. As late as 1965, only 24 countries had either banned its use outright or ceased its use in practice. By 2008, however, approximately 90 countries had abolished capital punishment, and another 30 had not executed anyone in at least a decade. The span of these four decades arguably represents the most radical shift in social attitudes toward the use of capital punishment in the course of written history.

This shift is perhaps most acutely a geographic one. Western Europe has seen the most complete shift away from the use of capital punishment, to the extent that no western European nation currently allows for its use. Following the breakup of the Soviet Union, a majority of eastern European states have followed in this direction as well, with only Belarus, Russia, and Latvia still allowing for its use. The second largest shift in the last 40 years has been within Central and South American countries, particularly in the increased democratization of Central and South American states following years of repressive governments. Today, a majority of South and Central American states have discontinued its use, although a majority of Caribbean states still retain it.

The effect of these regional shifts toward abolition or desistance has been that an increasing number of the world's executions are concentrated in a smaller number of regions, mostly in Africa, Asia, and the United States. Accordingly, in the last decade, roughly 90 percent of all executions have occurred in a handful of countries—China, Iran, Iraq, Pakistan, Saudi Arabia, Sudan, and the United States. The decreasing international distribution of capital punishment also represents its continued widespread use in Islamic as well as in authoritarian states. Within Islamic states, only Turkey, Turkmenistan, and Azerbaijan do not use capital punishment. Authoritarian states include communist nations such as China, Vietnam, North Korea, Cuba, and Laos; and other despotic or authoritarian governments such as Burma, Zimbabwe, Belarus, and Singapore. Of these states, China by far executes the most people; approximately 1,000 people in 2006, although official figures from China are inaccurately low.

Capital Punishment in the Contemporary United States

With the exception of the 1972 Supreme Court decision *Furman v. Georgia,* which temporarily barred most executions in the United States, capital punishment has been used with regularity since colonial times, for a variety of offenses. Today, state and federal laws, as well as the Military Code of Justice, recognize numerous capital offenses. By and large, such offenses include either premeditated murder and/or treason as a necessary part of a capital charge. Beginning in the 1990s, several states passed laws that allowed for aggravated sexual assault, kidnapping, hijacking, and other crimes to be punishable by the death penalty, but the recent 2008 Supreme Court ruling in *Kennedy v. Louisiana* has limited the use of the death penalty to crimes resulting in the death of the victim, and crimes against the state (i.e., treason or espionage).

Within the 20th and early 21st centuries, the use of capital punishment has ebbed and flowed in relation to a variety of political, economic, legal, and social considerations. In the first two decades of the 20th century—buttressed by a strong abolitionist movement—the use of capital punishment declined, and several states banned its use altogether. The influence of abolitionism waned in the 1920s and 1930s, however, in response to fears of communism following the Russian Revolution, the rise of Prohibition and corresponding organized crime, and the Great Depression, and the 1930s saw the highest rates of executions on record, at about 167 per year.

Support for capital punishment remained strong throughout World War II and the 1940s, only to shift again within the context of the postwar boom of the 1950s. The difference between the two decades is notable, where the number of executions decreased by almost half, from 1,289 in the 1940s to 715 in the 1950s. By the 1960s, public support for capital punishment hit an all-time low in the United States, where in 1964, a Gallup poll reported that only 42 percent of Americans supported it use, and by the end of the decade, executions had come to a virtual standstill.

The limiting of executions coincided with the landmark Supreme Court case *Furman v. Georgia* in 1972, which halted the use of capital punishment de facto on Eighth Amendment grounds in finding that its use was "arbitrary and capricious." Many opponents assumed this represented the end of capital punishment in the United States, but in 1976, the Supreme Court upheld the constitutionality of capital punishment in *Gregg v. Georgia*, which set forth capital sentencing guidelines through which states could reinstate its use. Notably, the Court also ruled against the defendants in *Gregg* that capital punishment was not unto itself "cruel and unusual," as long as it is applied within the use of objective criteria that allows for consideration of the defendant's character and record. Almost immediately, states revised their laws in accordance with these guidelines, and the number of death sentences began to rise, particularly as increases in crime rates and growing social unrest in the 1970s shifted public support increasingly in favor of capital punishment.

The election of Ronald Reagan in the 1980s was achieved in part on a "tough on crime" platform, and in the early 1980s, both the public and state legislatures returned en mass to supporting the use of capital punishment. By 1984, public support for the death penalty reached an all-time high of 75 percent, and the number of people sentenced to death increased markedly—although executions rose more gradually as a result of the mandatory appeals process for capital sentences. Beginning in the 1990s, public support for capital punishment slowly tapered to around 62 percent in 2007. However, the number of executions rose throughout the decade to a high of 98 in 1999, largely due to the exhausting of appeals from the increase in capital sentences beginning in the 1980s, as well as to a general decrease in the use of clemency, particularly in Texas. Since this time, the number of executions has generally decreased, with 52 executions in 2009.

Legally, the Supreme Court has heard over 30 cases regarding specific applications of capital punishment since its reintroduction in *Gregg v. Georgia* in 1976. In 1987, the Court ruled in *McClesky v. Kemp* that racial disparities in capital sentences, while problematic, did not constitute a violation of "equal protection of the law." In *Atkins v. Virginia* (2002), the Court overturned the use of capital punishment for mentally challenged offenders. *Roper v. Simmons* (2005) overturned the practice of executing those who had committed crimes as minors. In 2008, the Supreme Court upheld the use of lethal injection in *Baze v. Rees*, and ruled in *Kennedy v. Louisiana* to restrict the use of the death penalty to crimes resulting in the death of the victim, treason, or espionage.

The current composition of the Supreme Court suggests that capital punishment will not face any serious challenges to its overall constitutionality in the near future. Politically, the federal government is probably even less likely to propose legislation to prohibit its use, and the last major presidential candidate to oppose its use, Michael Dukakis in 1988, was roundly derided as being soft on crime, a perception that most believe cost him the election. On the state level, however, several states have recently proposed legislation barring the use of capital punishment, and in 2009, New Mexico banned its use in all future cases. As of 2010, 15 states had laws barring the use of capital punishment.

The most common method of execution in the United States is lethal injection, with 36 states and the federal government allowing for its use. Nine states allow for electrocution, five allow for the gas chamber, two for hanging, and one state (Utah) still allows for the use of the firing squad. Since the reintroduction of capital punishment in 1976, lethal injection has been used in approximately 85 percent of the total executions.

Pro: Arguments in Favor of Capital Punishment

The two primary arguments most commonly put forth by proponents of capital punishment are that such punishments are effective in deterring crime and saving lives; and that such punishments are necessary for achieving and maintaining justice for victims, as well as more generally for society itself.

The Deterrence Effect

Deterrence arguments are based on the premise that the use of capital punishment reduces rates of serious violent crimes, particularly homicides. Within modern legal theory, deterrence is one of the four primary justifications for the depravation of liberty (the other three being incapacitation, rehabilitation, and retribution). Theories of the use of punishment as a means of deterrence are nominally divided into categories of general and specific deterrence. The concept of general deterrence centers on the idea that the punishment of one person encourages other people to act in law-abiding ways, or at the very least induces them to commit lesser crimes in the furtherance of their criminal activities. The argument of specific deterrence, on the other hand, centers on the idea that punishment of an individual will discourage them from committing further criminal acts. Support for capital punishment takes the form of general deterrence insofar as the execution of a specific offender can be understood not as deterrence, but as an incapacitation of the offender by death.

The effectiveness of capital punishment in deterring others from committing similar crimes has remained one of the most enduring justifications for the continued support of its use in the United States, both by policymakers and the public. Public opinion polling data shows that until the end of the 1980s, deterrence was the most frequently cited reason for why Americans supported its use, and since the 1990s, it has remained the second most-popular reason, behind retribution. This has also been reflected in national politics, where no winning presidential candidate has opposed capital punishment since Jimmy Carter, and virtually all of them have cited its deterrent effect as a primary reason for doing so.

Yet research on the ability of capital punishment to save the lives of others did not concur with public opinion throughout the middle of the 20th century. Thorsten Sellin's major study of capital punishment in 1959 found no deterrent effect, and later studies even suggested a negative correlation between deterrence and capital punishment in the "brutalization effect." In 1975, however, Isaac Ehrlich published a seminal study using multivariate regression analysis that purported to find a small but statistically significant negative correlation between capital punishment and homicides in the United States between 1933 and 1969, concluding that on average, each execution saved between six and seven lives.

The effect of Ehrlich's research was profound in its effect on policymakers, as well as on setting forth a program of research for further econometric studies into the link between executions and deterrence. His findings, though controversial, were nevertheless immediately popular among proponents of capital punishment. Ehrlich's work was cited in *Gregg v. Georgia* (1976) as evidence of the "inconclusive" state of research on the question of deterrence, but his assumption of murder as a more or less rational decision was itself influential within the emerging rational-choice school of thought in criminology that included notable criminologists such as James Q. Wilson and Charles Murray. Wilson would become an advisor to Ronald Regan, and by the 1980s, the assumptions of rational-choice theories of crime—including those of the deterrent effect of capital punishment—were part and parcel of the policy movement away from rehabilitation toward tough-on-crime policies, including the increase in many states of the use of capital punishment.

Ehrlich's work has been followed by a larger number of econometric studies in the 1990s and 2000s that have used newer statistical methods such as panel data to support the relationship between capital punishment and deterrence. Research from Hashem Dezhbakhsh, Paul Rubin, and Joanna Shepherd in 2003 utilized county-level data (seen as more accurately able to reflect relationships between executions and homicide rates than state or national-level data) and concluded that on average, executions saved about 18 lives in terms of reduced homicides. Other studies have found similarly significant negative correlations between executions and homicides, and within the last decade in particular, there have been over a dozen major peer-reviewed studies that have published similar findings.

A Deserved Punishment

Yet, the idea that capital punishment saves lives is not the only primary justification for its continued use within the United States. Perhaps ironically, as Ehrlich and other econometricians were building a case for its deterrent effect, the 1980s also saw an important shift in why Americans supported this type of punishment. Beginning in 1990, Americans who supported capital punishment increasingly did so because they believed it was deserved, regardless of whether or not it had a deterrent effect on others.

The idea that some people deserve to die is rooted in the legal premise of retribution. Retribution has roots in the *lex talionis* ("law of the same kind" or "measure for measure") of the Judeo-Christian and Near East religions, in the moral philosophies of Hegel and Kant, and more recently in the contemporary work of Andrew von Hirsch and John Rawls. The word itself stems from the Latin *retribuere,* meaning "to hand back" or "to recompense," and within retributive theories of justice it is argued that crime causes harms to victims and to society that result in an imbalance of justice. The point of retribution, argue supporters, is thus not revenge, but rather a return of the net balance of justice that has been upended through crime.

Thus, even where many people who support capital punishment do so for reasons of both retribution and deterrence, theoretically, they are dissimilar.

The concept of retribution contrasts starkly to that of deterrence insofar as the former focuses on what has already happened, while the later is premised on what may come in the future. Retribution, and in particular modern forms of just-deserts theories, argue that punishment is only justified for the reason of restoring this net balance, and as such, must be applied only to guilty people in a manner proportional to the offense. Application of punishment for other reasons, in particular for utilitarian reasons of crime prevention or social welfare, violates the net balance of justice insofar as it may apply either less or more punishment that is recompense for the offense.

The work of Andrew von Hirsch in particular has been instrumental in the resurgence of the idea that punishment is only justified as a result of one's just deserts—namely, under conditions where guilt has been established, and where the punishment corresponds to the level of harms caused to victims. In this regard, the use of capital punishment is seen as not only ethically permissible, but necessary, insofar as the net imbalance caused by the taking of a life cannot be returned by life imprisonment or other less equal punishments. In this regard, argue proponents, the question of whether or not capital punishment deters future offenders is immaterial; and on the grounds of deterrence alone, it cannot be justified.

Con: Arguments in Opposition to Capital Punishment

Opponents of capital punishment argue that there is little evidence to support a deterrent effect, and that any net balance that may be theoretically achieved through its use is offset by a variety of ethical and practical problems. Opponents also argue that capital punishment disproportionally targets minorities (particularly African Americans), and on average costs more than life imprisonment.

Lack of Proof of Deterrent Effect

In response to the argument that capital punishment deters crime, opponents point to a substantial body of research that suggests otherwise. Prior to Ehrlich's work and the subsequent application of econometric methods to the question of deterrence, few criminologists believed that there was strong evidence to support this argument. Recent surveys of criminologists have found that they still overwhelmingly believe that capital punishment does not deter crime; in 2009, a study of leading American criminologists found that 88 percent thought the death penalty was not a deterrent.

Critics point out that a large number of studies on the topic have found no deterrent effect, and that the attitudes of criminologists reflect this evidence. Sellin's work on the deterrent effect in 1959 was one of the first primary studies that compared states with similar populations and crime rates, and found that those with the death penalty had, on average, no significant decreases in homicide rates. This work was followed by dozens of published studies that compared states with or without the death penalty, and notably after 1972, compared homicide rates before and after the halting of executions within specific states, and concluded there was little deterrent effect.

Beginning in the 1970s, there has also been a substantial body of work that has focused more extensively on rebutting the methodologies and findings of Ehrlich and later econometricians. In response to Ehrlich's findings, the National Academy of Sciences appointed a panel of experts to review his work and concluded in 1978 that his methodology was flawed, and his conclusions were not sustainable. Critics have pointed out that his findings were largely dependent upon the specific variables he chose to include in his studies, as well as the specific time frames he focused on, and even minor changes to these inputs and parameters have resulted in radically different outcomes. More recently, the work of Jeffery Fagan and several colleagues has demonstrated that the use of econometric methods by researchers who have found a link between executions and deterrence are equally susceptible to large variances through small changes to variables or time frames.

Aside from the argument that capital punishment does not deter crime, critics also argue that the death penalty does not in fact result in increased justice for either victims or society. Many critics are opposed to the idea of retribution on moral or religious grounds, and argue that for a variety of reasons, the death penalty constitutes a violation of the Eighth Amendment's ban on cruel and unusual punishment. Another common argument against the use of capital punishment as a morally or socially necessary form of recompense is the fact that for centuries, modern Western societies have substituted other forms of punishment in lieu of the specific types of offenses committed by criminals. When a person is found guilty of rape, they are not raped in return. Nor do arsonists have their houses burned down. In this sense, critics see capital punishment as nothing more than a thinly veiled form of vengeance.

Wrongful Convictions and Social Inequality

To the degree that retributive theories of justice demand that the guilty, and only the guilty, be punished, critics also point to numerous cases where those on death row have been exonerated, or in a smaller number of cases, found innocent after they have been executed. Since the reinstatement of the death penalty, over 100 people have been exonerated from death row in the United States, and at least 10 have been found to be innocent after they were executed. Concerns over the execution of the innocent were central to the decision of Illinois Governor George Ryan to commute 156 capital sentences in 2003, calling the death penalty system in that state "arbitrary and capricious." Here, critics frequently point to judge William Blackstone's famous dictum in the late 18th century that it is "better that 10 guilty persons escape than that one innocent suffer."

The argument that capital punishment disproportionally targets minorities, and in particular African Americans, is most immediately related to social inequality in the United States, but as many legal theorists have argued, it also intersects with retributive theories to the degree that they assume a requisite net balance of justice. Critics point out that since the reinstatement of the death penalty, 35 percent of those executed have been black, within a general African American population of about 13 percent in the United States. Moreover, since 1976, data on interracial homicides suggests that blacks who kill whites have received the death penalty on average 15 times for every time a white person has killed a black person. Moreover, critics point to the concentration of executions in U.S. states since 1976, with approximately 80 percent of all executions occurring in the south. In this respect, data on the disproportional use of capital punishment on black and other minorities, particularly when the race of victims is taken into account, demonstrate a continuance of a two-tiered system of justice that critics argue stretches back to slavery. Such a two-tiered system not only impugns the legitimacy of the death penalty, but more broadly the concept of a net balance of justice itself.

Finally, critics argue that capital punishment is, contrary to popular belief, more expensive that life imprisonment. They point to numerous studies on individual states such as California, Indiana, and North Carolina, as well as comparative studies, which have found that on average, the costs of initial capital trials, lengthy periods of incarceration on death row, mandatory appeals, and the execution itself generally exceed those of life incarceration. Such monies, argue critics, could be better spent on furthering the reduction of crime through increased law enforcement or other proven avenues of reduction.

❖

See Also: 2. Clemency; 3. Cruel and Unusual Punishment; 11. Life
Sentence; 12. Mentally Ill and Mentally Challenged Inmates.

Further Readings

Bedau, Adam Hugo, and Paul G. Cassell. *Debating the Death Penalty: Should America Have Capital Punishment? The Experts on Both Sides Make Their Best Case.* New York: Oxford University Press, 2004.
Ehrlich, Isaac. "The Deterrent Effect of Capital Punishment: A Question of Life and Death." *The American Economic Review,* v.65 (1975).
Hood, Dennis. *The Death Penalty: A Worldwide Perspective,* Third Edition. New York: Oxford University Press, 2002.
Sarat, Austin. *When the State Kills: Capital Punishment and the American Condition.* Princeton, NJ: Princeton University Press, 2002.
Steiker, Carol. "Capital Punishment and American Exceptionalism." *Oregon Law Review,* v.81 (2004).
Zimring, Franklin E. *The Contradictions of American Capital Punishment.* New York: Oxford University Press, 2003.

2

Clemency

Jeffrey Crouch
American University

Clemency, also known as the *pardon power*, is the capability of an executive officer to forgive violations of criminal laws. Official forgiveness or pardoning is an ancient concept that has existed as long as formal systems of punishment have been used in societies. In the United States, clemency is a check-and-balance power that the chief executive may use to trump decisions made by the judiciary. Early presidential use and Supreme Court precedents hold that clemency may be used either as an "act of grace" or "for the public welfare," although recent presidents have at times arguably abused clemency to further their personal legal or financial interests in a few high-profile cases.

Still, barring a famous recipient or a scandal, most clemency actions are barely noticed by the public. Even in the most notorious circumstances, Congress has just two Draconian tools with which to check the clemency power: impeaching the president or amending the U.S. Constitution. The legislature does hold a number of indirect pressure points, however, such as holding hearings, demanding documents, issuing subpoenas, and cutting funding. Controversial clemency decisions by "lame duck" (end of tenure) presidents George H.W. Bush, Bill Clinton, and George W. Bush have raised questions about the effectiveness of current checks on the clemency power. Typical pardon decisions by recent presidents have excused such crimes as tax evasion, embezzlement, making a false statement to a government entity or a bank, and moonshining. Only the president of the United States has the power to forgive federal offenses.

State governors may grant clemency for violations of state law. The clemency power is usually held by the governor alone, though he or she may act with or without the assistance of a clemency board. A few modern state clemency decisions have earned headlines: New Mexico Governor Toney Anaya commuted the death sentences of all five of his state's death row prisoners in 1986 because of his personal opposition to the death penalty; and in 2003, outgoing governor George Ryan commuted the death sentences of all 167 Illinois death-row inmates amid concerns about fairness in the administration of justice. More recently, former Arkansas governor and ex-presidential hopeful Mike Huckabee penned an op-ed for the *Washington Post* titled "Why I Commuted Maurice Clemmons's Sentence," a move spurred by criticism over Huckabee's 2000 decision to grant clemency to Clemmons, a longtime criminal suspected of killing four police officers in November 2009.

Types and Methods of Clemency

Article II of the U.S. Constitution gives the chief executive the power to "grant reprieves and pardons for offenses against the United States, except in cases of impeachment." In order to be eligible for clemency, an offender must have committed a federal crime and may not be undergoing formal removal from an official position. On its face, the Constitution contemplates only "reprieves and pardons," but these are just two of several forms of clemency available to the president. Supreme Court precedents have determined that the president should have flexibility to fashion clemency decisions to fit the particular circumstances of a crime. Thus, the president's pardon power may assume a number of forms.

Full Pardon, Commutation, and Amnesty

The most wide-ranging form of forgiveness is a full pardon, which forgives the offense and may restore the recipient's rights to vote, serve on a jury, or own a gun. A pardon may be absolute or conditional, whereby the intended recipient is required to act or refrain from doing something in order for clemency to take effect. Perhaps the most famous single pardon in American history was President Gerald Ford's decision to pardon former president Richard Nixon for any crimes he may have committed while president.

A commutation of sentence may reduce a recipient's prison time, but does not remove the legal stigma from a criminal conviction. President George W. Bush's decision to commute the prison sentence of Vice President Dick Cheney's former chief of staff, I. Lewis "Scooter" Libby, is the most visible recent example of this version of the clemency power. Nearly all clemency decisions by recent presidents are either pardons or commutations. More infrequently used versions of clemency include remittance of fines and forfeitures, and reprieve or respite, which merely puts off punishment without reducing or eliminating it.

Finally, amnesty is a form of clemency that is often given after a war to a distinct group of offenders who may have yet to face prosecution. Perhaps the most famous amnesties were granted by Civil War presidents Abraham Lincoln and Andrew Johnson, who hoped to entice confederates to rejoin the Union. In more modern times, both Gerald Ford and Jimmy Carter offered amnesty to Vietnam War draft evaders.

Obtaining a Pardon

One may obtain a presidential pardon in two ways. The first method is a direct appeal to the president. Most people do not have the access to the president that is necessary for this approach to work. The majority of clemency seekers are left with the second method of requesting clemency, which is to file a petition with the pardon attorney, an officer in the Department of Justice charged with processing clemency appeals.

The pardon attorney's screening process can protect the president from making a politically costly mistake. The president may grant clemency whenever he wishes, but usually does not do so until he receives a recommendation from the pardon attorney. Federal regulations require applicants to wait five years from the end of their conviction or prison sentence (whichever is later) to file a request with the pardon attorney. Then, the pardon attorney's office will initiate an investigation into the criminal case and make a recommendation to the deputy attorney general, who will communicate a recommendation to the president. Internal clemency information is kept confidential, but the overwhelming majority of applicants are unsuccessful.

Clemency has become less common since 1900, and even more rare since the 1960s. Among other factors, intense media scrutiny following President Gerald Ford's highly volatile pardon of former president Richard Nixon and controversial pardons by Ford's successors has helped to discourage acts of presidential mercy.

Legal Precedents

Even though several legal cases have helped to define the nature, extent, effect, and limits of the clemency power, the nature of clemency remains uncertain today. A unanimous 1833 U.S. Supreme Court decision in *United States v. Wilson* established that the pardon power is an "act of grace" shown to an individual. Almost 100 years later, another unanimous Court ruled in *Biddle v. Perovich* (without overruling *Wilson*) that the pardon power is not an "act of grace;" rather, it is a decision that the president makes as "part of the Constitutional scheme" and for the public, not the individual in question. The extent of the clemency power is broad: the Court decided in *Ex parte Garland* (1866) that it may be granted at any time after an offense is committed—the offender is not required to have been convicted of, or even charged with, a crime. Decisions in other cases have found that the effect of a pardon can be to restore state and federal civil rights and excuse criminal, but not civil, contempts of court.

The pardon power, however, has some limits: it cannot interfere with other constitutional protections or clauses (such as the Takings Clause of the Fifth Amendment and the Spending Clause in Article I, Section 9). It does not expunge or erase court records on the pardoned offense, and it does not blot out the existence of a criminal indictment.

The courts have generally protected the pardon power from congressional efforts to block or limit its effect. The most aggressive moves by Congress to control presidential clemency occurred in the Civil War era, when radical Republicans in Congress passed legislation to interfere with President Abraham Lincoln and President Andrew Johnson's clemency offers to confederates they hoped to entice back to the Union. In a series of Reconstruction-era cases, the courts generally sided with the president and in favor of a broad clemency power.

The History of Clemency Before the Founding

As long as formal codes of punishment have existed, so has official forgiveness. Clemency can be traced back to the first legal code known to man, the Code of Hammurabi, used by the Babylonians in about 18th century B.C.E. Both the ancient Greeks and ancient Romans exercised a clemency power, with perhaps the most famous example recorded in the Hebrew Bible of Pontius Pilate's pardon of Barabbas instead of Jesus Christ. In the 17th and 18th centuries, monarchs—including the king of England—used clemency to excuse transgressions committed by friends, attack their opponents, raise funds, and so on. A royal pardon was viewed as an "act of grace." The English colonial governing authorities in the New World were granted wide-ranging clemency powers by the king, but these were hewed down in the years leading up to the drafting of the American Constitution. Few governors enjoyed a clemency power—it was either shared with the legislature or held by the legislature alone. The Articles of Confederation were silent about a national clemency power.

John Rutledge scribbled language regarding a pardon power into the margin of the Virginia Plan, and this is how the subject entered the debate at the Constitutional Convention in 1787. The framers were concerned about whether and how to implement a clemency power, a particularly touchy subject given their recent history: should a nation that just broke away from a tyrannical monarch vest this kingly power in a single individual? Key issues discussed included whether the president alone should have the clemency power, or whether he should share it with the Senate; if the president should be limited to pardoning offenses only "after conviction;" and finally, the danger of a president who might use the power to excuse treason committed by executive branch officials. The framers entrusted clemency to the president in Article II, made it wide-ranging enough to include both pre- and post-conviction offenses, and decided that the danger of abuse would be adequately addressed by the threat of impeachment.

The framers decided that, on balance, it made the most sense to vest the pardon power in the president. As Alexander Hamilton argued in *Federalist* No. 74, someone had to be trusted to correct judicial errors because "without an easy access to exceptions in favor of unfortunate guilt, justice would wear a countenance too sanguinary and cruel." What is more, Hamilton argued that one person would be able to act quickly to confront national emergencies: "in seasons of insurrection or rebellion, there are often critical moments when a well-timed offer of pardon to the insurgents or rebels may restore the tranquility of the commonwealth." In fact, the first well-known pardons issued by an American president were George Washington's pardons of two Whiskey Rebels.

Clemency From the Founding to Watergate

George Washington's Whiskey Rebel pardons were the first widely seen example of presidents using the clemency power for political reasons. Other early presidents followed suit: John Adams pardoned participants in Fries's

Rebellion, while Thomas Jefferson pardoned everyone who had been prosecuted under his predecessor's Alien and Sedition Acts.

In the 20th century, presidents used clemency to address controversial political leaders who ran into trouble with the law but remained popular with their constituencies. President Warren G. Harding commuted the sentence of Socialist presidential candidate Eugene Debs because Harding considered his opponent—who won about a million votes—to be a special case. President Calvin Coolidge commuted the prison time of African American civil rights activist Marcus Garvey. President Harry Truman commuted the sentence of his would-be assassin, Puerto Rican nationalist Oscar Collazo. President Richard Nixon offered conditional clemency to labor leader Jimmy Hoffa: Nixon would commute the sentence as long as Hoffa agreed not to participate in his labor-management activities until the end of his punishment.

These highly visible cases are the exception, not the rule. In most clemency cases, few beyond the pardoned individuals and their families even notice. The Department of Justice may issue a press release, but most cases—barring a famous recipient or connection to a scandal—pass almost completely under the media radar. Not only are pardons barely noticed, but since 1900, the number of pardons has also dropped precipitously. Among the causes are a society that is less tolerant of crime, a clemency screening process that is less generous, longer waiting periods, a higher rate of clemency applications, and changes in the criminal justice system to address problems formerly only addressed by the clemency power. Not to be discounted is the lasting impact of Watergate and the Nixon pardon. Since President Gerald Ford's fateful decision to pardon Richard Nixon for all of his potential Watergate crimes, the media and the public watch presidential clemency decisions for signs of corruption more carefully than ever.

Watergate and the Nixon Pardon

The Watergate scandal, particularly revelations of the Nixon administration's complicity in the coverup of a break-in at the Democratic National Committee headquarters located in the Watergate office complex, rocked the political world in the early 1970s and led to President Richard Nixon's resignation in disgrace to avoid impeachment. Watergate angered and frightened the American public, and strained the relationship between elected officials and their constituents. Sensitive to this situation, investigative journalists viewed public officials with new skepticism and scrutiny.

Just a month after taking office following Richard Nixon's resignation, Gerald Ford shocked the world by granting Nixon a full pardon for any crimes he may have committed as president. The decision, which reopened the wounds of Watergate that were just starting to heal, was made before Nixon had stood trial or even been charged with a crime. Ford's initial public explanation for his decision was handled clumsily and raised a number of questions about the decision.

One key question had to do with the legality of the Nixon pardon. Was Ford on solid legal ground pardoning Nixon before he had even been indicted? The Supreme Court had ruled in an earlier case that a president may exercise the clemency power as soon as a crime is committed. Another concern was whether Ford acted to help out his predecessor or for the good of the country. Though his initial public explanation was mixed, Ford argued that he pardoned Nixon for the good of the country, and to clear space and time to govern. The public was skeptical, and continuing negative media attention hurt Ford's image as his approval rating plummeted from 71 percent to 49 percent in the weeks following the pardon. In the years to come, a majority of the public would come to see things Ford's way, but too late to save Republicans in the 1974 election, who lost in droves; and Ford, whose own presidential bid in 1976 was frustrated by Democrat Jimmy Carter.

Clemency Since Watergate: The Bush and Clinton Years

President Ford's successors, Jimmy Carter and Ronald Reagan, created few sparks with their clemency decisions. However, Presidents George H.W. Bush, Bill Clinton, and George W. Bush each made at least one extraordinarily controversial clemency call.

George H.W. Bush pardoned former defense secretary Caspar Weinberger and five other Iran-Contra figures once it became apparent that Weinberger would have to stand trial and may have called Bush to testify. Bush exercised his pardon power and avoided embarrassment, acting after he had lost his reelection bid to Bill Clinton.

Bill Clinton offered conditional clemency to members of the FALN, a Puerto Rican terrorist organization, despite the unified opposition of law enforcement. At the time of Clinton's offer, his vice president, Al Gore, was preparing to run for president; and his wife, Hillary Rodham Clinton, was contemplating a run for New York senator. An advisor had emailed top Clinton officials that pardoning members of the FALN would play well with Puerto Rican voters in New York.

In his final hours as president, Clinton granted clemency to 176 people, including his half-brother, Roger Clinton, Whitewater figure Susan McDougal, and fugitive financier Marc Rich. Following a newspaper investigation, it became known that Rich's ex-wife, Denise, had donated half a million dollars to Clinton's presidential library fund and had participated in a secret, widespread campaign to secure a pardon for Rich.

Coming on the heels of Clinton's clemency scandal, the hallmark of clemency decisions in the George W. Bush administration was political safety. Nearly all of Bush's 200 clemency decisions involved older offenses and nonviolent crimes, such as theft and fraud. Bush and his recent predecessors generally shared a reluctance to pardon, preferring not to deplete their political capital on a potentially risky decision that would bear little fruit for their personal standing.

Even so, Bush commuted the prison sentence of I. Lewis "Scooter" Libby, Vice President Dick Cheney's former chief of staff. Libby had been swept up in an investigation into whether any Bush administration officials had leaked the secret CIA identity of Valerie Plame to the press. Plame's husband, former ambassador Joseph Wilson, had published a widely read opinion that took issue with the Bush administration's official explanation for entering into war with Iraq, and many believed that the leak of Plame's identity was retribution for Wilson's op-ed.

The actions in these cases illuminate a surprising paradox in modern clemency practices: while a preoccupation with political safety has kept presidents from pardoning many offenders, each of the nation's last three presidents (excluding Barack Obama, who had by late 2010 not yet exercised clemency) has made at least one clemency decision, arguably to further his own personal interest, that triggered a public outcry. Some observers have advocated changing the clemency power to address this situation, while others defend the status quo.

Pro: Arguments Supporting the Presidential Pardon

The arguments for the president to hold and exercise the existing clemency power are straightforward. Clemency is one of the few kingly, exclusive powers granted to the chief executive in the U.S. Constitution. The framers wanted to create a way to mitigate overly harsh judicial decisions in general and, in unusual circumstances, to provide a "safety valve" to relieve societal tension, especially in cases of rebellion or revolt. As history has shown, it has served these purposes. Clemency has allowed presidents to defuse civil unrest, as demonstrated by the examples of Washington and the Whiskey Rebels, and Lincoln and Johnson and the confederates. In lower-profile cases, clemency has allowed presidents to forgive thousands of offenders, demonstrating that mercy is possible in our society.

The vast majority of clemency cases are not controversial, and may not even be noticed by the general public. Many clemency recipients have served their time and need a pardon to simply get on with their lives. It is the exceptional cases—Nixon, Weinberger, Rich, and Libby—that give the clemency power a bad name. Most of these decisions were made in high-profile cases by lame-duck presidents, and are far from the ordinary course of pardon business.

The president has the office of the pardon attorney to help protect him from making an error, and he actually protects his political standing by using this bureaucratic filter and making regular, generous clemency decisions. Once the public has a sense for how the president uses clemency and who receives it, they are more apt to forgive a mistake as long as the regular procedures are followed. In this sense, using clemency regularly and generously may actually protect the president's political capital. With a strong overall track record, the clemency power has proven its value. Proponents argue that any proposal to amend the Constitution to address a few isolated abuses would be wrong-headed.

Con: Arguments Against the Presidential Pardon

Critics of the executive pardon argue that no one is entitled to clemency, and anyone who needs clemency is usually a criminal—*Burdick v. United States* (1915) suggests that accepting presidential clemency implies guilt. Thus, there is no compelling reason for presidents to pardon anyone. At the same time, the special treatment that several of the last few presidents' former executive branch allies, donors, and supporters have enjoyed raises the question of a two-track legal system. Just because a few criminals have had access to the president should not mean that they receive special treatment. The temptation to abuse clemency—especially when protected from punishment at the ballot box—has proven too tempting for these presidents to resist, and will continue to be a problem unless the framers' setup is adapted to current times.

There are at least two proposed solutions that would address the pardon power's shortcomings: Former senator Walter Mondale (D-MN) proposed amending the Constitution to give Congress the power to overturn a pardon if it can muster a two-thirds vote in each chamber, while Rep. Barney Frank

(D-MA) suggested barring the president from using the pardon power near the end of his term. The administration of the clemency power in recent years has been tweaked as federal regulations governing clemency applications have been modified to require the Attorney General to notify victims that an offender in their case has asked for clemency. Still, unless there is a catastrophe that spurs a long-lasting reform movement, neither plan seems likely to garner sufficient support to overcome the practical obstacles to amending the Constitution.

See Also: 5. Early Release; 11. Life Sentence.

Further Readings

Armstrong v. United States, 80 U.S. 154 (1872).

Armstrong's Foundry, 73 U.S. 766 (1868).

Becker, Benton. "The History of the Nixon Pardon." *Cumberland Law Review*, v.30 (2000).

Belli, Melvin. "The Story of Pardons." *Case and Comment*, v.80/3 (1975).

Bernard Hibbitts, ed. "Presidential Pardons." *Jurist: The Legal Education Network.* http://jurist.law.pitt.edu/pardons.htm (Accessed January 2010).

Biddle v. Perovich, 274 U.S. 480 (1927).

Bjerkan v. U.S., 529 F.2d 125 (C.A. Ill. 1975).

Boudin, Leonard. "The Presidential Pardons of James R. Hoffa and Richard M. Nixon: Have the Limitations on the Pardon Power Been Exceeded?" *University of Colorado Law Review*, v.48 (1976).

Boyd v. United States, 142 U.S. 450 (1892).

Brown v. Walker, 161 U.S. 591 (1896).

Buchanan, G. Sidney. "The Nature of a Pardon Under the United States Constitution." *Ohio State Law Journal*, v.39 (1978).

Burdick v. United States, 236 U.S. 79 (1915).

Cannon, Carl, and David Byrd. "The Power of the Pardon." *National Law Journal*, v.32 (2000).

Carannante, Jerry. "What to do About the Executive Clemency Power in the Wake of the Clinton Presidency?" *New York Law School Law Review*, v.47 (2003).

Carlesi v. New York, 233 U.S. 51 (1914).

Carlisle v. United States, 83 U.S. 147 (1872).

Crouch, Jeffrey. *The Presidential Pardon Power.* Lawrence: University Press of Kansas, 2009.

Dinan, John. "The Pardon Power and the American State Constitutional Tradition." *Polity,* v.35 (2003).

Duker, William. "The President's Power to Pardon: A Constitutional History." *William and Mary Law Review,* v.18/3 (1977).

Eksterowicz, Anthony, and Robert Roberts. "The Specter of Presidential Pardons." *White House Studies,* v.6 (2006).

Ex parte Garland, 71 U.S. 333 (1866).

Ex parte Grossman, 267 U.S. 87 (1925).

Ex parte Wells, 59 U.S. 307 (1855).

Feerick, John. "The Pardoning Power of Article II of the Constitution." *New York State Bar Journal,* v.47 (1975).

Firestone, Bernard, and Alexej Ugrinsky, eds. *Gerald R. Ford and the Politics of Post-Watergate America.* Westport, CT: Greenwood Press, 1993.

Fisher, Louis. "The Law: When Presidential Power Backfires: Clinton's Use of Clemency." *Presidential Studies Quarterly,* v.32 (2002).

Haase, Paul. "'Oh My Darling Clemency': Existing or Possible Limitations on the Use of the Presidential Pardon Power." *American Criminal Law Review,* v.39 (2002).

Hamilton, Alexander, James Madison, John Jay, and Clinton Rossiter, ed. *The Federalist Papers.* New York: Mentor, 1961.

Hart v. United States, 118 U.S. 62 (1886).

Hoffa v. Saxbe, 378 F.Supp. 1221 (D.D.C. 1974).

Hoffstadt, Brian. "Normalizing the Federal Clemency Power." *Texas Law Review,* v.79/3 (2001).

In re Abrams, 689 A.2d 6 (D.C. 1997).

In re North, 62 F.3d 1434 (C.A.D.C. 1994).

Johnson, Scott, and Christopher Smith. "White House Scandals and the Presidential Pardon Power: Persistent Risks and Prospects for Reform." *New England Law Review,* v.33 (1999).

Kalt, Brian. "Pardon Me? The Constitutional Case Against Presidential Self-Pardons." *Yale Law Journal,* v.106 (1996).

Knote v. United States, 95 U.S. 149 (1877).

Kobil, Daniel. "The Quality of Mercy Strained: Wresting the Pardoning Power From the King." *Texas Law Review,* v.69 (1991).

Koh, Harold. "Begging Bush's Pardon." *Houston Law Review,* v.29 (1992).

Krent, Harold. "Conditioning the President's Conditional Pardon Power." *California Law Review,* v.89 (2001).

Lardner, George. "The Role of the Press in the Clemency Process." *Capital University Law Review,* v.31 (2003).

The Laura, 114 U.S. 411 (1885).

Love, Margaret, ed. "Pardon Law." http://www.pardonlaw.com/index.html (Accessed January 2010).

Moore, Kathleen. "Pardon for Good and Sufficient Reasons." *University of Richmond Law Review,* v.27 (1993).

Morris, Ernest. "Some Phases of the Pardoning Power." *American Bar Association Journal,* v.12 (1926).

Murphy v. Ford, 390 F.Supp. 1372 (D.C. Mich. 1975).

Office of the Pardon Attorney, Department of Justice. http://www.justice.gov/pardon (Accessed January 2010).

Ohio Adult Parole Authority v. Woodard, 523 U.S. 272 (1998).

Osborn v. United States, 91 U.S. 474 (1876).

Peterson, Todd. "Congressional Power Over Pardon and Amnesty: Legislative Authority in the Shadow of Presidential Prerogative." *Wake Forest Law Review,* v.38 (2003).

Public Citizen v. U.S. Dept. of Justice, 491 U.S. 440 (1989).

Ruckman, P. S. Jr., ed. "Pardon Power." Available at: http://pardonpower.com (Accessed January 2010).

Ruckman, P. S. Jr., and David Kincaid. "Inside Lincoln's Clemency Decision Making." *Presidential Studies Quarterly,* v.29 (1999).

Schick v. Reed, 419 U.S. 256 (1974).

Sisk, Gregory. "Suspending the Pardon Power During the Twilight of a Presidential Term." *Missouri Law Review,* v.67 (2002).

Steiner, Ashley. "Remission of Guilt or Removal of Punishment: The Effects of a Presidential Pardon." *Emory Law Journal,* v.46 (1997).

Strasser, Mark. "Some Reflections on the President's Pardon Power." *Capital University Law Review,* v.31 (2003).

United States v. Klein, 80 U.S. 128 (1871).

United States v. Wilson, 32 U.S. 150 (1833).

United States v. Padelford, 76 U.S. 531 (1869).

U.S. v. Noonan, 906 F.2d 952 (C.A. 3 1990).

Walsh, Lawrence. "Political Oversight, the Rule of Law, and Iran-Contra." *Cleveland State Law Review,* v.42 (1994).

Werth, Barry. *31 Days.* New York: Nan A. Talese, 2006.

Whitford, Andrew, and Holona Ochs. "The Political Roots of Executive Clemency." *American Politics Research,* v.34 (2006).

3

Cruel and Unusual Punishment

Christopher E. Smith
Michigan State University

The prohibition on cruel and unusual punishments is presented in the Eighth Amendment of the U.S. Constitution. The Eighth Amendment is one of the 10 amendments that make up the Bill of Rights, ratified in 1791 to protect individuals against potentially excessive actions by the federal government. The American authors of the Constitution and Bill of Rights borrowed the phrase "cruel and unusual punishments" from the English Bill of Rights of 1689, a statute enacted by the British Parliament. In the United States, the meaning and specific nature of protections provided by the Cruel and Unusual Punishments Clause of the Eighth Amendment are defined by judges, especially the justices of the U.S. Supreme Court. Over the course of American history, new judicial interpretations have limited governmental authority by expanding the meaning of cruel and unusual punishments to provide protections against actions by state government, certain applications of capital punishment, and harsh prison conditions. Because the words "cruel and unusual punishments" are vague and lack any clear or inherent meaning, debates continue about when and how to apply this legal protection to limit government's power to impose punishments. Among the justices of the contemporary Supreme

27

Court, significant disagreements exist about how the phrase should be interpreted and applied.

American History of Cruel and Unusual Punishment

When the authors of the Bill of Rights borrowed the phrase "cruel and unusual punishments" from the 1689 English Bill of Rights when choosing the specific legal protections to list in the Eighth Amendment, they knew from history that many governments and rulers used harsh, physical punishments such as beheadings, torture, and burning at the stake as a means to terrorize and control their subjects. The founders of the new governing system in the United States intended to prohibit these sorts of punishments, but they did not specify precisely which punishments were barred. Instead, they placed into the Eighth Amendment a vague phrase that would inevitably be subject to interpretation.

Significant Eighth Amendment Cases

Through the end of the 19th century, in the relatively few cases concerning the Eighth Amendment decided by the U.S. Supreme Court, the justices interpreted the phrase "cruel and unusual punishments" as prohibiting punishments that were similar to torture. By contrast, judges in Great Britain, who also utilized the phrase in their own court cases, were concerned about punishments that they regarded as disproportionate to a crime.

In *Wilkerson v. Utah* (1878), the Supreme Court discussed the meaning of the Eighth Amendment in a case concerning a man convicted of murder who had been sentenced to death by firing squad in Utah Territory. The Court emphasized that the Cruel and Unusual Punishments Clause prohibits punishments that inflict torture. It referred to historical documents citing burning at the stake and slicing open the stomachs of live people as actions causing painful, lingering deaths that would be prohibited as cruel and unusual. The Court's decision observed that execution by firing squad did not constitute slow, painful torture and therefore did not violate the Eighth Amendment.

The Supreme Court expanded the protections of the Eighth Amendment in *Weems v. United States* (1910). The justices reinterpreted the phrase "cruel and unusual punishments" as prohibiting disproportionate punishments as well as torturous punishment. Weems, who worked for the U.S. government in the Philippines, was convicted of making false entries concerning small amounts of money in accounting books for the payment of wages to lighthouse workers. For this crime, he was sentenced to 15 years of imprisonment, including hard labor in ankle chains throughout the sentence, followed by a lifetime of limitations on his citizenship rights. The justices concluded that the sentence was excessive and imposed a punishment that was far too severe for the crime, especially when examined in light of lesser sentences sometimes imposed for far more serious crimes. After the decision in *Weems*, judges called upon to interpret the meaning of "cruel and unusual punishments" in individual cases could consider both aspects of the phrase, whether a punishment was disproportionate to the crime and whether it constituted a form of torture.

Actions of State and Local Governments

For most of American history, the Eighth Amendment's protection against cruel and unusual punishments applied only against punishments imposed by the federal government. The Supreme Court declared in *Barron v. Baltimore* (1833) that the Bill of Rights was intended to protect individuals against federal actions, but not against actions by state and local governments. The very first words in the Bill of Rights are "Congress shall make no law ...," thus indicating the authors' intent to stop the federal legislature and other elements of the national government from undertaking actions that would violate individuals' rights. The original presumption underlying the federal focus of the Bill of Rights was that state constitutions and other state laws would protect individuals against abusive actions by state and local governments. Most state constitutions have language parallel to that in the Eighth Amendment that prohibits cruel and unusual punishments, so it was presumed that state judges could use that language to prevent improper and excessive punishments within their own state court systems.

After the ratification of the Fourteenth Amendment in 1868, language was added to the Constitution that was intended to protect individuals against actions by state and local government. Within that amendment are the key words that "no state shall" deny "due process of law." Beginning in the late 19th century and continuing through the first seven decades of the 20th century, lawyers argued that the Fourteenth Amendment should be interpreted to include the individual protections, such as freedom of speech and right to counsel, that are listed in the Bill of Rights. Through a series of Supreme Court decisions in the middle decades of the 20th century, the justices of the nation's highest court announced that most, but not all, of the specific rights in the Bill of Rights now also provide protection against state and local action as a result of the right to due process in the Fourteenth Amendment.

It was not until 1962, in the case of *Robinson v. California*, that the Supreme Court declared that the Eighth Amendment's protection against cruel and unusual punishments applied to actions by state and local government officials. The *Robinson* case challenged a California law that made it a crime to be a drug addict. Robinson was convicted under the law and sentenced to incarceration solely because he had needle-mark scars on his arms that were consistent with those widely seen on the arms of intravenous drug users. The Supreme Court invalidated the California law by applying the Eighth Amendment. The Court declared that states cannot criminalize a status, such as the status of being a drug addict or a prostitute. Instead, crimes must focus on actions or planned actions, such as trafficking, possessing, or carrying drugs. A majority of justices concluded that it is cruel and unusual to punish people for their status, especially because the status of being a drug addict, for example, may not be the fault of the individual addicted to drugs. For example, a baby can be born addicted to drugs if his or her mother was addicted to drugs during the pregnancy. Similarly, a physician who prescribes an improper dosage of painkillers can lead an innocent patient to become dependent on those prescription painkillers. The justices did not want to permit such individuals to be prosecuted through the criminalizing of a status rather than an action.

While the *Robinson* case focused on the issue of criminalizing a specific status, the most significant enduring impact of the decision was the application of uniform cruel and unusual punishment protections against state and local governments as well as the federal government. Subsequently, federal judges have interpreted and applied the Eighth Amendment in examining the permissibility of state sentencing statutes, including capital punishment procedures, as well as conditions and practices in state prisons.

Defining Cruel and Unusual Punishments

The Case of Trop v. Dulles

The U.S. Supreme Court decision that gave the most enduring guidance to judges about the interpretation of the Eighth Amendment phrase was *Trop v. Dulles* (1958). Trop was a native-born American serving in the U.S. Army in North Africa during World War II. Trop escaped from the military jail in Casablanca, where he was confined for violating military rules. After walking along the road for a day, he surrendered to the occupants of a passing army vehicle and was returned to the military jail. Based on his action, he was convicted of desertion and sentenced to three years of confinement with hard labor and given a dishonorable discharge. He served his sentence at a military prison in the United States and then reentered civilian life. In 1952, he applied for a passport in order to travel overseas, but his application was rejected by the U.S. State Department. He was informed that the law under which he was convicted for wartime desertion also mandated the forfeiture of his American citizenship. He filed a legal action against the law by claiming that the forfeiture-of-citizenship penalty violated his Eighth Amendment right against cruel and unusual punishments.

In ruling in favor of Trop's claim, the Supreme Court's opinion, written by Chief Justice Earl Warren, conceded that the Court "has had little occasion to give precise content to the Eighth Amendment." He went on to say that the "basic concept underlying the Eighth Amendment is nothing less than the dignity of man" and that "the Amendment stands to assure that [the governmental] power to punish be exercised within the limits of civilized standards." Warren then observed that the meaning of the Eighth Amendment "is not static" and that "the Amendment must draw its meaning from the evolving standards of decency that mark the progress of a maturing society."

In other words, the meaning of the phrase "cruel and unusual punishments" would change over time as society's values changed. Punishments that were accepted as standard penalties for crimes during one era could later be declared unconstitutional violations of the Eighth Amendment if judges decided that society's values had changed. This standard has guided the decisions of judges since 1958, as evidenced by the Supreme Court's citation to the *Trop* case as the governing standard for the Eighth Amendment in its 2008 decision in *Louisiana v. Kennedy* forbidding the use of the death penalty in cases of child rape.

The Court's Interpretive Debate: Arguing for a Fixed Meaning

The evolving definition of "cruel and unusual punishments" articulated in *Trop v. Dulles* is highly controversial, despite the fact that it continues to be endorsed and utilized by a majority of justices on the U.S. Supreme Court. Critics claim that the vague, changing standard simply permits judges to rule in any way that they wish by claiming that society's values have changed. Thus, the standard arguably permits judges to simply apply their own values in deciding whether criminal sentences or prison conditions violate the Eighth Amendment. To critics, this invites judges to overstep their appropriate judicial roles by dictating the punishment policies for society, a task normally performed by elected members of legislatures.

U.S. Supreme Court Justices Antonin Scalia and Clarence Thomas argue that in order to limit judges' freedom of decision, the Eighth Amendment should be defined by the original intentions of the people who wrote and ratified the amendment from 1789 to 1791. In effect, these justices argue that "cruel and unusual punishments" should be treated as having a fixed meaning that cannot be changed by the whims and preferences of modern judges. The thought of permitting the full range of late 18th-century punishments, such as hanging for a wide array of offenses, is unsettling to many modern-day observers. Even Justice Scalia admits that he would be uncomfortable with the thought of a state returning to the use of whipping as a punishment for convicted criminals, although his interpretive approach would permit a state to take that approach since whipping was considered legally acceptable in 1791.

An additional criticism of the *Trop* standard raised by Justice Scalia focuses on the general presumption that this standard will lead to the use of increasingly humane punishments. Chief Justice Warren's phrase in *Trop* referred to "decency" and the "progress of a maturing society." Moreover, Eighth Amendment rulings have generally limited the range of punishments carried out by governmental officials by, for example, reducing the crimes eligible for punishment through the death penalty and requiring improvements in prison conditions. As Justice Scalia points out, however, a flexible standard that can change according to judges' values could actually lead to harsher and physically brutal punishments if judges in a future generation decide that society's values have changed in a direction that indicates greater acceptance of the infliction of physical pain upon convicted offenders.

Another interpretive debate focuses specifically on the word *punishments* within the phrase "cruel and unusual punishments." The U.S. Supreme Court has adopted a narrow view of the word *punishments* as referring on to governmental actions directed at people convicted of crimes. If a person is not a convicted offender, then the Eighth Amendment's protections do not apply to him or her. For example, many people held in local jails are criminal suspects who are awaiting various pretrial hearings and trials. They are presumptively innocent and therefore do not benefit from the Eighth Amendment unless and until they are convicted of the crimes for which they stand accused. Pretrial detainees are protected against abusive governmental treatment by rights under the Due Process Clause. Meanwhile, they may be sharing a jail cell with someone serving a six-month sentence for a minor offense. The convicted offender sharing the same cell is protected by the Eighth Amendment by virtue of experiencing "punishment" from a criminal conviction.

Questions about the interpretation of the word *punishment* and the attendant applicability of the Eighth Amendment have arisen in other contexts. In 1978, the U.S. Supreme Court decided *Ingraham v. Wright*, a case concerning middle school students who were struck with a two-foot wooden paddle by an assistant principal because they responded too slowly to a teacher's instructions. One student needed medical attention for a resulting hematoma, and another temporarily lost the use of one arm. They filed a lawsuit against school officials that asserted a violation of the Eighth Amendment right against cruel and unusual punishments. The Court rejected the claim because the students did not experience "punishment" in Eighth Amendment terms, since the justices had limited that word's definition to apply only to convicted criminal offenders.

Proportionality and Non-Capital Sentences

The U.S. Supreme Court has addressed several cases asserting Eighth Amendment claims about the length of prison sentences. In *Solem v. Helm* (1983), Solem was convicted of passing a "no account" check for $100 in 1979. He had six prior convictions for nonviolent felonies dating back to 1964, including grand larceny, driving while intoxicated, and obtaining money under false pretenses. Normally, his conviction for a no-account check would draw a maximum sentence of five years in prison. However, his prior convictions made him eligible for South Dakota's habitual offender law. Thus, he was sentenced to life in prison without possibility of parole. When his claim of an Eighth Amendment violation reached the Supreme Court, the justices examined whether the punishment was disproportionate to the crime by examining three factors: (1) the gravity of the offense and the harshness of the penalty; (2) the sentences imposed on other criminals in the same state; and (3) the sentences imposed for the commission of the same crime in other jurisdictions. After applying these factors to Helm's cases, a majority of justices concluded that his right against cruel and unusual punishments had been violated because the sentence was excessive and out of proportion to his crime. This decision appeared to conflict with an earlier decision of the Supreme Court that rejected an Eighth Amendment claim by a Texas offender who was given a life sentence as a habitual offender for three separate thefts over the course of nine years that gained him a total of $229. However, in the prior case, *Rummel v. Estelle* (1980), the offender had the possibility of parole. Thus, the Court's decision in *Solem v. Helm* stood for the proposition that a sentence of life without parole could violate the Eighth Amendment when imposed on someone who committed a series of nonviolent, lesser offenses.

In *Harmelin v. Michigan* (1991), the Court examined Michigan's law that mandated a sentence of life in prison without possibility of parole for anyone convicted of possessing 650 or more grams of cocaine. Because Michigan does not have the death penalty, this severe sentence was the same as the punishment mandated for people convicted of first-degree murder, the act that is typically considered the most serious crime under state law. Harmelin was a first offender with no prior criminal record. He claimed that his sentence was disproportionate to the crime when he was caught carrying a large quantity of cocaine, but he had never committed an act of violence or any other prior crime. Part of his argument rested on the fact that no other American court system punished this crime so severely. If Harmelin had been prosecuted in federal court, he would have received a sentence of only 10 years' imprisonment.

Despite the fact that Michigan's sentence for this offense was far more severe than comparable sentences elsewhere in the United States, a majority of justices said that Michigan could choose to impose such sentences without violating the Eighth Amendment. In this case, the majority of justices accepted the harshest possible noncapital sentence for a single nonviolent crime because it was a serious crime, and the Court appeared to defer to states on determining the length of sentences in such circumstances. Justice Scalia even argued that the Court should no longer consider proportionality of criminal sentences to be potential Eighth Amendment violations, except if the death penalty is applied to lesser offenses. However, he could not persuade a majority of his colleagues to adopt his argument about limiting noncapital applications of the Cruel and Unusual Punishments Clause to torturous punishments and not disproportionate punishments.

The proportionality issue returned to the Supreme Court in *Lockyer v. Andrade* (2003), which challenged California's three-strikes law designed to give long sentences to repeat offenders. Andrade was convicted of petty theft for attempting to steal videos from a store by sticking them in the waistband of his pants. Because he had prior convictions over the previous 13 years for misdemeanor theft, burglary, and transporting marijuana, he was sentenced to two consecutive terms of 25 years to life in prison, meaning he would need to serve at least 25 years of the first sentence before he could begin serving the second sentence that would also last at least 25 years. A slim majority of justices accepted the sentence as permissible under the Eighth Amendment, presumably because there was the possibility of parole, albeit not until at least 50 years had passed. Overall, the *Lockyer* decision reinforced the idea that the Supreme Court would find prison sentences to be disproportionate to a crime only in rare, extraordinary circumstances, such as life without parole for lesser offenses.

Capital Punishment

The Cruel and Unusual Punishments Clause is frequently interpreted and applied in cases concerning capital punishment. Judicial decisions have reduced the range of crimes and offenders eligible for death penalty. In *Coker v. Georgia* (1977), the Court declared that the imposition of the death penalty was excessive and disproportionate to the crime when applied as a punishment for the rape of an adult woman. In 2008, the justices reached the same conclusion about the application of capital punishment for the rape of a child (*Louisiana v. Kennedy*). As a result, the Court used the Eighth Amendment to narrow the application of the death penalty to the crime of murder.

For the crime of murder, the Supreme Court narrowed the categories of offenders eligible for the death penalty. In *Atkins v. Virginia* (2002), a majority of justices declared that it is impermissibly cruel and unusual to sentence mentally challenged murders to death. Similarly, in *Roper v. Simmons* (2005), the Court decided that states violate the Eighth Amendment if they impose death sentences on convicted murderers who committed their crimes prior to the age of 18. In both decisions, the Court's majority relied on the *Trop v. Dulles* standard by concluding that society had changed in a manner that made such death sentences inconsistent with dominant, contemporary values. Dissenting justices vigorously disagreed with this conclusion in each case.

Methods of execution in capital punishment have also been the focus of legal disputes about the meaning and applicability of the phrase "cruel and unusual punishments." In the final decades of the 20th century, several lower federal courts and state supreme courts ruled that both the gas chamber and the electric chair violated the right against cruel and unusual punishments. Although these decisions only affected the specific federal districts or states under the jurisdiction of these courts, those decisions spurred states throughout the nation to reexamine their methods of execution and pushed a widespread movement toward using lethal injection as the preferred means of execution.

When the Supreme Court examined an Eighth Amendment claim about the permissibility of lethal injection as a method of execution in *Baze v. Rees* (2008), the justices ruled that there was not enough evidence about infliction of pain to prove that lethal injection constituted impermissible cruel and unusual punishment.

Beginning in the late 20th century, several justices argued that capital punishment is always unconstitutional. Most notably, Justices Thurgood Marshall (Supreme Court service: 1967–91) and William Brennan (Supreme Court service: 1956–90) argued that the death penalty is inherently cruel and unusual punishment when judged in light of contemporary social values. Opponents of the death penalty have long harbored the hope that someday a majority of the Court's justices would eventually adopt that perspective. Because only one 21st-century justice, Justice John Paul Stevens, was openly opposed to capital punishment, it seems likely that Eighth Amendment disputes about the death penalty will continue to focus on specific aspects of this criminal punishment rather than on the general concept of capital punishment. For example, Justice Stevens and Justice Stephen Breyer have argued that it can violate the right against cruel and unusual punishment to have long delays of many years between the conviction and execution of a convicted murderer, such as in *Johnson v. Bredesen* (2009). Such specific issues are likely to be presented to the Supreme Court in future cases.

Prison Conditions

Lower federal courts first began to apply the Cruel and Unusual Punishments Clause of the Eighth Amendment to conditions in prison during the 1960s. For example, in *Jackson v. Bishop* (1968), the U.S. Court of Appeals for the Eighth Circuit ruled that prison officials violated the Eighth Amendment when they whipped prisoners as punishment for violating prison rules. Thus, contemporary American prison officials must use penalties such as loss of privileges or confinement in isolation cells to punish prisoners for rule violations; they can no longer administer beatings to prisoners, as was commonly done in many prisons throughout American history prior to the 1960s.

The U.S. Supreme Court first applied the Cruel and Unusual Punishments Clause to prison conditions in *Estelle v. Gamble* (1976). In that case, the Court ruled that prison officials violate the Eighth Amendment when they are deliberately indifferent to prisoners' serious medical needs. The Court's decision effectively communicated to lower court judges that they could examine complaints about prison living conditions by examining whether those conditions violate the Eight Amendment's standard from *Trop v. Dulles* of "evolving standards of decency that mark the progress of a maturing society." In *Estelle v. Gamble*, the Court effectively decided that deliberate indifference to prisoners' serious medical needs violates society's evolving standards of decency.

Subsequently, the same standard was applied to examinations of food, shelter, sanitation facilities, and other aspects of prison conditions. As a result, federal judges throughout the country used interpretations of the Eighth Amendment as the basis for ordering prison officials to correct deficiencies in prison conditions. In a few states, federal judges found the conditions to be so bad that the judges effectively took control of the prison system. For example, in *Pugh v. Locke* (1976), a federal judge took control of Alabama's prison system after hearing evidence about filthy conditions, exposed electrical wires, insects in the food, prisoner-on-prisoner violence and rapes, and other conditions that made certain prisons, according to an inspection by an official from the U.S. Public Health Service, "unfit for human habitation." The Cruel and Unusual Punishments Clause became the vehicle through which federal judges pushed for improvements in prison conditions nationwide.

Sexual Violence, Confinement, and Use of Force

Congress sought to address the issue of sexual violence in prisons through enactment of the Prison Rape Elimination Act (2003). The act sought to mandate zero tolerance for sexual assaults in prisons and help prison officials to develop training and procedures to address the problem. Eighth Amendment violations occur when corrections officials are deliberately indifferent to either prisoner-on-prisoner sexual assaults or staff-on-prisoner sexual abuse, the latter being a serious problem that persisted in the victimization of women offenders by male corrections officers in many states. The act mandated that a federal commission study and develop recommendations for addressing such problems. In light of the information and resources made available under the act, any institution's failure to take steps to prevent sexual abuse and violence would provide grounds for a lawsuit by victims.

Prisoners are kept in solitary confinement for short periods as punishment for violating institutional rules, or for years when placed in super-maximum-security prisons. Decisions by federal appellate courts make clear that officials must provide these prisoners with proper food, blankets, clothing, ventilation, sanitation, and exercise in order to avoid violating the Cruel and Unusual Punishments Clause. Prisoners are often removed from their cells and placed alone in a small, cage-like recreation area so that they may walk and do exercises for one hour each day in order to fulfill judges' interpretations of Eighth Amendment requirements for exercise.

The Eighth Amendment also governs the use of force by prison officials. An excessive use of force against prisoners constitutes a violation of the protection against cruel and unusual punishments. In *Whitley v. Albers* (1986), the Supreme Court decided that prisoners can sue corrections officers for Eighth Amendment violations when those officers cause injuries through the use of force that was applied "maliciously and sadistically for the very purpose of causing harm."

Standard of Proof

One of the biggest debates about how to interpret the Cruel and Unusual Punishments Clause and apply it to prison conditions concerns the standard of proof that prisoners must fulfill to demonstrate an Eighth Amendment violation. In *Estelle v. Gamble* (1976), the Court declared that prisoners must prove "deliberate indifference" to serious medical needs; and in *Whitley v. Albers* (1986), the Court required proof that corrections officers used force "maliciously and sadistically." Both of these tests are subjective tests because they require proof of the thoughts or intentions of corrections officials in order to prove a rights violation. In *Wilson v. Seiter* (1991), a slim majority of justices required proof of "deliberate indifference" for all alleged Eighth Amendment violations concerning prison conditions, such as inadequate food, overcrowding, and unhealthy sanitation. By contrast, other justices argue that the Court should use an objective standard that simply asks, "are these conditions or deprivations so bad as to constitute cruel and unusual punishment?" without concern about corrections officials' thoughts and intentions.

Pro: Arguments in Support of the Subjective Standard

Advocates of the subjective standard argue that prison officials receive limited resources from state legislatures and local governments with which to run corrections facilities. From this viewpoint, it would be unreasonable to permit judges to impose idealistic standards for living conditions that no corrections administrator could possibly fulfill. Thus, prison officials should be expected to do the best that they can in maintaining a humane and safe environment. For example, the *Estelle v. Gamble* standard seeks to ensure that corrections officials do not ignore prisoners' serious medical needs, but it does not operate in an unreasonable fashion by requiring that prisoners have immediate access to expensive medical specialists or other idealized measures that are not even available to the general public. In addition, advocates of the subjective standard do not believe that prison officials should be held liable and possibly be forced to pay compensation for rights violations when there are inadvertent deprivations or situations otherwise out of the control of prison administrators.

What if, for example, a city's water system suffers a problem and the entire city is temporarily without water for a few days while the problem is being fixed? Should prison officials be subject to lawsuits for Eighth Amendment violations because prisoners temporarily are unable to take showers or flush toilets, just like all citizens in that particular city? As long as prison officials are doing everything that they can to provide bottled water, install portable chemical toilets in the prison yard, and take other measures to alleviate the problem, advocates of the subjective standard do not believe that they should be found liable for being temporarily unable to provide for the expected human need of hot and cold running water, toilets, and showers. Thus, advocates would limit liability to those situations in which prison officials ignore or otherwise indicate that they do not care about the conditions experienced by prisoners.

Con: Arguments Against the Subjective Standard

Critics of the subjective standard complain that two prisoners can suffer identical deprivations, but only the prisoner who can prove "deliberate indifference" will be regarded as suffering an Eighth Amendment violation. For example, imagine two prisoners at separate institutions who each suffer serious discomfort as the result of a painful skin infection that risks spreading elsewhere on their bodies. At one institution, the corrections officials say, "we don't care—that's your problem;" therefore, the Eighth Amendment right is violated. At the other institution, the corrections officials say, "we care, but we never made any plans to have the medication that you need stocked in the prison pharmacy." The second prisoner suffered identical unnecessary physical pain, but the corrections officials' statement "we care" may prevent this situation from being regarded as a rights violation. Furthermore, it raises the possibility that corrections officials will simply claim they care about every situation that arises, along with an excuse about not having enough money to fix a problem, as a means to avoid meeting expectations about minimum humane prison conditions.

In addition, it can be very difficult, and often impossible, for prisoners to prove the nature of corrections officials' thoughts and intentions. If corrections officials carelessly shoot innocent prisoners while trying to break up a knife fight in the prison yard, how would a severely injured, innocent prisoner prove whether the shooting was done "maliciously and sadistically?" The innocent prisoner, who suffered severe and potentially permanent injuries because of careless actions by corrections officers, would need to prove the very difficult assumption that the officers had evil intentions at the moment that they fired their weapons. Critics argue that this is the sort of excessive use of force that should be considered cruel and unusual punishment—and that each situation should be examined without regard to intention by considering whether deprivations of human needs and inflictions of physical pain constitute violations of the Cruel and Unusual Punishments Clause by being inconsistent with contemporary values for decency and human dignity.

See Also: 1. Capital Punishment/Death Penalty; 4. Due Process Rights of Prisoners; 9. Healthcare and Medical Assistance for Prisoners; 11. Life Sentence; 12. Mentally Ill and Mentally Challenged Inmates; 19. Sex Offender Treatment; 20. Shaming Penalties.

Further Readings

Berkson, Larry C. *The Concept of Cruel and Unusual Punishment.* Lexington, MA: Lexington Books, 1975.

Crouch, Ben M., and James W. Marquart. *An Appeal to Justice: Litigated Reform of Texas Prisons.* Austin, TX: University of Texas Press.

Feeley, Malcolm M., and Edward L. Rubin. *Judicial Policy Making and the Modern State: How Courts Reformed America's Prisons.* New York: Cambridge University Press, 1998.

Fliter, John A. *Prisoners' Rights: The Supreme Court and Evolving Standards of Decency.* Westport, CT: Greenwood Press, 2001.

Melusky, Joseph A., and Keith A. Pesto. *Cruel and Unusual Punishment.* Santa Barbara, CA: ABC-CLIO, 2003.

Smith, Christopher E. *The Rehnquist Court and Criminal Punishment.* New York: Garland Publishing, 1997.

Yackle, Larry W. *Reform and Regret: The Story of Federal Judicial Involvement in the Alabama Prison System.* New York: Oxford University Press, 1989.

4

Due Process Rights of Prisoners

Kenneth C. Haas
University of Delaware

The Fourteenth Amendment to the U.S. Constitution prohibits state actions that deprive "any person of life, liberty, or property without due process of law." The U.S. Supreme Court has consistently held that people cannot be deprived of life, liberty, or property without adequate procedural due process. However, specifying the particular procedures and quantifying the precise amount of protection required by the Due Process Clause is decided on a case-by-case basis by the judiciary. Questions of "how much process is due" a person who faces or has already suffered one or more deprivations of liberty or property controversial, and have been the focus of ongoing debate and interpretation.

The right to due process of law, like other constitutional rights, has never been distributed equally to all segments of the population. The rights enumerated in the Constitution, for example, have never been fully extended to those who are incarcerated. The history of prisoners' rights is maligned with cases of indifference and neglect. The problems of determining the particular protections afforded by the Due Process Clause are especially difficult in the context of imprisonment, which by design, curtails inmate liberty.

Prior to the 1960s, federal and state courts typically refused to review cases brought by prisoners complaining of harsh conditions of confinement, arbitrary punishments imposed without due process protection, or other prison policies or practices that were constitutionally questionable. In declining jurisdiction over litigation involving prisons, the courts relied upon a policy generally known as the hands-off doctrine. This approach to inmate lawsuits reflected the views that a convicted prisoner was a "slave of the state" without enforceable rights, and that the courts lacked the expertise and authority to intervene in prison management. In practice, the hands-off doctrine made it virtually impossible for prisoners to seek judicial relief from alleged mistreatment at the hands of prison officials.

In the 1960s, many federal courts and a few state courts began to relax their traditional hands-off attitude toward the legal rights of prisoners. The early 1970s were years of growth and development in prison litigation. Although most cases were decided in favor of prison authorities, prisoners nevertheless prevailed in a number of well-publicized cases finding that inmates had been subjected to arbitrary beatings; contaminated and nutritionally inadequate food; poor sanitation; severe overcrowding; and prolonged confinement in filthy isolation cells that were lacking light, ventilation, and any means of maintaining bodily cleanliness. The Supreme Court enlarged the scope of prisoners' rights of access to the courts, expanded inmate rights to religious freedom and decent medical care, and for the first time held that prisoners are entitled to procedural due process during prison disciplinary hearings.

Due Process Rights of Parolees and Probationers

Wolff v. McDonnell

The Supreme Court did not address the question of whether prisoners are constitutionally protected by the Due Process Clause of the Fourteenth Amendment until its landmark 1974 decision in *Wolff v. McDonnell*. However, two earlier decisions marked the Court's first efforts to determine the extent to which people under correctional supervision are entitled to due process when they are charged with offenses that could subject them to additional punishment. The Court's first venture into these legal waters came in the 1972 case of *Morrissey v. Brewer*. In *Morrissey*, the Court addressed (1) the question of whether the Fourteenth Amendment's requirement of due process applies to parolees facing revocation of their parole status and a return to prison; and (2) if so, what process is due parolees who find themselves in this situation.

After answering the first question in the affirmative, the Court reasoned that the government has a legitimate interest in returning a potentially dangerous parolee to prison without the burden of a full-fledged criminal trial, and that the parolee has a legitimate interest in avoiding reimprisonment and having the opportunity to show that he has done nothing to deserve losing his parole status. Consequently, the revocation of parole does not require the full panoply of rights accorded to defendants in criminal trials. However, it does require a "simple factual hearing" in which the parolee has a reasonable opportunity to convince officials that he should not be returned to prison. Writing for the majority, Chief Justice Burger held that the Due Process Clause requires, first, a preliminary hearing to determine whether there is probable cause to believe that the parolee has committed a new crime or otherwise violated his parole conditions; and second, a final hearing within a reasonable time to decide whether he has violated these conditions and should be returned to prison.

An independent officer or official is to preside over the hearings. This hearing officer need not be (but could be) a judge or magistrate, but must be someone not directly involved in the case (perhaps a parole officer other than the one who recommended revocation). The chief justice added that at each hearing, the parolee is entitled to notice of the violations alleged and the evidence against him; an opportunity to be heard in person and to present witnesses and documentary evidence; and the right to confront and cross-examine adverse witnesses, unless the hearing officer finds that a potential witness would be exposed to a significant risk of harm. Furthermore, the decision whether to revoke parole is to be made either by the hearing officer or a "neutral and detached" hearing body such as a traditional parole board. Finally, the decision maker must give the parolee a written statement as to the evidence relied upon and the reasons for revoking parole, and there must be a written record of the hearing.

The *Gagnon* Court

The very next year, the Court considered whether those on probation were entitled to due process protections before their probation could be revoked. In *Gagnon v. Scarpelli* (1973), the Supreme Court held that a probationer's sentence can only be revoked after both a preliminary and final revocation hearing. The *Gagnon* Court found that probationers are similarly situated to parolees in that they enjoy partial, supervised freedom in the community and would be sent to prison if found to have violated their probation. Accordingly, the Court held that before probationers can have their probation revoked, they must be afforded all of the same due process rights that *Morrissey* extended to parolees charged with violating the conditions of their parole. In *Gagnon*, the Court also addressed a question that was not addressed in *Morrissey*—whether indigent probationers and parolees have the right to be represented by appointed counsel during probation or parole revocation hearings.

The Court, however, refused to provide a clear yes or no answer to this question. Citing the importance of giving correctional officials flexibility in conducting revocation hearings, the Court held that the decision as to the need for counsel was to be made on a case-by-case basis by probation and parole officials. Thus, it was not necessary for the Court to impose a detailed set of guidelines to be followed when indigent probationers and parolees request the assistance of an attorney during revocation proceedings. In *Gagnon*, the Court instructed correctional officials to tell those undergoing a revocation hearing that they had a right to request counsel. The Court next told officials to consider whether the probationer or parolee appeared to have a reasonable claim that he either did not violate the rules, or that a violation of the rules should not result in his imprisonment. If so, according to the Court, officials making the decision whether to provide counsel should take into account such factors as the complexity of the case and whether the probationer or parolee was capable of speaking effectively for himself.

Although *Gagnon* dealt with the case of an indigent probationer who requested appointed counsel, the *Gagnon* guidelines also apply to nonindigent probationers and parolees who request the right to be represented by retained counsel in a revocation hearing. Nearly 40 years later, *Morrissey* and *Gagnon* remain the law of the land. The Supreme Court still has not answered the question of whether nonindigent probationers and parolees have the right to be represented by a retained attorney in revocation hearings in which an indigent would not have the right to appointed counsel. Another important unanswered question concerns the standard of evidence (or proof) that needs to be established to revoke a probationer's or parolee's freedom. In the absence of a definitive Supreme Court ruling, most federal and state courts permit revocation on the basis of the preponderance of the evidence standard, and some permit it on the basis of an even lower standard.

Prisoners' Due Process Rights in Disciplinary Hearings

After outlining the due process rights to be extended to parolees and pro-bationers who faced revocation of their conditional freedom, the Court in 1974 reviewed its first case raising the question of what, if any, due process rights must be extended to prisoners facing disciplinary action for alleged violations of prison regulations. In *Wolff v. McDonnell*, the Court heard a class-action claim brought by Nebraska inmates who asserted that disciplinary procedures in the state's prisons fell short of the Fourteenth Amendment's requirement of due process of law.

Prior to *Wolff*, the courts took diverse positions on the question of whether prisoners accused of violating prison rules were entitled to any due-process protection before being punished. A few federal courts called for a brief, nonadversarial hearing at which the accused inmate could speak for himself. But most courts permitted prison officials to impose summary punishments with no procedural protections for prisoners. For the most part, prison officials and custodial staff were free to serve as arresting officer, prosecutor, judge, and sentencer when inmates were suspected of any kind of prison misconduct. Prisoners accused of any kind of offense, from offensive language to possession of contraband to first-degree murder, simply were not constitutionally entitled even to an informal hearing at which they could make a case for innocence, extenuating circumstances, or mitigating factors.

Due Process for Major Punishments

Writing for the *Wolff* majority, Justice White began by making it clear that prisoners were not constitutionally entitled to due-process safeguards when they were accused of minor misconduct such as dress code violations, swearing, rude gestures, and pushing or shoving among inmates that ends promptly and without injury. Such behavior could be dealt with swiftly and informally, and would typically result in a relatively mild punishment such as a reprimand, withdrawal of privileges, limitations on visitation or work assignments, or a change in cell location or classification status. The imposition of these kinds of punishments is constitutionally de minimis; they are routinely administered in the prison setting and are not considered to be harmful enough to trigger the need for constitutional protection.

But according to Justice White, the situation is different and the Due Process Clause is implicated in cases where a prisoner faces a major punishment—typically the loss of previously earned credits toward an earlier release (good-time credits) and/or the imposition of solitary confinement. Justice White stressed that the loss of good time, like the imposition of solitary confinement, is of considerable importance to the inmate. The first of these punishments postpones the date of parole eligibility and extends the maximum term to be served, and the second has the effect of further restricting the inmate's freedom by removing him from the general population and placing him in a smaller, more uncomfortable cell with little or nothing to do. These punishments, Justice White contended, are significant enough to trigger the need for due-process safeguards. Thus, when an inmate faces such a punishment—either because he allegedly has engaged in multiple instances of minor misconduct or committed a single act of serious misconduct (such as possession of contraband or assault on a staff member or another prisoner)—he is entitled to at least minimal due process protection. Justice White conceded, however, that prison disciplinary hearings are conducted in prisons—places where tension, resentment, and despair are prevalent, and where confrontation, retaliation, and violence are common. Accordingly, he concluded, prisoners facing serious disciplinary charges are entitled to some, but not all, of the due process rights accorded to parolees and probationers in *Morrissey* and *Gagnon*.

Opportunity to Appear at a Hearing

Specifically, the *Wolff* majority ruled that the Due Process Clause of the Fourteenth Amendment obligates prison officials to give inmates who are accused of serious misconduct an opportunity to appear before an administrative hearing board or hearing officer and to discuss or challenge the charges against them. Hearing officers typically would be prison staff members, but *Wolff* requires them to be "impartial," which means at the very least that the inmate's accusers may not serve as hearing officers. *Wolff* also requires prison officials to give the inmate written notification of the charges against him at least 24 hours prior to the hearing.

At the hearing, the prisoner is permitted to present documentary evidence and call witnesses in his defense, although the hearing board has discretion to disallow a witness when it believes that permitting him to testify would jeopardize institutional security. Further, if the case is unusually complex, or if the accused is illiterate or otherwise unable to speak for himself, he is entitled to a "counsel substitute," likely another inmate but perhaps a staff member, to assist him during the hearing. Finally, *Wolff* obliges the hearing board to provide a written statement explaining the decision, the evidence relied upon, and the reasons for any disciplinary action.

To the dismay of prisoners and the dissenting justices, the *Wolff* majority went no further and, in fact, argued that the unique problems of preventing violence and maintaining order in prisons justified clear limitations on inmates' due process rights. Justice White's majority opinion stressed that inmates are never entitled to a retained or appointed lawyer, only to "counsel substitute" in special cases. Most important, the majority held that accused inmates have no constitutional right to confront or cross-examine hostile witnesses. The *Wolff* Court was silent with respect to any other due-process issues that were likely to arise in prison disciplinary proceedings. Since correctional officials were obligated to give accused inmates only the specific protections listed in *Wolff*, inmates still have none of the evidentiary protections routinely afforded defendants in criminal courts. Hearsay evidence is admissible, and inmates have no right to a Miranda warning and no right to the exclusion of evidence seized in violation of the clause addressing search and seizure in the Fourth Amendment.

Raising More Questions From Wolff

Like many Supreme Court decisions, *Wolff* raised more questions than it answered. Today, federal and state courts continue to struggle with many unanswered questions. What constitutes an adequate statement of the evidence relied upon and the reasons for disciplinary action? What rules should govern the admissibility of hearsay evidence or evidence from anonymous informants? Is a prison policy that allows the inmate's requested witnesses to submit written statements but not to testify in person constitutional? Is "lack of necessity" a justifiable reason for the hearing board to deny a prisoner's request for a particular witness? Under what circumstances can the hearing board deny an inmate's request for a particular inmate to serve as counsel substitute?

Although many post-*Wolff* issues remain unsettled, the Supreme Court has answered several important questions. For example, in *Baxter v. Palmigiano* (1976), the Court ruled that a prison hearing board can consider an inmate's silence during a disciplinary hearing as evidence of guilt. In *Ponte v. Real* (1985), the Court held that the hearing board does not have to tell the accused inmate its reasons for denying him the right to call a particular witness at the time of the hearing. The *Ponte* Court concluded that the hearing board doesn't have to explain its reasons unless and until the inmate challenges the denial by filing a lawsuit.

Some Evidence: The Surprising Hill Decision

Also in 1985, the Court finally answered what arguably is the most important question about the fairness of inmate disciplinary hearings: How much evidence is constitutionally sufficient to find an inmate guilty of serious misconduct? In *Superintendent v. Hill*, the Court unanimously concluded that there must be "some evidence" of the inmate's guilt. Many legal scholars were surprised by the *Hill* ruling, and inmates and their supporters were both surprised and dismayed by the holding. While there was no expectation that the Court would require "proof beyond a reasonable doubt" or even "clear and convincing evidence" to support a hearing board or hearing officer's finding of guilt, most legal observers assumed that the Court would require a finding of guilt to be supported by a preponderance of the evidence, enough to allow a reasonable person to conclude that it is more likely than not that the inmate is guilty. Prior to *Hill*, many prisons and jails used the preponderance standard in their disciplinary proceedings. Others predicted that the Court might require only probable cause, not a preponderance of evidence, but enough to support an arrest warrant or a search warrant in the American criminal justice process.

Since *Hill*, many legal scholars—and even federal judges—have criticized the Court's decision. Some legal commentators claimed that the "some evidence" standard was intended only as the standard that appellate courts were to apply when reviewing inmates' claims of denial of due process in disciplinary hearings, and that the standard for the actual hearing should be more demanding than a mere finding of "some evidence." However, a close reading of Justice O'Connor's *Hill* opinion, subsequent holdings by federal and state courts, and the lack of subsequent clarification by the Supreme Court make if entirely clear that the "some evidence" standard is constitutionally acceptable both as the standard for a finding of guilt by a prison disciplinary tribunal and for the rejection of a prisoner's due-process suit by a federal or state court. The *Hill* holding is considered a major setback for prisoners and the cause of prisoners' rights.

Since *Hill*, the Supreme Court has continued to weaken the procedural protections available to inmates accused of disciplinary infractions. The Court's decision in *Sandin v. Connor* (1995) provides a good example of this trend. In *Sandin*, the Court held that a state prisoner in Hawaii who had been given 30 days in segregated confinement for an alleged disciplinary infraction could not bring a *Wolff*-type lawsuit challenging the constitutionality of his disciplinary hearing. A 5–4 majority reasoned that 30 days in the Hawaii segregation unit did not impose an "atypical and significant hardship" on this inmate, in part because he was serving a sentence of 30 years to life in a maximum-security prison. According to Chief Justice Rehniquist's majority opinion, the inmate's 30-day punishment was "within the range of confinement to be normally expected" while serving such a sentence. The chief justice added that prisoner complaints that are nothing more than complaints about "the ordinary incidents of prison life" should not be accorded constitutional status by federal judges. *Sandin* did not overrule *Wolff*. However, *Sandin* has made it more difficult for prisoners to bring constitutional challenges against prison disciplinary proceedings or against transfer and classification decisions made by correctional officials. The main result has been more confusion, as lower courts decide on a case-by-case basis whether or not an inmate's grievance involves an "atypical and significant hardship."

Pro: Arguments in Favor of Limited Due Process

Prison officials and others who defend the legal status quo argue that the Supreme Court has achieved a workable balance between the requirements of institutional security and the need to protect the due process rights of prisoners. Some correctional officials initially were concerned that the 1974 *Wolff* holding might hamper their ability to maintain discipline behind bars. Nearly four decades later, however, few complaints are heard from wardens or their staff. Conducting a *Wolff*-type hearing has become as routine in prisons as reading the Miranda warning has become in the nation's police stations. These is no reason to believe that *Wolff* and its progeny have led to weakened supervisory control or to an increase in prison violence. No social science study has shown that *Wolff* has contributed to prison management problems. Moreover, there has been no organized effort by state or federal prosecutors to develop a "stalking horse" case that the current Court could use to overrule *Wolff*.

From the viewpoint of prison officials, however, there has been a much-needed legislative effort to curtail prisoners' ability to file lawsuits in federal courts. The 1995 Prison Litigation Reform Act (PLRA), signed into law by President Clinton in 1996, was not specifically aimed at *Wolff*, but the law makes it more difficult for prisoners to have any kind of grievance adjudicated by a federal court. Among other things, the PLRA requires that before a prisoner can file a civil rights suit in a federal court, he must exhaust all available administrative remedies, including any inmate grievance system the prison may have. Moreover, an inmate who sues in federal court will now have to show that he suffered a physical injury in order to recover monetary damages for mental or emotional injury suffered while in custody. The PLRA also contains its own three-strikes provision. It prohibits a prisoner from filing an in forma pauperis petition (which allows an indigent litigant to proceed with his case when the court determines that he lacks the funds to pay the filing fee) if he has previously filed three or more federal petitions that were dismissed as frivolous, malicious, or for failing to state a claim for which relief can be granted.

Additionally, the PLRA provides for sanctions, including the possible loss of previously earned good-time credits, to be imposed on federal prisoners who are found to have presented false evidence in a lawsuit or to have filed suit for malicious reasons. The PLRA has led to the dismissal of hundreds of inmate lawsuits, and this is a result that many public officials applaud. For prison officials, most of whom already seemed comfortable with the *Wolff* requirements, the PLRA could only be considered as giving them more leeway to conduct disciplinary hearings with little fear of inmate retaliation through lawsuits. Correctional administrators are quick to point out that the PLRA has no effect on the substantive law established by *Wolff* and other major cases involving inmate due-process rights. Typically, they concede that the PLRA has made it more difficult for inmates to challenge disciplinary hearings on due process grounds, but they contend that they nevertheless strive to be fair and they argue that the PLRA is very much in line with the Supreme Court's post-*Wolff* jurisprudence.

Prison administrators and their supporters maintain that *Baxter v. Palmigiano, Ponte v. Real, Superintendent v. Hill,* and *Sandin v. Connor* prove that they have complied with the mandates of *Wolff* in good faith and in a thorough manner. As they see it, the Supreme Court's unwillingness to go any further than *Wolff* itself in safeguarding the due process rights of inmates is, in effect, an acknowledgement that additional due process requirements are unnecessary. The minimal requirements of *Wolff* and the Court's subsequent approval of a mere "some evidence" standard as sufficient to find an inmate guilty of major misconduct are viewed as judicial approval for the way in which prison discipline is imposed. If there had been reason to believe that *Wolff*-type hearings were ineffective or underused, they contend, surely the Supreme Court would have strengthened or added to the *Wolff* requirements. Instead, the Court has decided every major post-*Wolff* case to the advantage of prison administrators and to the disadvantage of inmates.

The Court's decisions, according to correctional officials, are not only a vindication of existing policies, but are reflective of the greater problems prison staff face in light of the sharp growth in the American inmate population, the problems posed by prison gangs, and the difficulties of hiring and training personnel who can deal with inherently dangerous people crammed into overcrowded and dilapidated facilities. Extending more due-process protections to prisoners, it is argued, would not only undermine prison discipline; it would subvert efforts to create and manage effective rehabilitation programs. Statistics on prison violence and other disruptive incidents are notoriously unreliable. It cannot truly be known whether the per-capita rate (or severity) of assaults or other cases of major misconduct are in decline or on the rise. Prison officials, nevertheless, can point to anecdotal evidence that the minimal due-process requirements imposed by the courts have given them the discretion and flexibility they need to maintain control of overcrowded institutions and to protect inmate and staff safety. It has been 30 years since the United States has witnessed a prison riot on the scale of the 1971 rebellion at New York's Attica Prison (33 inmates and 10 guards killed) or the 1980 riot at the Penitentiary of New Mexico in Santa Fe (33 inmates killed). That is reason enough, as far as prison officials are concerned, to go no further to protect the due process rights of prisoners.

Con: Arguments in Opposition to Limited Due Process

Prisoners and their advocates were disappointed by the *Wolff* holding and are even more disappointed by the Supreme Court's post-*Wolff* jurisprudence. In response to claims that minimizing inmate due process protections and the resulting tough disciplinary policies have helped to curb prison riots and other manifestations of inmate violence, they point out that dozens of major riots have taken place in recent years, although none resulted in as many fatalities as the Attica and New Mexico catastrophes. In fact, the longest prison riot in American history occurred in 1993 at the Southern Ohio Correctional Facility in Lucasville, Ohio. During an 11-day siege, nine inmates and one guard were killed. Ironically, this is the same prison that was at the center of another famous decision by the U.S. Supreme Court. In 1981's *Rhodes v. Chapman*, the Court rejected the claim that this prison's policy of double-celling—assigning two inmates to a 63-square-foot cell built to house only one inmate—violated the Cruel and Unusual Punishment Clause of the Eighth Amendment. This decision permitted the Lucasville prison to continue to house far more inmates than it was designed to accommodate, and when the riot occurred, 1,820 inmates were crammed into a facility built to max out at 1,540. The disciplinary regime at Lucasville was tightly run, as permitted by the loose standards of the *Wolff* line of cases. Arguably, it is more likely that one of the major causes of this riot was the pervasive overcrowding allowed by a Supreme Court decision favoring prison officials, not any loss of disciplinary control by prison officials.

Many legal scholars and social scientists believe that the Supreme Court's refusal to expand the due process rights of prisoners actually contributes to an atmosphere in which rule-breaking and violence are prevalent and rehabilitation efforts are fruitless. Arbitrary discipline and harsh punishments, it is argued, succeed only in confirming prisoners' perceptions of a hostile and unjust society, thereby making them more cynical about the intentions of authorities and discouraging them from participating in a meaningful way in rehabilitation programs. Similarly, disciplinary procedures viewed by inmates as unfair are likely to aggravate behavioral problems by spurring the anger, hostility, and contempt for the law that are inevitable by-products of rules, regulations, and punishments regarded as unreasonable and one-sided.

Social scientists have conducted studies that confirm what is generally known as the theory of procedural justice. When the procedures used to resolve disputes or charges of wrongdoing are both fair and perceived by the participants as fair, everyone involved, even those who disagree with or are disappointed in the outcome, are more likely to feel satisfied by the outcome and accept it as legitimate. In his seminal work *A Theory of Justice* (2005), political philosopher John Rawls discussed various notions of procedural justice at length and argued that both in a moral and practical sense, procedural justice was most likely to be achieved when a decision-maker or tribunal establishes independent criteria for reaching a fair and just outcome and then consistently follows these criteria to reach a decision. Studies have shown that both criminal defendants and civil litigants are more inclined to accept unfavorable verdicts when they feel that they have been given the chance to speak for themselves and confront opposing parties during a fair and transparent hearing held before and decided by an impartial judge or jury. An inmate accused of violating prison rules will be more inclined to accept the decision of a disciplinary hearing panel and less inclined to react with anger or retaliatory violence when he or she believes that the disciplinary process was truly fair.

Safer Prisons

Supporters of rights for prisoners also can point to recent studies finding that adding to the legal protections accorded prisoners leads to improved inmate behavior and fewer attacks on prison staff. Surveys of correctional administrators have found that many wardens believe that the demise of the hands-off doctrine, as well as the Supreme Court decisions that increased inmates' right of access to the courts, actually proved helpful in maintaining safe prisons. A surprising number of supervisory-level respondents acknowledged that prisoners who discovered that they could bring lawsuits to contest their convictions, sentences, or conditions of confinement were less likely to express their frustrations by provoking a violent confrontation with a guard or another inmate. Access to the courts arguably supplies a valuable outlet for inmates' stress and frustration. Many prison officials have conceded that prisoner legal assistance programs mandated by courts have led to a decrease in disciplinary problems and provided inmates with positive experiences that are conducive to rehabilitation programs.

Advocates of extending greater due process protection to prisoners charged with disciplinary violations also can cite a long tradition of sociological studies of prisons. Beginning with Donald Clemmer's 1940 classic *The Prison Community*, sociologists have demonstrated that prison discipline is maintained not by the total power and dominance of custodial officials, but through complicated informal relationships between guards and inmates. Guards typically refrain from strictly enforcing institutional regulations in exchange for the cooperation of inmate leaders in preventing widespread rulebreaking and major outbreaks of rebellion or violent protest. These findings cast doubt on the claim that minimizing inmate rights and inflexible administration of the rules are indispensable to the maintenance of safe prisons.

The Court's Inadequate Due Process Protections

Perhaps the most fundamental argument against the current state of the law as it pertains to the due process rights of prisoners is that it simply is not substantial enough to give prisoners a fair and full opportunity to contest arbitrary deprivations of their liberty and property by correctional officials. Although American courts have consistently emphasized that lawful confinement necessarily limits prisoners' entitlement to the full range of constitutional protections, the Fourteenth Amendment itself draws no distinction between the due process rights of those who are free and those who are incarcerated. Respect for the values underlying the U.S. Constitution, it is argued, should lead the courts to expand *Wolff* and its progeny to the point where inmates will have a realistic opportunity to mount a defense against serious accusations that can lead to harsh punishments.

Critics of the *Wolff* holding continue to press the same major argument advanced by Justices Marshall, Brennan, and Douglas in the *Wolff* dissenting opinions—that the rights of confrontation and cross-examination are indispensable to fairness in prison disciplinary hearings. If anything, these rights are just as crucial in the prison disciplinary context as in a criminal trial. Disciplinary hearings often turn on disputed questions of fact, and prisons by their very nature are places where witnesses may be motivated by vindictiveness, prejudice, or malice. Cross-examination thus is necessary not only to reveal such common human frailties as a faulty memory or a mistaken identification, but the very real possibility that a testifying inmate may be seeking revenge or that the guard filing the charges may primarily be concerned about vindicating his power and advancing his career. As Justice Marshall argued in his dissenting opinion, there may be some cases where it is vital to protect inmate informers by keeping their identity confidential. However, giving hearing board officers absolute and unfettered power to preserve the secrecy of all witnesses is unnecessary in the vast majority of cases where the accused inmate already knows the identity of the guard or guards who brought the charge against him. In these cases, shielding witnesses from confrontation and cross-examination does nothing more than deprive inmates of their only legitimate means of testing the believability of adverse witnesses.

Advocates of prisoners' rights also have been highly critical of the Supreme Court's post-*Wolff* decisions. In particular, the *Ponte* and *Hill* holdings in 1985 are viewed as weakening the few due-process protections secured in *Wolff*. *Ponte*, by permitting hearing board officials to refuse to explain why they would not allow an accused inmate to call defense witnesses unless and until the inmate successfully files a lawsuit about the issue, needlessly undermines due-process rights; aggravates tension between inmates and staff; and encourages more, not fewer, lawsuits. The *Hill* decision, permitting disciplinary boards to find inmates guilty merely on the basis of "some evidence," has been the target of a great deal of criticism by legal scholars. The "some evidence" standard of proof is the Court's lowest level of proof ever considered adequate to protect individuals' Fourteenth Amendment due process rights in administrative hearings, at which government officials seek to deprive a person of life, liberty, or property.

A few federal courts have refused to interpret *Hill* in a literal manner. In theory, the "some evidence" standard would support a guilty finding even if there were a one percent chance that the inmate was guilty. Yet, in 2001's *Broussand v. Johnson*, the U.S. Court of Appeals for the Fifth Circuit reversed a prison disciplinary committee's finding that an inmate was guilty of possession of contraband because the contraband was found in an area to which 100 inmates had access. However, the Seventh Circuit held in 1992 in *Hamilton v. O'Leary* that a 25 percent chance of guilt (contraband was found in a vent in a cell shared by four inmates) was more than enough to satisfy the "some evidence" standard.

Prisoners' rights supporters contend that the Supreme Court's unwillingness to go beyond (and willingness to lessen) the due-process regimen established for disciplinary purposes in *Wolff* is especially harmful in light of the Court's consistent holdings that prisoners have virtually no constitutionally protected due process rights in any other context of prison administration. For example, in the 1979 case of *Greenholtz v. Inmates of Nebraska Penal and Correctional Complex*, the Court ruled that the Fourteenth Amendment in and of itself provides no due process protection for parole-eligible inmates seeking a full and fair hearing before a parole board. Chief Justice Burger, writing for the Court, declared that parole is a privilege granted by the legislature, not a right protected by the Constitution and enforced by the courts. Parole release, he added, should not be confused with parole revocation, and it requires none of the protections mandated by *Morrissey* and *Gagnon*. Accordingly, states are free to abolish parole altogether and are obligated only to protect "state-created liberty interests"—the procedures that state legislatures are willing to make available to prisoners seeking parole. In the *Greenholtz* case, the Court held that there was no need to hold a formal hearing for every parole-eligible inmate, and no need for the Nebraska Parole Board to provide those denied parole with a statement of the reasons for denial.

Limited to Serious Punishment

The Supreme Court also has ruled that the limited due-process rights listed in *Wolff* apply only when a prisoner faces serious punishment as a result of an accusation that he has violated prison rules or regulations. Serious punishment, as defined by the aforementioned *Sandin v. Connor* decision, consists of the loss of "good time," more than 30 days in solitary confinement, or some other type of substantial or extraordinary penalty.

Since its 1976 decision in *Meachum v. Fano*, the Court has made it clear that a decision to transfer an inmate to a higher security prison with harsher conditions of confinement for purely administrative, not punitive, reasons is well within the discretion of prison officials and requires no Fourteenth Amendment safeguards. The only due-process protections available are the particular procedures, if any, that the state itself chooses to give prisoners in its statutes or administrative regulations. The Supreme Court has taken the same approach in cases where an inmate seeks to file suit to recover damages for the loss of liberty or noncontraband property caused by the negligence of prison officials.

In a controversial 1986 decision, *Daniels v. Williams*, Chief Justice Rehnquist authored a majority opinion that has been described as a major reinterpretation of the Fourteenth Amendment. In a case in which an inmate sought monetary damages for serious injuries (long understood as a loss of liberty in American jurisprudence) that resulted from a guard's negligence, Rehnquist's majority opinion asserted that the Due Process Clause protects prisoners only from deliberate or intentional deprivations of life, liberty, or property. Mere carelessness or negligence on the part of prison officials, he concluded, does not amount to a violation of prisoners' due-process rights. Thus, prisoners have no right to bring such a claim to a federal court. They may be able to file a due-process action in a state court, but only if the state has a statute that permits such lawsuits.

In short, as prisoners and prisoners' right advocates see it, *Wolff* and subsequent Supreme Court decisions have drastically limited the scope of due-process protections available to prisoners. These limitations, critics believe, are not necessary to the maintenance of prison discipline. Instead, they create resentment and frustration among inmates and undermine inmates' respect for authority and the potential for achieving rehabilitation. Prisons and jails can be managed effectively and made safer, according to supporters of inmate rights, without abrogating the due-process protections guaranteed by the Fourteenth Amendment.

See Also: 3. Cruel and Unusual Punishment; 6. Free Speech Rights of Prisoners; 8. Gangs and Violence in Prison; 9. Health Care and Medical Assistance for Prisoners; 10. Legal Assistance for Prisoners; 14. Prison Labor; 15. Prison Overcrowding; 18. Religious Rights.

Further Readings

Alpert, Geoffrey P., ed. *The Legal Rights of Prisoners*. Beverly Hills, CA: Sage, 1980.

Baxter v. Palmigiano, 425 U.S. 308 (1976).

Board of Pardons v. Allen, 482 U.S. 369 (1987).

Branham, Lynn S., and Michael S. Hamden. *The Law and Policy of Sentencing and Corrections*. St. Paul, MN: West Publishing, 2009.

Broussard v. Johnson, 253 F. 3d 874 (5th Cir. 2001).

Carlson, Peter M., and Judith Simon Garrett. *Prison and Jail Administration: Practice and Theory*. Sudbury, MA: Jones and Bartlett, 2008.

Clemmer, Donald. *The Prison Community*. New York: Holt, Rinehart and Winston, 1940.

Connecticut Board of Pardons v. Dumschat, 452 U.S. 458 (1981).

Conover, Ted. *Newjack: Guarding Sing Sing*. New York: Random House, 2000.

Cooper, Phillip J. *Hard Judicial Choices: Federal District Court Judges and State and Local Officials*. New York: Oxford University Press, 1988.

Daniels v. Williams, 474 U.S. 327 (1986).

DiIulio, John J. *Courts, Corrections, and the Constitution: The Impact of Judicial Intervention on Prisons and Jails*. New York: Oxford University Press, 1990.

Gagnon v. Scarpelli, 411 U.S. 778 (1973).

Greenholtz v. Inmates of Nebraska Penal and Correctional Complex, 442 U.S.1 (1979).

Hamilton v. O'Leary, 976 F. 2d 341 (7th Cir. 1992).

Harvard University Law School. "Two Views of a Prisoner's Right to Due Process: *Meachum v. Fano*." *Harvard Civil Rights and Civil Liberties Law Review*, v.12 (1977).

Hay, Bruce. "Procedural Justice—*Ex Ante vs. Ex Post*." *UCLA Law Review*, v.44 (1997).

Hewitt v. Helms, 459 U.S. 460 (1983).

Jackson, Michael. *Prisoners of Isolation: Solitary Confinement in Canada*. Toronto: University of Toronto Press, 1983.

Jacob, Sharif. "The Rebirth of *Morrissey*: Towards a Coherent Theory of Due Process for Prisoners and Parolees." *Hastings Law Journal*, v.57 (2006).

Kentucky Department of Corrections v. Thompson, 490 U.S. 454 (1989).

Martin, Steve J., and Sheldon Ekland-Olson. *Texas Prisons: The Walls Came Tumbling Down*. Austin, TX: Texas Monthly Press, 1987.

Matthews v. Eldridge, 424 U.S. 319 (1976).

McCool, Amy. "An Unbalanced Approach to Prisoners' Procedural Due Process Rights." *Creighton Law Review*, v.30 (1997).

Meachum v. Fano, 427 U.S. 215 (1976).

Merolli, Mark Adam. "*Sandin v. Connor's* 'Atypical and Significant Hardship' Signals the Demise of State-Created Liberty Interests for Prisoners." *St. Louis University Public Law Review*, v.15 (1995).

Morrissey v. Brewer, 408 U.S. 471 (1972).

Olim v. Wakinekona, 461 U.S. 238 (1983).

Pollock, Jocelyn M. *Prisons and Prison Life: Costs and Consequences*. Los Angeles: Roxbury, 2004.

Ponte v. Real, 471 U.S. 491 (1985).

Rawls, John. *A Theory of Justice: Original Edition*. Cambridge, MA: Harvard University Press, 2005.

Rhodes v. Chapman, 452 U.S. 337 (1981).

Sandin v. Connor, 515 U.S. 472 (1995).

Schmalleger, Frank, and John Ortiz Smykla. *Corrections in the 21st Century*. New York: McGraw-Hill, 2011.

Superintendent v. Hill, 472 U.S. 445 (1985).

Surrette, Robert A. "Drawing the Iron Curtain: Prisoners' Rights From *Morrissey v. Brewer* to *Sandin v. Connor*." *Chicago-Kent Law Review*, v.72 (1997).

Sykes, Gresham M. *The Society of Captives*. Princeton, NJ: Princeton University Press, 1958.

Werner, Tiffany A. "Is the Court Washing Its Hands of Prisoners' Due Process Rights?" *Seton Hall Law Review*, v.28 (1997).

Wilkinson v. Austin, 545 U.S. 209 (2005).

Wolff v. McDonnell, 418 U.S. 539 (1974).

5

Early Release

Danielle S. Rudes
Faye S. Taxman
George Mason University

arly release from prison is not as simple as the words *early* and *release* might suggest. Historical analysis of prison release policies and practices yields a wealth of penal thinking that dates back nearly 140 years. Part of the difficulty in discussing early release stems from the variety of types of release and the legal, political, and social contexts surrounding release decisions. Early release—also commonly called controlled release, conditional release, and/or discretionary release—is the discharge of a prison or jail inmate prior to the end of their legally imposed sentence. This includes (1) compassionate release, for terminally ill inmates who generally cannot care for themselves any longer; (2) parole or probation, which is discretionary or mandatory release to a period of post-incarceration supervision; (3) earned or discretionary release without post-release supervision; (4) exoneration, for a prisoner later found not guilty; (5) commutation or clemency, a governmental release without forgiving crime; and (6) pardon, a governmental release with crime forgiveness.

The History of Early Release

Founded in the Pennsylvania Quaker system under the guidance of William Penn, America's first prisons were designed to produce a reflection of sins and a recommitment to societal norms. Penitents entered penitentiaries to reform themselves during a pre-arranged length of stay (a flat sentence). At the end of their time, they were released under an assumption of repentance but without any formal assessment. Philadelphia's High Street Jail (1682) and Pennsylvania's Western (1818) and Eastern (1820) State Penitentiaries are good examples of these types of prisons. A slightly different penal ideology emerged out of New York's Auburn Prison (1816). Auburn worked on a step-model, where prisoners were initially isolated but were later allowed contact with other inmates. After a rash of suicides and other mental illnesses among inmates that many claimed erupted from sustained, forced isolation, Auburn switched to a system that allowed silent labor among other prisoners during the day and forced isolation only in the evenings. In both New York and Pennsylvania, inmates served the entire length of their sentence without any discretionary or early release.

Influenced by early prison reformers both inside and outside of the United States, early release developed as a result of the need for incentives within institutional environments. In the United States, good-time laws emerged as early as 1817 in New York State, when prison administrators began asking their state legislatures for a way to reward well-behaved inmates. By the mid-1800s, nearly half the states had good-time laws in place. Abroad, Captain Alexander Maconochie, the Scottish Warden of Norfolk Island—a notoriously rough Australian prison—developed the mark system, where inmates could earn their freedom early through hard work and good behavior. At the same time, Sir Walter Crofton, director of an Irish prison, began to question how penitentiaries were achieving repentance if inmates were never ascribed this status and given release as reward. Crofton developed what he called "the Irish system," where inmates progressed through various custody stages from solitary confinement, to group work, and finally to a type of halfway house where they reestablished relations with their community. If prisoners completed the stages successfully, they were said to have earned a "ticket of leave." Crofton took his version of early release a step further by having community members supervise former inmates post-incarceration as a component of their conditional release.

A Declaration of Principles

As prison populations rose dramatically in the United States during the late 1800s and early 1900s, American prison administrators began implementing some of these early release ideas in their institutions. In the 1860s,

Reverend Enoch Wines and Theodore Dwight were commissioned by a private watchdog group to inspect American and Canadian prisons. They wrote a *Report on the Prisons and Reformatories of the United States and Canada* in 1867, chronicling the problems with both countries' prison systems and declaring that there was no reform occurring anywhere. With American outcry over this report's findings, Wines formed an international conference on prison reform, which met in Cincinnati in 1870. The group, the National Congress on Penitentiary and Reformatory Discipline, included delegates from 24 states. Various prison reformers in the United States and abroad (including Crofton) discussed reintroducing reform as the primary goal of prison. From this meeting, the group drafted a Declaration of Principles that outlined correctional policies for years to come. Some of their principles called for training and education within prison and putting an end to contract labor. They advocated using a medical model approach to inmates, suggesting that prison was a place to treat the illness of criminality. The declaration also demanded the use of a mark system so prisoners could earn release. These reformers also suggested that determinate sentences (fixed) should replace indeterminate (discretionary) ones for the sake of fairness.

Following the National Congress, New York State was the first to pass a law limiting judicial discretion on sentencing for youth offenders, noting that prison officials would "mark" the youths once they had been incarcerated. Ohio enacted America's first parole system in 1885, whereby inmates could receive early release at the discretion of prison officials. By the 1920s, 47 states (except Florida, Mississippi, and Virginia) had parole systems designed as indeterminate sentences, and nearly half of all releases were made by parole boards. As indeterminate sentencing systems developed, community reentry and reintegration became a primary goal of prison custody.

Indeterminate Sentencing Systems and Truth-in-Sentencing

Sentencing structures state-to-state—albeit indeterminate or determinate—are intricately linked with early-release decisions. Historically, flat or determinate sentences were used by criminal justice agencies to impose and maintain strict or complete sentences on offenders. A determinate sentencing system provides offenders with a release date at the time of judicial sentencing. Inmates are expected to serve their entire sentence and are released upon completion. In contrast, indeterminate sentencing removes some sentencing discretion from judges and relocates it to parole or probation boards and prison officials. In this system, judges give offenders a range of years they will serve in custody for their offense. Then, inmates can earn early release through good behavior and/or participation in prison programs such as education, training, and therapy or treatment. Parole or probation boards make discretionary decisions on a case-by-case basis for individual offenders. Early release, with the exception of conditional release or exoneration, is possible in an indeterminate sentencing system via a parole board or in a determinate sentencing system combined with good-time policies. Today, though most states maintain indeterminate sentencing structures, at least 16 states have abolished discretionary parole release (mostly during the 1980s tough-on-crime years), and two states—Virginia and Maine—have abolished post-release supervision via parole altogether. State policies like mandatory minimums, three-strikes, life without parole (LWOP), and truth-in-sentencing are all examples of determinate sentencing structures.

As a mechanism of controlling or curtailing early discharge from custody, truth-in-sentencing (TIS) is a crime policy intricately linked with early-release decisions. TIS emerged in 1994 as part of the Violent Crime Control and Law Enforcement Act under President Bill Clinton. This program tied federal funding for prison building and maintenance to state policies, mandating that inmates must serve 85 percent of their imposed sentence. As states adopted TIS laws to ensure federal funding, early-release options became more limited in both determinate and indeterminate sentencing states. In the years since TIS was introduced, studies have consistently shown increases in state prison spending, increases in amount of time served, and little or no significant reduction in crime within states that have adopted all or partial TIS policies.

For some, early release is a back-end solution to a broad and critical social problem. For others, early release represents a counter-solution to the just-deserts model, arguing that inmates should only remain incarcerated until they are ready and able to return to their communities and remain crime free.

Pro: Arguments in Favor of Early Release Programs

Proponents of early release argue six main positive effects. They contend that early release: saves money, relieves overcrowding, increases motivation and incentives for inmates in custodial environments, decreases inmate violence, decreases opportunities for criminogenic effects in prison, and allows innovation. However, despite these common themes, supporters of early release do not holistically agree on how release decisions should be made, by and for whom they should be made, and under what guidelines and rules.

Prison Cost Savings

First among the most popular arguments for early release is the possible cost savings afforded by letting some offenders out of prison early. States typically spend nearly 10 times more to incarcerate an average inmate than to keep them in the community on parole or probation supervision. For example, in California in the 2000s, it cost the state roughly $40,000 to supervise an inmate in a medium-security correctional institution for one year, but approximately $4,000 to supervise that same offender in the community on parole. Proponents of early release contend that the value of this cost savings cannot be understated. In times of economic recession, states look for ways to balance budgets more fervently than in more prosperous years. The economics of early release present a powerful ally to politicians and lawmakers who are sorely in need of spending reductions during tight economic times.

Lowering Prison Populations

Following the "tough on crime" sentiment of the 1980s and 1990s, the resulting prison boom yielded an unprecedented increase in prison populations. America saw the number of prisoners quadruple after 1980, regardless of increases or decreases in crime rates. Today, with over 2.3 million in custody in the United States and a large portion of institutions at or above maximum capacity, correctional administrators and politicians are looking for ways to whittle down those numbers. This desire stems not only from financial concerns, but also from safety concerns, such as increased potential for riots, violence, passage of communicable diseases, and from sheer space issues. Well past double bunking, several states are now quadruple bunking in common areas of their prisons that were once used for exercise and eating, such as gymnasiums and cafeterias. One prison in southern California even reported, via local news media, that they temporarily housed some inmates on an outdoor basketball court during the spring and summer months when they had exhausted all available space inside their institution. As such, early release presents a viable option for reducing the number of persons behind bars.

Early release not only releases a number of inmates before their sentence expires, it also limits the number of inmates that other inmates can converse with and potentially learn from. Numerous studies have suggested a criminogenic effect in prisons, whereby offenders learn new crimes and/or hone their crime-related skills in the company of other inmates. When inmates are exposed to large numbers of other criminals for an extended period of time, they often learn or hone their skills in ways that are not only ultimately detrimental to themselves, but also to the community at large. For example, a bank robber can learn new tricks and techniques from a more experienced or polished bank robber within the same institution, or an inmate incarcerated for drug-related crimes can learn better ways to fool urine drug tests from other, more experienced inmates. Early release limits the number of offenders within prison, which in turn decreases the number of potential networks inmates can make while incarcerated.

Improved Behavior

Early release supporters suggest that the very possibility of shaving some time off a prison sentence is enough to motivate inmates to better themselves and/or behave better while in custody. They argue that when institutions provide fair and sound incentives to inmates, many inmates will work toward their release in ways that will benefit them and their communities exponentially. For example, some studies suggest that inmates trying to earn their release are more likely to attend in-custody drug or alcohol treatment programs. They are also more likely to participate in correctional employment; pre-release planning; therapeutic justice courses such as anger management, parenting skills, and victimology; and job training and other educational opportunities, such as skills training and high school or college courses. All of these courses and trainings have the potential for helping offenders reintegrate back into their communities post-release. Additionally, they also increase overall cooperation within social control environments.

In addition, the old adage "idle hands are the devil's work" may have some bearing within prison environments, where boredom and lack of structured activity often leads inmates to make poor choices. Through regular and sustained activity motivated by early release, inmates can increase their self-perception and self-worth while also staying busy. This leaves them less time for engaging in unproductive activities such as fighting, sexual misconduct, property damage, and use of illegal substances.

Innovation and Technological Advances

Finally, early release contributes to innovation within prison environments. Technological advances in electronic and GPS monitoring as well as developments in home-confinement strategies often emerge as a derivative of early-release programs. Despite popular opinion, early release is not synonymous with free and clear. Released offenders are commonly supervised post-release via probation or parole by means of probation or parole officers and/or via equipment-based supervision. Early release then can be said to drive innovation, as supervised release strives to develop new ways to manage released offenders using sound, yet cost-saving means.

Despite these potential benefits, proponents of early release do not fall into one unified group, and research on early release shows positive effects in a variety of different early release schemes. One study in Washington State showed that early release coupled with work release yielded some positive results. Others argue for coupling Intensive Supervision Programs (ISP) with early release, pointing to a decrease in the number and seriousness of criminal activity when the two were used simultaneously. Most early release supporters argue for the use of risk-assessment tools and instruments in conjunction with early release programs.

Some take this a step further, including both static (unchangeable factors such as demographic factors and criminal history) with dynamic factors (changeable factors such as gang affiliation and treatment program participation) in any risk-assessment protocol. Likewise, early-release advocates assert that release is not risk-free at any time. Predicting the possibility of criminal activity is the stuff of science fiction, but not real life. Keeping an inmate in custody for some additional number of days is unlikely to be the one factor that makes a difference in the majority of recidivism cases. Some scholars and practitioners suggest that less concern should be placed on the timing of release, but rather on what is being done pre- and post-release to help offenders successfully reintegrate within their communities, ultimately lowering the likelihood that they will reengage in criminal activity. Preventing future crime may not be dependent on a release date. Rather, the preparation for and support during release may be what matters most.

Con: Arguments Against Early Release

The most powerful argument against early release is recidivism. Richard Allen Davis, the man who raped and murdered Polly Klaas in California in 1993, is one of many important examples for early-release naysayers. While Davis's extremely violent crime draws attention for its horror, other more symbolic, political, and/or emotional denials of early release also make it seem like a risky proposition. Famous athletes like Michael Vick, the NFL star convicted of illegal dog fighting, and infamous murders like Susan Atkins—one of the Manson family girls convicted of several murders—have publicly been denied early release on a variety of grounds, and Americans have largely supported these decisions. At its core, then, public safety is a primary argument against early release, and one that fits well with the legacy of incapacitation and tough punishment laws and policies that have reigned in the United States for the past several decades, and continue today. In various states and the federal system, there are several examples of policies and practices guarding against early release: (1) New Jersey's No Early Release Act of 1996, (2) the amendment to the Federal Compassionate Release Law to include the words "extraordinary and compelling circumstances," and (3) the condition that early release is not to be used with LWOP. Each case provides a good example of recent justice tightening coupled with a lower tolerance for repeat offenders. In support of these claims, some prior studies have noted some increase in criminal activity among early-released cohorts (as compared to control groups), though this varies dramatically from one locale to another.

Risk of Public Safety

Early-release opponents take direct aim at the cost-savings arguments presented by early-release advocates, noting that risking community safety to save money is both morally and socially wrong. They suggest that early release is a direct slight to victims of crimes who thought the offenders in their cases would be summarily punished, but in fact are given a second chance before the completion of their court-imposed punishment. Additionally, further crime and the legal infrastructure it takes to detect, try, convict and reincarcerate for these crimes may lead to more time, money, and additional resources than keeping them in custody.

Subsequently, there are two additional reasons opponents frequently cite when disputing early release. First, some scholars and criminal justice professionals contend that early release lowers both the specific (among offenders) and general (among the noncriminal public) deterrent effects of incarceration, arguing that early release is a form of reward for bad behavior. They suggest that releasing an offender prior to the end of their imposed sentence contributes to recidivism, subsequently putting public safety at risk. Second, politicians often view early release as political suicide. Take for example, the 1988 presidential election candidacy of Michael Dukakis.

When the now-infamous Willie Horton case came to light during his campaign, Willie Horton, while serving a life sentence for murder without the possibility of parole, was released on a weekend work furlough (a form of early release) in Massachusetts, on a program Dukakis had argued was rehabilitative. He did not return after his release, and while out, he committed rape, robbery, and armed assault. Dukakis saw his political capital plummet and abandoned any hope of becoming president. Though cost savings and rehabilitative and humanitarian goals are important to politicians, when it concerns prisoners, the only successful stance in recent decades has been one that includes a tough-on-crime message.

Conclusion

There are no easy answers to questions raised by both proponents and opponents of early release. On one hand, if the primary goal is to keep communities safe, violent offenders might never be released. On the other hand, if it is considered important to lower recidivism, violent offenders such as murderers might be the first ones that are released, as they often have extremely low recidivism rates due to their propensity toward heat-of-passion crimes that usually occur once in a lifetime.

Throughout the U.S. prison system (both state and federal), over 90 percent of inmates are released back into their communities. This may occur with or without parole board approval as inmates earn their way out or max out of penal institutions. Noting the words of criminologist Jeremy Travis, "but they all come back," early release or prison release at any point is a controversial and challenging issue.

See Also: 2. Clemency; 7. Furlough and Work Release Programs; 11. Life Sentence; 15. Prison Overcrowding; 17. Punishment Versus Rehabilitation.

Further Readings

Austin, James. "Using Early Release to Relieve Prison Crowding: A Dilemma in Public Policy." *Crime and Delinquency*, v.32 (1986).
Giertz, J. Fred, and Peter F. Nardulli. "Prison Overcrowding." *Public Choice*, v.46 (1985).

Morris, Norris, and David J. Rothman, eds. *The Oxford History of the Prison: The Practice of Punishment in Western Society.* New York: Oxford University Press, 1995.

Petersilia, Joan. *When Prisoners Come Home: Parole and Prisoner Reentry.* New York: Oxford University Press, 2003.

Pilato, Stacey L. "New Jersey's No Early Release Act: A Band-Aid Approach to Victim's Pain and Recidivism." *Seton Hall Legislative Journal* (1997–98).

Sims, B., and J. O'Connell. "Early Release: Prison Overcrowding and Public Safety Implications." National Institute of Justice (NCJ 098130) paper, 1985.

Steiner, Benjamin D., William J. Bowers, and Austin Sarat. "Folk Knowledge as Legal Action: Death Penalty Judgments and the Tenet of Early Release in a Culture of Mistrust and Punitiveness." *Law and Society Review*, v.33/2 (1999).

Travis, Jeremy. *But They All Come Back: Facing the Challenges of Prisoner Reentry.* Washington, DC: Urban Institute Press, 2005.

Travis, Jeremy, and Joan Petersilia. "Reentry Reconsidered: A New Look at an Old Problem." *Crime and Delinquency*, v.47/3 (2001).

Wooten, James. "Truth in Sentencing—Why States Should Make Violent Criminals Do Their Time." *University of Dayton Law Review,* v.20 (1994–95).

6

Free Speech Rights of Prisoners

Julie A. Beck
California State University, East Bay

Freedom of speech, religion, and freedom from arbitrary punishment are among the basic established rights of U.S. prisoners, but they have not always been. Prisoners' rights were won in the United States as a result of decades of struggle within the prisons, through social movements, and in the courts. There are many countries where rights to free speech for prisoners are not recognized and inmates are punished for speaking out, such as China, Egypt, Libya, and Cuba. Conversely, prisoners in Europe, Canada, and the United States have gained certain rights to free speech. Human rights in general are essential for all human beings, including those who are incarcerated. Globally and in the United States, the battle over prisoners' free speech rights continues.

Because the United States relies on imprisonment far more heavily than most other countries, it has a rich history of social and legal discourse surrounding prisoners' freedom of speech rights. The First Amendment to the U.S. Constitution protects freedom of expression such that the government cannot censor speech based on the content of this speech alone. Rather, speech can only be limited by the place, time, and manner it is exercised. However, prisoners are not afforded all of the rights of nonincarcerated free citizens. Their First Amendment rights are more limited, and prison authorities can restrict and even ban certain kinds of literary content entering and leaving prisons, including restricting correspondence among inmates, through the Internet, and with the media. While prisoners do possess constitutional rights, these rights are balanced with the security interests of individual prison administrations.

The free speech rights of prisoners have evolved since the earliest 19th-century U.S. prisons, where prisoners enjoyed virtually no rights of free speech; in fact, they were forbidden to speak at all, and a regimen of absolute silence was imposed inside prisons. Prior to the 1970s, in the absence of active federal court involvement regarding prisoners' First Amendment rights to speech, the treatment of prisoners and the administration of prisons were left almost completely up to prison officials. In the mid-1970s, however, within the context of the social movements of the era, including the prison reform movement, the U.S. Supreme Court passed a landmark decision affecting prisoners' First Amendment rights. This marked the beginning of an era of Court involvement in prisoners' rights of free speech, including rights to access the media, which courts have ruled must be balanced with prison security. The course of progress toward more rights for prisoners has not been linear. Instead, it has been filled with gains and losses, often dictated by the changing composition of the Supreme Court. From the mid-1970s through the 1980s, Supreme Court decisions have significantly curtailed, though not completely revoked, prisoners' speech rights.

American society has gained an increasing recognition of prisoner free-speech rights, which have been brought to light by several key federal court decisions. Within the struggle for free speech rights, prisoner rebellions and responses by prison officials have been a significant factor. Specific areas of free speech that have been examined include: correspondence among prisoners and with the media; access to books and other written materials, including indirect interfacing with the Internet; the prison press (prison newspapers); the right to provide legal advice to fellow inmates; and the right to redress grievances in federal court. Finally, there are pro and con positions within current debates over free speech rights for prisoners, which illustrate the tenuous balance between free speech rights for prisoners and prison security and safety concerns.

From Imposed Silence to First Amendment Protections

Freedom of speech for prisoners is a relatively recent development. Auburn Prison, established in 1816 as the first state prison in New York, imposed a regimen of absolute silence at all times. Prisoners possessed no rights to speak whatsoever, neither among themselves nor with prison guards or other officials. In addition, extreme isolation in the form of solitary confinement for all prisoners was mandated at all times. Prisoners could also be subjected to physical punishment. As a result of this extreme deprivation of human speech and communication, if was not uncommon for prisoners to eventually go mad: prisoners at Auburn frequently suffered from mental illness, including depression, and there was a high incidence of suicide. Later, the Auburn policy of isolation through solitary confinement was reformed such that prisoners could work and eat together in a common area of the prison, but they were still required to go through their day and otherwise function in complete silence.

Later, in 1829, the Eastern Penitentiary System was opened in Pennsylvania. This new prison promoted extreme isolation and silence, but with no communal work and dining areas like those at Auburn. The radial floor plan prevented inmates from seeing each other in the surrounding cells. This extreme lack of human contact and correspondence among prisoners, including with anyone outside the prison, like at Auburn, led to mental illness among the inmates. The regimen of silence in the Pennsylvania System, like the Quaker-based Auburn System, was influenced by religious beliefs, the idea that such austere practices would offer the prisoners the time and the motivation to reflect upon their crimes and to repent for them (hence the term *penitentiary*). Eventually, the Auburn "congregate" prison system, where prisoners were housed in separate cells but could eat together and were forced to work together in silence, was favored as the U.S. model of incarceration. The general code of silence in prisons had eventually been lifted. By 1913, The Eastern Pennsylvania Prison had switched to the congregate prison model until it closed in 1971.

During the wide-scale social movements of the 1960s and 1970s, such as the civil rights movement, prisoners also experienced gains in civil rights. Their speech rights were broadened and improvements were made in prison conditions, such as the introduction of rehabilitation programs and college classes into the prisons. Many of these reforms were influenced by the emergence of a prisoners' rights movement and by the federal courts' new commitment to hearing cases about prison issues.

Today, in addition to basic speech privileges, such as the ability to converse among themselves and telephone calls to family members, prisoners have some rights to offer each other legal help ("jailhouse lawyers"); are permitted to correspond in writing with individuals outside the prison; can operate prison presses; and within limits, may correspond with reporters and the media. Prisoners' free speech rights also include access to courts. These rights allow them to redress grievances and to establish new rights, including access to adequate medical care; broader access to the press; better treatment by correctional officers; and amelioration of prison overcrowding, among other demands. Prisoners' free speech rights have played an important role in bringing about prison program improvements, including rehabilitation and education programs, which decrease recidivism.

Politicized Prisoners and Free Speech Rights

Between 1969 and 1972, there was also a series of prison rebellions or riots led by prisoners. Of the many prison rebellions that occurred, five attracted considerable media attention: the riots at Attica prison in New York, Leavenworth prison in Texas, San Quentin Prison in California; and prison uprisings in Michigan and New Mexico. Prisoners demanded better prison conditions, protesting an array of problems inside the prisons, including brutality by guards, inadequate healthcare, arbitrary punishments, and the disproportionate numbers of incarcerated people of color.

The largest and bloodiest prison riot took place in Attica Prison in New York in 1971, when unarmed prisoners led protests inside the prison, took guards hostage, and set up negotiations over a list of written demands for prison reforms, which they presented to the commissioner of correctional services. These included the demand to improve prison conditions, which they described as "degrading." The prisoners' unarmed takeover of the prison and failed negotiation attempts lasted for four days before Governor Nelson Rockefeller sent in state troopers and corrections officers, who carried tear gas and rifles into the prison; this offensive resulted in the deaths of 29 prisoners and 10 prison guards.

After the Attica rebellion (and a subsequent class-action lawsuit by prisoners over increased brutality toward prisoners in retaliation for the uprising), reforms were instituted in prisons across the country. Among these was the introduction of more rehabilitation programs and college classes in prisons. University professors typically volunteered to teach these classes, which were often originated by prisoners. The new prison education programs exposed inmates to academic and political ideas, including racial oppression and improving prison conditions. In Leavenworth Federal Penitentiary, for example, prisoners started a prison newspaper and a political organization, and advocated for a cultural studies class. In addition, literature and pamphlets from outside social movements circulating in the prisons helped forge a sense of connection for many prisoners for African American and Hispanic rights.

The U.S. Supreme Court's new willingness to hear cases concerning prisoners' rights might be understood within this context of the social movements of the 1960s and 1970s, which were characterized by a surge in politicized demands for prisoners' rights, both by inmates and outside the prisoner-rights movement. The federal courts' traditional "hands off" policy toward prisons had entailed leaving problems regarding prison administration, including issues of prisoners' free speech, out of the courts and up to prison authorities. However, between 1964 and about 1984, the hands-on doctrine came into effect when the Supreme Court began to rule on the issue of prisoners' First Amendment rights. The Court sought to balance the freedom of speech of prisoners with the government's interest in maintaining security in prisons. The Courts' new hands-on approach, which was reflected in a series of rulings surrounding the First Amendment, in effect determined that prisoners do not forfeit all constitutional protections, even if they do not possess the full range of freedoms as free citizens. The Supreme Court emphasized that the goal of prison security should be balanced with First Amendment rights stated in the U.S. Constitution, thus setting a precedent for free speech rights for prisoners.

Legal Developments in Free Speech Rights of Prisoners

In the landmark *Procunier v. Martinez* decision in 1974, the Supreme Court abandoned its hands-off policy with regard to prisons and First Amendment rights of prisoners, and ruled on the issue of censorship of prison mail. Prisoner plaintiffs claimed that prison authorities had restricted mail in a way that was aimed at suppression of inmate complaints and of what prison officials perceived to be inflammatory political and other opinions. The Supreme Court ruled that such regulations on the part of the prison administration were overly broad and unconstitutional. Invoking the First Amendment rights of inmates, coupled with the full free-speech rights of those outside of prison who wished to communicate with prisoners, the Court barred prison authorities from censoring prison mail—both incoming and outgoing—even in cases where prison officials believed this mail to be inappropriate, to be complaining, to express inflammatory views, or to defame prison officials. That is, any regulation of mail, the ruling stated, must not be aimed at the suppression or censorship of prisoners' opinions or other kinds of expression. The Court also required a high standard of justification by the prison for regulation (or censorship) of mail, such that any regulation of mail must be shown to further an important or substantial government interest of security, order, and rehabilitation, and must involve an infringement on First Amendment rights no greater than is necessary or essential to the protection of the particular governmental interest involved.

This landmark decision was favorable to prisoners' First Amendment rights to free speech. Within the framework of this decision, however, prison authorities were also left with significant discretionary power to adopt institutional policies regarding speech rights that accorded with the maintenance of security and order in the prison. The pendulum would swing backward in the courts on the issue of the free speech rights of prisoners in the years and decades that followed.

Correspondence Between Prisoners and With the Media

In the same year that *Procunier* was decided, the Supreme Court also upheld a California state regulation prohibiting personal interviews between media personnel and individual, named inmates (*Pell v. Procunier*, 1974). This ruling was also extended to federal prisons that same year. The ruling held that prisoners and news reporters have no explicitly stated First Amendment right to face-to-face interviews if the media has alternative means of obtaining information about prison policies and conditions (for example, through the mail, or talking to attorneys or family members who visit inmates). Favoring the government's interest in prison security, the Court argued that the security interest of the prison and the possibility of exploitation of media access by certain prisoners justified restraining media access.

Several years later, in a case that involved controversy over conditions of incarceration, specifically over solitary confinement in the security housing unit (SHU) inside the prison (*Houchins v. KQED*, 1978), a television broadcaster sued for access to the prison. The prison in question had barred the press from entering the prison, restricting all opportunity for the press to talk to the inmates and all tours of the controversial SHU. The Supreme Court sided with the prison authorities' interest in prison security, ruling that the media have no special rights of access to the prison in question above those of the general public. In another important ruling (*Turner v. Safley*, 1987), the Court upheld Missouri prison regulations that barred certain kinds of correspondence between inmates, but it struck down a prohibition on inmate marriages. The Court used a lesser standard of review than in that past; the question would now concern whether regulations by prison authorities were reasonably (as opposed to substantially) related to a legitimate penological interest. One factor determining the reasonableness of a prison restriction is the presence of alternative means of exercising a given right.

Incoming Books and Prison Newspapers

A series of rulings would allow prisons to restrict written materials entering the prison using the reasonable standard—that is, if prison authorities believed they posed a reasonably (rather than substantially) threat to the prison's penological goals and to prison security. For example, in 1989, the Court ruled that while inmates were still allowed to subscribe to or receive periodicals or books without prior approval, wardens were now permitted to reject incoming items that they deemed detrimental to institutional security, order, or discipline. In addition, any item excluded could be excluded entirely (as opposed to only certain segments of the material). These regulations were upheld as being reasonably related to legitimate penological interests (*Thornburg v. Abbott,* 1989).

Earlier, the Supreme Court had barred inmates in a North Carolina prison from holding labor union meetings and from receiving or distributing packets of union publications that had been mailed in bulk (*Jones v. North Carolina Prisoners' Labor Union,* 1977). The Court also upheld a ruling that forbade inmates in New York City from receiving hardbound books from sources other than publishers, book clubs, and bookstores, finding this to be a reasonable response to prison officials' belief that hardbound books could be used more easily than paperback books and magazines for smuggling contraband items into the prison, and therefore posed a security threat. In sum, prisoners' First Amendment rights can be limited for security purposes. Both incoming and outgoing mail and literature can be restricted to different degrees, and prison officials may deny many types and sources of reading materials.

Prison authorities are also permitted to edit and censor, to a certain degree, the prison press. Prison newspapers, written and edited by inmates, have been permitted in prisons despite the authoritarian nature of the prison institution. However, the prison press has been a source of tension between inmates and prison authorities. The struggle has centered on whether and to what extent prison authorities can regulate the content of prison newspapers. Federal and state courts have generally sought to protect the content of prison newspapers and magazines insofar as it does not disrupt the prison administrations' interest in prison security, order, and rehabilitation. For example, when the prison administration halted publication of *The Luparar,* a prison newspaper published by inmates at the Vermont State Prison, claiming that it attacked prison officials' personalities, the Vermont district court ruled that the newspaper did not threaten any legitimate penological objectives; it allowed the prison to limit the newspaper's content only insofar as these restrictions were no broader than necessary to protect a legitimate penological interest. Later, a U.S. appeals court also supported inmates' First Amendment rights to speech, stating that censoring the content of prison newspapers violates the First Amendment. The ruling also required that a newspaper review board that included inmate input should be created.

However, the courts have also left much discretion up to prison officials to regulate newspaper content. For instance, in this latter decision, the court did not specify where the line would be drawn between what is inflammatory and what is dangerous to prison administration or security. Overall, judicial responses to the prison press have been inconsistent. Courts have tended to grant much discretion to prison authorities through newspaper review boards. For example, when prisoners challenged the censoring of an inmate magazine, a federal court held that the free speech rights exercised in this prison publication could disrupt prison order or interfere with the penological objectives of the prison (*Pittman v. Hutto,* 1979). However, in another case in which inmates challenged the constitutionality of prior review of prison newspaper content, a Virginia district court limited the prison review board's ability to censor speech in the prisons' newspaper except in cases where it might lead to violence, including interracial violence (*Burk v. Levi,* 1975).

When inmates challenged prison authorities' ban of a cartoon and a photograph in a prison newspaper (*Huston v. Pulley,* 1984), the California Court of Appeal held that since neither item could be found obscene or a threat to prison security, the ban deprived inmates of their First Amendment free-speech rights. The California Supreme Court ruled in favor of an inmate editor of the *Soledad Star* when he challenged Soledad prison officials' rejection of two articles they believed to be an attack on the prison administration. The court held that prison authorities cannot suppress or censor newspaper content written by prisoners simply because they disagree with it, if the prisoner is criticizing the prison's policy, or because they are seeking to avoid discussion of controversial topics. However, it also held that they may continue to regulate prison newspaper content or ban publications they perceived to be a threat to prison security (*Bailey v. Loggins,* 1982).

While these courts have maintained that prisoners cannot be denied their First Amendment rights to speech, they have also left prison authorities with broad powers to exercise suppression of prison newspapers in the interest of maintaining prison order and security.

Jailhouse Lawyers and Access to the Courts

The First Amendment free-speech rights of prisoners also include legal correspondence and filing grievances in court. Most attorney–client correspondence, including mail related to prisoners' rights to access the courts, cannot be limited. However, legal correspondence between inmates may be restricted. jailhouse lawyers are inmates seeking to assist fellow convicts with legal issues surrounding their cases. The extent to which prisoners can offer legal assistance to fellow inmates is generally left up to individual prison administrations' estimation of whether such speech or information poses a reasonable threat to the security interests and penological aims of the prison. Inmates can also be prevented from consulting with one another without prior approval. In 2001, a prisoner in Montana brought a lawsuit against the state, claiming that restrictions against providing legal assistance to fellow inmates violated his First Amendment rights (*Shaw v. Murphy,* 2001). The Supreme Court decided that legal correspondence was similar to regular prisoner-to-prisoner communication, and that jailhouse lawyers' correspondence with fellow inmates could be limited if the restriction imposed by prison officials was reasonably related to legitimate and neutral government objectives, such as prison security.

A related issue is the ability of prisoners to seek redress in court for complaints and to file lawsuits that challenge their conditions of confinement. Such legal challenges by inmates include media access, medical care, physical abuse, conditions of solitary confinement, and unfair punishment. As early as 1964 (*Cooper v. Pate*), the Court opened the way for prisoners to petition federal courts about conditions of confinement, which led to a key ruling in 1970. In *Holt v. Sarver*, the Court responded to prisoners' complaints about prison conditions by ruling that conditions inside the Arkansas penitentiary system, "in overall effect," constituted cruel and unusual punishment. However, within 25 years of this decision, the right of prisoners to exercise free speech through seeking redress for complaints or injury in court had been vastly curtailed. With the passage of the Prison Litigation Reform Act (1996 and 2001) by Congress, prisoners are now required to exhaust all prison remedies before filing a petition in federal court. In addition, inmates would have to pay federal filing fees (unless they were paupers), limits on awards of attorneys' fee were imposed, and judges were permitted to dismiss what they deemed frivolous lawsuits. The decision also bars prisoners from suing federal governments for mental or emotional injury, unless there is also physical injury.

In sum, since the 1970s, the courts have begun to establish First Amendment speech rights for prisoners, stating that prisoners should possess rights to free speech unless the speech poses a reasonable threat to the penological goals of the prison and prison security. Although many of prisoners' rights to free speech have been significantly restricted since the 1974 *Procunier v. Martinez* decision, they have not been altogether eliminated. In addition, there is an established precedent of prisoners' free speech rights today.

Current debates about the pros and cons of free speech for prisoners center on the nature and extent of prisoners' First Amendment rights. Recent struggles over free speech rights of prisoners have focused on press and Internet access, including the right of prisoner advocacy groups to post the stories and pen-pal requests of prisoners on the Internet. Opponents of broad rights of free speech for prisoners hold that such speech rights threaten prison security and can retraumatize crime victims. On the other hand, civil rights attorneys, prisoner rights advocates, and prisoners' family members argue that free speech rights are necessary in order to maintain inmates' constitutional rights and to expose substandard and criminally negligent prison conditions and abuses.

Pro: Arguments in Support of Free Speech for Prisoners

Advocates of unrestricted free speech for prisoners hold that because prisons are hidden from the public's view and access, freedom of speech for inmates is a crucial vehicle both for exposing civil rights violations and abuses inside prisons as well as for information-sharing between inmates and outside organizations seeking to reform prisons. The voices of prisoners through writings and press interviews can also help to dispel stereotypes about prisoners. Overall, proponents of broadening prisoners' First Amendment free-speech rights claim that these rights to free speech should only be limited in cases where they could pose a legitimate security threat to the prison.

Exposing Neglect and Abuse

Proponents argue that restrictions on prisoners' free speech cover up negligent and abusive conditions in prisons. For example, in the mid 1990s, inmates and prison reform organizations filed the *Shumate v. Wilson* class-action lawsuit against the California Department of Corrections and Rehabilitation (CDCR), exposing gross medical neglect inside two California women's prisons. The history of abuses documented in the lawsuit included neglect by prison doctors and prison officials that caused the death of inmates who had easily treatable illnesses. Retaliation by guards for prisoners complaining about mistreatment, or for simply seeking medical care, was also documented. In one instance, a letter written by a woman prisoner exposing mistreatment was smuggled out of Chowchilla Women's Prison by a guard who hoped for justice. This prompted an investigation of medical neglect by the press and attorneys.

The exposure of criminal neglect in these women's prisons through prisoners' letters and complaints, as well as by the media, prompted Human Rights Watch and Amnesty International, as well as news reporter Ted Koppel, to come to California to investigate other forms of human rights abuses in the state's prisons, including conditions of solitary confinement at another women's prison. Unprecedented legislative hearings held inside one of the women's prisons in 2000 were also scheduled, in which female inmates could offer additional testimony to legislators, reporters, and the media. The result of this and other lawsuits filed by men's prisons was a federal court order mandating federal oversight of healthcare in California's prisons. Advocates of free speech rights for prisoners argue that the medical neglect in California prisons would have remained a secret if correspondence between inmates had been suppressed. Civil rights advocates argue that the Shumate case, among many others, attests to the need for prisoners' unhindered access to the media, public forums, and the courts.

Access to News Media and Literature

Civil liberties groups and prisoners' rights organizations also argue that restricting inmates' access to the press and radio is a way to silence politically outspoken prisoners such as death row inmate Mumia Abu Jamal (born Wesley Cook). A writer, former Black Muslim Nationalist, and outspoken prison reform advocate with a large following, Abu-Jamal began offering radio commentaries in 1994 and has written books from death row. His exercise of free-speech rights, when it has been permitted by prison authorities, has exposed his case to the public, both in the United States and internationally. Abu-Jamal is asking for a retrial on the grounds that he is innocent, his due process rights were violated, and that he is a victim of racism. Through the Prison Radio Project and independent media radio program, Abu-Jamal has been allowed to read his written social commentary pieces to the public (through a Plexiglas wall, while in shackles). When shortly after one such reading, the Pennsylvania State Department of Corrections passed new rules forbidding journalists from bringing cameras and audio-video equipment into interviews with prisoners, among other restrictions, civil rights attorneys and anti-death penalty and other prisoner advocacy groups claimed that the ban was an attempt to silence Abu-Jamal and was unrelated to prison security goals.

Newspaper reporters, individual inmates, and community organizations complain that California's 1996 law banning journalists from interviewing specific prisoners face-to-face (although they are still allowed in the prison and could randomly interview prisoners on the spot), creates substantial obstacles for reporters seeking to get inside prisons and interview inmates. Reporters complain of long wait lines; press passes (they now must be on the prisoner visitor list); and restrictions that prohibit pen, paper, or recording devices during interviews.

Journalists, scholars, activists, and artists seek access to interviews and to prisons in order to offer inmates opportunities for individual expression, claiming that this can dispel myths about convicts and humanize prisoners to the public. For example, in 1998, playwright and activist Eve Ensler was granted access to Bedford Hills, a maximum-security prison for women in New York, to direct a prison-writing project illuminating the voices of female prisoners. She turned this into a documentary film to illustrate seldom talked-about issues such as incarcerated women's histories of sexual and physical abuse, and women who have killed to protect themselves from domestic violence.

In addition, criminology scholars and free speech proponents have taken up cases concerning prisoners' rights to books. In 2002, prisoners challenged and won a case against the California Department of Corrections and Rehabilitation (CDCR) concerning a rule requiring books received from vendors to have a special shipping label attached. The CDCR claimed that they were upholding prison security and safety by reducing the chance that contraband could be smuggled into the prison in book packages. Prisoners' rights advocates agreed with the court's decision, however, which held that since the prison already routinely screened books for contraband, the regulation was arbitrary and unnecessarily restricted inmates' First Amendment right to freely read books.

Internet Access

More recently, civil liberties and other prisoner advocacy groups maintain that restricting inmates' free speech over the Internet violates their First Amendment rights and undermines the efforts of prison reform groups. In 2002, the Arizona legislature, for example, passed a law totally blocking prisoners' access to the Internet; that is, banning handwritten letters from prisoners that request organizations or individuals to post photos and information about their cases or their stories on the Internet, including for those prisoners who allege they have been wrongly convicted. Inmates do not possess the right to directly access the Internet, but prisoners' rights groups sometimes post their photos or information about their cases, or allow them to seek pen pals on their groups' Websites. The Arizona law also allowed for disciplining and possibly lengthening the sentence of any inmate who sought to access a service Website and post information on it. Following the law's passage, the Arizona Department of Corrections had contacted anti-death penalty and other groups demanding that prisoners have their names and faces removed from these Websites.

The American Civil Liberties Association (ACLU), the Canadian Coalition Against the Death Penalty, and other advocates of prisoners' rights and free speech claimed this law was unconstitutional. They protested that the state was suppressing information flowing from prisoners to the outside, and that the Arizona law also suppressed the advocacy work and free speech rights of anti-death penalty and other political organizations. The ACLU claimed that the U.S. Constitution does not allow censorship of speech just because it may be considered offensive (for example, an inmate's accessing the Internet to disseminate a negative message), for this would simultaneously jeopardize the speech of inmates alleging their innocence or exposing prison conditions. The U.S. District Court judge in Phoenix declared the Arizona law that banned all Internet exchange unconstitutional in 2003. He argued that abusive Website postings could still be stopped with existing regulations that prohibit inmates from sending or receiving that sort of material through the regular mail. Prisoner rights advocates claimed this ruling as a victory for civil liberties, prisoners, and all American citizens.

Con: Arguments Opposing Free Speech for Prisoners

Prisons administrations, law enforcement representatives, and victims' rights organizations advocating for restrictions on prisoner speech rights, on the other hand, argue that allowing prisoners to exercise a broad range of free speech rights can pose a security threat to the prison, and undermine the authority of the prison administration. They claim that prisoners' free speech places crime victims at risk for retraumatization through the photos and stories of prisoners in the media and on the Internet. Opponents also maintain that inmates' free speech allows some prisoners to manipulate and scam citizens through such postings, and that essentially, prisoners' free speech contradicts the idea that prisoners' offenses against society justify steep restrictions on their rights.

Internet Access

Prisoners are forbidden from mail correspondence (including direct computer access) that could pose a public safety or prison security threat such as orchestrating crimes or threatening witnesses. However, inmates have used their right to correspond through the regular mail to contact prison advocacy and legal organizations who can then post their stories and cases on their Websites. Opponents argue that crime victims and their families must be protected from such affronts. They point out that the Web allows inmates to have access to hundreds of people on the outside instead of just a few, as in the past. Moreover, through outside organizations, prisoners can have pen-pal postings and have personalized Web pages that include photos of themselves and their writings and artwork. Opponents, including prison officials, argue that certain prisoners post offensive materials on Websites operated by shady individuals. They propose that these Websites can glorify criminals and their crimes, manipulate unsuspecting citizens monetarily, or in some instances, coerce people into romantic relationships.

For example, a death row inmate's column *Deadman Talkin,'* which appeared online, has since spurred more such Web postings by other inmates, and opponents of prisoner free speech argue that some of these postings have been highly offensive to the families of murder victims. Similarly, convict Beau Greene's Web page on a pen-pal site depicted him in a photo as a friendly man holding a cat, which offended the widow of the man he had killed. She complained that the Internet can offer a convenient way for prisoners, who are sometimes "manipulative and sociopathic," to prey on people. This and other complaints by victims' rights groups led to the Arizona law that attempted to ban prisoners' stories or photos from appearing on the Internet. Arizona legislators, Arizona Department of Corrections spokespersons, and victims' rights groups justified the ban by the need to protect families of murder victims. Victims' rights organizations were angered when a federal court struck down the Arizona law on the grounds that it violated inmates' First Amendment rights and did not threaten prison security.

Similarly, in 2004, the mother of one of Jack Trawick's victims, filed a lawsuit against the individual who maintained a Website populated by Trawick's material, as well as against the Alabama Department of Corrections. Trawick, an Alabama death row inmate, wrote hateful stories that glorified his criminal offenses, including his own drawings of mutilated women, which were posted on a Website operated by an individual citizen. Several states, with the support of victims' rights advocates, have passed laws opposing prisoners' free speech rights regarding Web access. However, because such laws also restrict the First Amendment rights of prisoner advocacy organizations and other individuals outside prison, they have not generally been upheld in court, as in the Arizona case.

Prison Safety and Order

Prison officials also argue that certain forms of freedom of speech would undermine prison safety, order, and security. Courts have maintained that prisoner speech can be restricted if it poses a legitimate threat to the penological objectives or security of a prison. A specific example of potentially dangerous speech in prisons is that by hate or extremist groups. The Anti-Defamation League (ADL) and other opponents of broad inmate free-speech rights argue that hate speech and literature could negatively influence inmates, some of whom are already involved in white supremacist and other kinds of prison gangs. Extremist groups pose a special security risk in prisons, they argue, because many tend to be strongly antigovernment, and by extension, may be against state prison authorities. In addition, opponents of this kind of speech in the prison environment argue that hate groups often encourage racial and ethnic hatred and violence, which could upset the already racially charged prison environment. The Aryan Brotherhood, for example, publishes what they call a "prison outreach newsletter" to facilitate recruitment and disseminates its literature to inmates. Prison libraries do not hold extremist groups' literature, nor is this literature allowed to enter the prison through the mail. However, regulation of written materials from inmates leaving the prison in the outgoing mail is more difficult to legally restrict based on content alone. The Supreme Court has ruled that restriction of outgoing mail could impinge on the First Amendment rights of nonprisoners receiving this mail (and outgoing mail generally does not pose the same threat to prison security). Prison officials cannot ban outright written communication from prisoners to hate groups based on its content alone. The only kind of outgoing prison mail content that can be entirely banned is that containing threats, blackmail, escape plans, and certain business transactions.

Harms to Society

Finally, some opponents of broad rights to free speech for inmates argue overall that the harms to society justify revocation of prisoners' First Amendment rights. For example, when former California governor Pete Wilson vetoed a bill in the legislature that would have required the California Department of Corrections and Rehabilitation to arrange for prisoners to have interviews with the press, he upheld a punitive stance over supporting prisoners' constitutional rights to speech, publicly stating that prisoners "should not be treated as celebrities" and that prison officials should prevent media coverage that allows criminal offenders to enjoy attention at other people's expense. In a similar vein, a representative of the Arizona legislature said that the judge's ruling that overturned Arizona's law banning prisoner access to the Internet was "shameful," because convicts have offended society such that they should not possess the rights of free citizens.

The California Department of Corrections and Rehabilitation (CDCR) has also responded to protests by prisoner rights and civil liberties groups by dismissing them as "fussing" about "perceived inconveniences" with regard to the 1996 ban on interviews with the press by specific inmates. The CDCR argues that the media interview ban in California is not restricting information to the public about operations of the state's prisons, and that the restriction on prisoners making appointments for interviews with reporters is reasonable because some other states have similar laws, and that criminal offenders should lose rights when they come to prison, such as special visitation privileges. The CDCR also justifies the media interview ban by claiming that the media, like certain inmates, can be manipulative. For example, it issued a public statement that shunned television talk and entertainment shows for being "opportunistic" by seeking to profit from sensationalizing violence, referring to a time years earlier when the TV shows had tried to interview incarcerated serial killer Charles Manson.

In summary, the tension between prisoners' rights and public safety has played out through federal court rulings, social movements, and public debates. The core question is how to maintain a balance between prisoners' established constitutional right to free speech, and the need for prison security and public safety. The debate grows louder with the growing number of U.S. prisoners. Restrictions on speech that are based on legitimate security threats must be distinguished from those that hide abusive practices or grant prison administrations excessive power.

See Also: 4. Due Process Rights of Prisoners; 10. Legal Assistance for Prisoners; 18. Religious Rights.

Further Readings

American Civil Liberties Union. "ACLU Challenges Arizona Law That Censors Anti-Death Penalty Web Sites." http://www.aclu.org/print/tech nology-and-liberty (Accessed January 2010).

American Civil Liberties Union. "CA Court Says Prisoners Have First Amendment Right to Receive 'Snail Mail' Printed From the Internet." http://www.aclu.org/print/prisoners-rights (Accessed January 2010).

Bagdikian, Ben. "Courts, Convicts and the Press." *The Nation* (August 31, 1974).

Baird, Russell N. *The Penal Press.* Evanston, IL: Northwestern University Press, 1967.

Belkin, Douglas. "Looking for Love From Lockup." *Boston Globe* (February 12, 2004).

Burgess, Susan. "The First Amendment Behind Bars." *News Media and the Law*, v.30/1 (Winter 2006).

Dobrin, Arthur, et al. *Convictions: Political Prisoners—Their Stories.* Maryknoll, NY: Orbis Books, 1981.

Feeley, Malcolm M., and Edward L Rubin. *Judicial Policy Making and the Modern State: How the Courts Reformed America's Prisons.* Cambridge, UK: Cambridge University Press, 1998.

Frankel, Geoffrey S. "Untangling First Amendment Values: The Prisoners' Dilemma." *The George Washington Law Review*, v.59/6 (August 1991).

Girardi, Michelle. "Locked Out." *News Media and the Law,* v.28/2 (Spring 2004).

Gomez, Alan E. "Nuestras Vidas Corren Casi Paralelas: Chicanos, Independentistas, and the Prison Rebellions in Leavenworth, 1969–1972." *Latino Studies,* v.6/1–2 (Spring 2008).

Greenhouse, Linda. "Supreme Court Roundup: Justices Question Broad Reach of 'Son of Sam' Law." *New York Times* (October 26, 1991).

Hudson, David L., Jr. "Pen Pals." *ABA Journal,* v.87/1 (January 2001).

Jacobs, James, B. "The Prisoners' Rights Movement and Its Impacts: 1960–80." *Crime and Justice,* v.3 (1980).

Johnson, Dirk. "Using Internet Links From Behind Bars." *New York Times* (August 1, 2000).

Kaleen, Jaweed. "Prisoner Pen Pal Services File Lawsuit Over Florida Ban." *Tribune News Service* (May 5, 2009).

Leslie, George. "Prison Interviews Versus the First Amendment." *News Media and the Law,* v.27/4 (Fall 2003).

Lucero, Linda K., and Jeffrey P. Bernhardt. "Substantive Rights Retained by Prisoners." *Georgetown Law Journal,* v.90/5 (May 2002).

McGraw, Carol. "Prisoner Pen Pal Sites Proliferate on Web—but Beware." *The Gazette* (October 17, 2004).

Rahimi, Shadi. "Outrage Over Prisoner's Right to Blog." *Press Democrat* (July 19, 2008). http://www.pressdemocrat.com/article/20080719/NEWS/807190312?p=1&tc=pg (Accessed January 2010).

Scarce, Rik. *Contempt of Court: A Scholar's Battle for Free Speech From Behind Bars.* Lanham, MD: AltaMira Press, 2005.

Sneed, Don, and Harry W. Stonecipher. "More Freedom for the Prison Press: An Emerging First Amendment Issue?" *Journalism Quarterly,* v.63/1 (Spring 1986).

Tonry, Michael. *Thinking About Crime: Sense and Sensibility in American Penal Culture.* Oxford, UK: Oxford University Press, 2004.

"While on Death Row, Inmates Find Freedom on the Internet." (January 25, 2004). http://www.nytimes.com/2004/01/25/us/while-on-death-row-inmates-find-freedom-on-the-internet.html (Accessed January 2010).

7

Furlough and Work-Release Programs

Brenda Vose
University of North Florida

In 2007, 751,593 offenders were admitted to state and federal penitentiaries. The same year, 725,402 offenders were released from state and federal penitentiaries. The influx of offenders into prisons and subsequent release of offenders into communities creates a unique set of challenges for policymakers, criminal justice practitioners, offenders, and communities. As such, the criminal justice system has developed a myriad of supervision options, referred to as the *continuum of care,* to manage the offender population and help offenders transition back into the community setting.

Furlough and work-release programs are one piece of the corrections continuum of care, designed for offenders nearing the completion of their criminal sentence. The purpose of these programs is to supervise offenders while providing an opportunity for the offender to maintain employment and gradually transition from supervision to release from custody. Work-release participants are permitted to leave the correctional institution during work hours and return to the correctional facility during nonwork hours. Going forward, the term *work release* is used here to refer to furlough and work-release programs.

The history of work release in the United States can be traced in three parts: first, the development of work-release programs in the early 20th century and subsequent growth in program popularity until the early 1970s; second, the paradigmatic shift that occurred in the late 1960s and early 1970s, which changed the way policymakers and criminal justice practitioners managed the offender population; and finally, the renewed interest in work release and offender reentry that has emerged in recent years.

There are also several benefits and drawbacks of work release. Benefits of work release include gradual reentry, enhanced vocational skills, individual income, correctional cost savings, paid restitution to victims, paid court orders, reduced prison overcrowding, improved well-being of offenders, and the building of positive peer networks. The drawbacks of work release include recidivism, hidden costs, the current economic condition, public sentiment, and the need for additional research.

History of Work Release in the United States

Development of Work-Release Programs

The late 1800s and early 1900s were marked by tremendous change in the social, cultural, economic, and political fabric of the United States. Until this time, the efforts of the criminal justice system were largely disorganized, and treatment of offenders was administered by criminal justice practitioners, members of the church, and volunteers from the community. However, as the country began to change, so too did the criminal justice system. During this time, penitentiaries were established in New York and Pennsylvania, the juvenile justice system was implemented in Illinois, and probation and parole were developed for juvenile delinquents and adult offenders.

The improvements in criminal justice practices in the early 20th century can be traced to the work of the Progressives. This group of educated and socially conscious reformers sought to improve the lives of Americans by reducing poverty, improving neighborhood conditions, and more generally, tending to the needs of individuals. The Progressives were also instrumental in the development of correctional initiatives across the country. Unlike what Feeley and Simon refer to as the "new penology," where emphasis is placed on the management of groups of offenders based on the seriousness of the crime committed, the Progressives believed that one-size-fits-all correctional treatment was inadequate. Instead, Progressives insisted that each offender be studied on a case-by-case basis so that a treatment plan could be implemented to meet the specific needs of each individual offender.

This highly individualized approach required the criminal justice system to allocate resources to assess, treat, and supervise offenders. Thus, probation officers, parole boards, and parole officers were introduced. Probation officers were employed to gather background information on each offender, determine the proper treatment, and to supervise low-risk offenders in the community. Given the indeterminate nature of treatment proposed by the Progressives, parole boards were established to review the treatment progress of each individual offender and determine when the offender was fit to return to the community. Offenders were not simply released into the community, but were rather placed under the supervision of a parole officer who duty continued to supervise, treat, and aid the offender in his or her effort to assimilate back into society.

Work-release programs were introduced in the 1920s as a mechanism to supervise offenders while allowing them to work and transition back into a community setting. Most work-release programs allowed offenders to leave the correctional setting for work purposes on the condition that they return to the correctional facility during nonwork hours. Other furlough programs granted offenders a weekend leave of absence from the facility. Although program characteristics varied across jurisdictions, the underlying theme of supervision in the community was rooted in the work of the Progressives.

Community correction and treatment efforts continued to grow in popularity from the 1900s through the early 1960s. The 1967 Presidential Forum on Crime Commission further endorsed the need to continue to develop community corrections, and urged that reintegration of offenders should be among the primary points of emphasis for the correctional system. Although the treatment or rehabilitation paradigm had dominated corrections for more than half a century, change was on the horizon, and so too was the temporary demise of offender rehabilitation through programmatic treatment.

Pragmatic Shift Changes Views of the Correctional System

The late 1960s and early 1970s were fraught with social and political change. The assassinations of Malcolm X, President Kennedy, Martin Luther King Jr., and Robert Kennedy; civil rights movement; deinstitutionalization movement; Bay of Pigs invasion; incidents of police brutality at the Democratic National Convention; Warren Court; hippie movement; Watergate; shootings at Kent State University; Vietnam War; the Beatles;

and riots at New York's Attica State Penitentiary—these were but a few of the events that polarized the nation's major political parties. Conservatives believed that the youth of the country had run amok and that the government and law enforcement needed to step in and reestablish order. Liberals, on the other hand, grew suspicious of the government because agents of the government were responsible for the shootings at Kent State University and killed guards and inmates at Attica State Penitentiary in New York. Despite their disagreement as to the root of the problem, both liberals and conservatives began to doubt the effectiveness of rehabilitation as the guiding philosophy of the correctional system.

The credibility of rehabilitation was further challenged by the publication of the *Martinson Report* in 1974. In this review of 231 treatment studies, Robert Martinson concluded that "nothing works" to reduce recidivism. Though he later recanted his now-famous statement, the American public heard the message that they had suspected for some time: rehabilitation did not work. Following the events of the late 1960s, early 1970s, and the publication of the *Martinson Report,* there was a move away from rehabilitation efforts. Instead, the public began to yearn for a more retributive approach to dealing with the offender population. To that end, liberals and conservatives collaborated to devise a plan to restore a sense of safety and equilibrium to the country.

Liberals and conservatives agreed upon a determinate sentencing model for offenders. This was a major shift from the previous indeterminate model of sentencing that allowed offenders to be supervised until the time at which the state believed the offender had been rehabilitated. Conversely, the determinate sentencing model would require judges to set a specific sentence length for convicted criminals prior to being admitted to an institution. Liberals agreed to this model on the basis that these changes would protect offenders from the abuse of power by government or state officials, thereby affording due process to offenders. Conservatives agreed to this model as a way to control crime by imposing harsher sentences. Given the social and political climate, the public embraced the conservatives' crime control model over the liberals' due-process model. Judges began to sentence offenders more harshly for their criminal acts. Instead of the short and definite sentences that liberals had hoped for, criminals were receiving longer sentences and parole boards were discouraged from granting early release. Conservatives believed that imposing longer, harsher sentences would teach criminals a lesson and deter them and potential offenders from committing crime in the future.

As a result of the new crime-control model, funding for treatment programs diminished, and emphasis was placed on punishment. The retributive approach continued to gain momentum through the 1980s with the advent of the "get tough on crime" movement. The public was no longer interested in rehabilitating offenders, but preferred to focus on punishing offenders. This move toward longer, harsher sentencing meant that funds previously designated for treatment programs were now being allocated to prison construction to accommodate the rapidly growing offender population.

The Furor Over Willie Horton

Work-release programs were also dealt a seemingly insurmountable setback in 1987 when Willie Horton, a convicted murderer in Massachusetts, committed crimes while on furlough for the weekend. During his time away from the institution, on April 3, 1987, Horton pistol-whipped, knifed, tied up, and gagged a man in Oxon Hill, Maryland, raped his fiancée twice, and stole their car. This tragic event resulted in an inordinate amount of bad publicity for work-release programs. Programs that had once been embraced by the public were now the target of public scrutiny. In turn, this fueled the collective interest to get tough on crime and do away with programs that might put the general public at risk.

The move away from treatment and toward more severe sentencing resulted in an increase in the prison population. In 1980, there were 1,842,100 inmates in state and federal prisons, but by 1990, the prison population had grown to 4,350,300. Throughout the 1980s and 1990s, the incarceration rate remained high, creating a tremendous burden on prisons and jails. In some facilities, inmates were housed in gymnasiums, lunchrooms, tents, and any space available because there were simply not enough cells to hold the burgeoning offender population.

The lack of space, coupled with the lack of financial resources to build additional prisons and jails to house the offender population, prompted lawmakers and corrections officials to explore alternatives to prison that would allow the state to supervise offenders in a manner that maintained public safety while reducing recidivism, prison overcrowding, and the overall cost of incarceration. To that end, intermediate sanctions were popularized across the country as a means to administer harsh punishment to offenders without housing them in penitentiaries.

Boot camps, electronic monitoring, house arrest, and shock incarceration were but a few of the intermediate sanctions implemented throughout the country. Initially, intermediate sanctions appeared promising, as they were less expensive to operate and expected to be punitive enough to prevent recidivism. While low recidivism and technical violations were the goals, policymakers did not accurately predict the effect that increased supervision would have. Instead of deterring offenders, the increased supervision and scrutiny offenders received from their probation officers simply resulted in the officers having more opportunities to catch their clients doing something wrong. As such, the increased supervision resulted in higher rates of recidivism. In some cases, the recidivism required the offender to be returned to prison. Thus, there was little or no financial savings, and the programs failed to significantly reduce prison crowding.

Offender Reentry Today

In the last 10 years, there has been a renewed interest in rehabilitation, with special emphasis on offender reentry that has emerged as a goal of the current correctional system. This is due in part to the failures of punitive intensive supervision, the expense of operating these programs, and overcrowded prisons and jails—the results of the "get tough" model of sentencing employed over the course of the last 35 years. Prisons and jails are overcrowded, and limited resources prevent the construction of new facilities to keep up with the high rate of incarceration. State and federal officials have been pressed to consider alternative ways to manage the offender population. To that end, the U.S. Department of Justice has embarked on the Serious Violent Offender Reentry Initiative (SVORI), which provides funding to states interested in developing offender reentry programs.

The current reentry efforts help to ease the transition from prison to community for the 600,000 or more offenders released from state and federal prisons each year. In years past, offenders were released from prison without the education or skills necessary to obtain gainful employment; therefore, the majority of individuals released from correctional supervision reoffended within three years. In attempt to reduce the likelihood of recidivism for offenders returning to the community, correctional agencies implement a gradual transition back into the general population, providing individuals with the educational, skill-building, and treatment opportunities needed to secure and maintain legitimate employment upon release from correctional supervision.

Research on the importance of matching offenders to treatment programs based on their individual risks and needs is abundant. So too is the research on the overall effectiveness of treatment programs at reducing the likelihood of recidivism. However, research on the effectiveness of reentry programs is only beginning to emerge. Early results suggest that aftercare plays an integral part in the likelihood of offender success in the community. A 2009 study by Anthony Braga, Anne Piehl, and David Hureau examined the effectiveness of the Boston Reentry Initiative (BRI) at reducing recidivism. This program assists violent adult offenders in reintegrating into the community after serving their jail sentence by providing them access to a variety of mentors, social services in the community, and skill-building opportunities. The results indicate that individuals who participated in the program had a 30 percent lower rate of recidivism than individuals who did not participate in BRI.

Pro: Benefits of Work-Release Programs

Despite the public's collective interest in punishing offenders, the reality is that 95 percent of all offenders in prison will eventually return to the community. Given this overwhelming number, proponents of work-release programs argue that it is imperative to provide services that will enable individuals to successfully transition from the prison setting to the general population. There are a number of positive benefits to work-release programs, including gradual reentry; improved vocational skills; financial gain to the offender, institution, victim, and offender's children; reduction in prison overcrowding; the impact of breaking up the ordinary prison routine; and the potential impact of socializing with a positive peer network.

Gradual Reentry

When an offender is incarcerated, he or she must go through a process that Donald Clemmer refers to as *prisonization*. This process requires offenders to learn and adapt to the informal and formal rules of the institution. Some inmates adapt relatively easily to their new surroundings, while others struggle with the transition to prison life. Just as there is a period of adjustment when an offender enters an institution, there is also a period of adjustment when an offender is released from supervision.

The difficulty prisoners have in adjusting to prison generally goes undetected by the general public. However, individuals who struggle with the transition from prison to the general population are far more visible, as their difficulties often appear in the form of rearrest or reconviction. In 1994, the Bureau of Justice Statistics examined recidivism in 15 states and found that 29.9 percent of prisoners released from prison were rearrested within six months. Forty-four (44.1 percent) were rearrested within one year, 59.9 percent were rearrested within two years, and 67.5 percent were rearrested within three years, with 25.4 percent returning to prison.

The high rate of recidivism and return to prison for offenders makes prisoner reentry a point of emphasis for the correctional system. Work-release programs provide offenders a bridge from prison to release that affords them structured flexibility as the offender finds his or her footing and adjusts to life on the outside. This gradual transition back into the general population may prove a more effective release mechanism for eligible offenders. That is, participation in work-release programs may help to reduce the likelihood of recidivism as compared to unconditional release into the community upon completion of a prison sentence.

Vocational Skills and Earnings

In many cases, offenders do not possess the vocational skills necessary to secure legitimate employment. Participating in work-release programs may teach offenders vocational skills that will make them competitive in the current job market. Moreover, offenders learn import life skills. For example, an offender is responsible for arriving for work on time and is required to be accountable for their individual job performance. Offenders are taught how to take instruction from an employer, and in many cases, how work as part of a team to accomplish common goals. These are valuable lessons that will serve the individual in their temporary work-release employment, but also in any professional work environment.

A 2001 study of Ohio inmates by Martha Henderson found that offenders view an inability to obtain employment as a reason to commit crime. Further, the majority of offenders sampled (68 percent) indicated a willingness to participate in programming that targets vocational skills and general employability. Henderson suggests that simply having a job may not be enough to prevent an individual from committing a crime. Rather, the individual's perception of the quality or meaning of the work must also be taken into consideration.

Work-release programs afford offenders the opportunity to learn vocational skills that may help individuals obtain and maintain quality employment upon release from prison. Not only do offenders acknowledge the need for employment, but they also articulate a desire to participate in programs that will enhance their vocational skills. Employment also allows the offender an opportunity to earn an income. Individuals who are gainfully employed tend to accumulate monetary, social, and material capital, and are consequently less inclined to participate in illegal activities that may put them risk for losing what they have accumulated. In other words, employed individuals have a greater stake in conformity than unemployed individuals.

Participation in a work-release program provides offenders the means to earn an income and amass savings prior to their release from prison. In turn, this savings may be used to rent an apartment, pay personal expenses, and tide them over until long-term employment can be obtained. Individuals released into the community without savings, a place to live, or employment will have far greater difficulty remaining crime-free than individuals who have established employment and are on solid financial ground.

Reduced Costs, Restitution, and Child Support

The Bureau of Justice Statistics reports that $29.5 billion was required to maintain adult correctional facilities in 2001. The cost to house an inmate in federal or state prison in 2001 was $22,632 and $22,650, respectively. Inmates who participate in work-release programs are required to pay a portion of their living expenses while at the correctional facility. As such, work-release programs alleviate some of the financial burden of housing the correctional population and can be reallocated for other correctional needs, such as staffing, treatment programs, and construction.

In addition to paying for their own room and board, work-release offenders are required to make restitution payments to their victims. Without work-release programs, the offender would have no source of income with which to pay restitution to their victims. Unpaid restitution may result in additional financial and emotional strain to the victim. Moreover, it may leave the victim feeling that justice has not been served. An offender's ability to pay restitutions helps him make amends to the victim and pay his dues to society.

In 1999, 55.4 percent of state prisoners and 63 percent of federal prisoners were the parents of at least one child under the age of 18. Offenders on work release are required to make all court-ordered payments of child support. Work-release programs allow offenders to financially contribute to their family while serving their sentence. This may alleviate some of the financial strain placed on the family due to the offender's incarceration.

Reduced Prison Overcrowding and Monotony

In 2007, 19 states and the federal prisons were operating over prison capacity. Still 19 more states were operating between 90 and 99 percent capacity. Removing offenders who are nearing the end of their sentence and eligible for participation in work release from the traditional prison setting frees up space to house serious offenders who require more supervision than is necessary for work-release offenders.

A day in the life of a prisoner is also highly supervised, and the entire prison operates on a strictly structured schedule. To that end, one day looks very much like the next. The monotony of life in prison may manifest itself in prison violence, mental illness, or other medical conditions. For these and other reasons, correctional institutions implement a variety of recreational, educational, and vocational programming to provide a change of scenery, release stress, stimulate minds through positive social interaction, and simply break up the day. Work-release programs afford the same opportunities. Offenders are allowed to leave the facility for the purpose of work, providing them with a change of scenery. The stress of confinement is temporarily relieved as the offender leaves the facility to work in the community. Although the type of employment varies across offenders, interacting with coworkers and engaging in work in a professional work environment will provide positive social interaction and mental stimulation that may not be available within the walls of the institution.

Positive Social Networking

Individuals whose friends engage in criminal activity are more likely to engage in criminal activity. Conversely, individuals who have few or no friends involved in criminal activity are less likely become involved in criminal activity. As such, it is common for rehabilitation programs to address a criminal's peer network—that is, emphasis is placed on breaking ties with people who influence the individual to commit crime. Individuals are encouraged to form social bonds with positive peers who engage in social activities and do not engage in criminal behavior.

Offenders involved in work-release programs work alongside other individuals in the community who are legitimately employed. It is likely that these individuals possess a more positive social lifestyle and outlook on the future than many of the peers with whom the offender associated prior to and during the early stages of their incarceration. In this sense, the offender starts to build positive ties with coworkers and the community to which he or she will soon be released. These positive influences will serve as protective factors to reduce the likelihood of recidivism.

Con: Drawbacks of Work-Release Programs

Although there are a number of benefits to work-release programs, there are also a number of drawbacks. Some of the concerns about work-release programs include the rate of recidivism, hidden costs, the current economic state, public sentiment, and the research regarding the effectiveness of work-release programs.

Recidivism

In criminal justice, it is common to hear the term *what works,* which generally refers to the effectiveness of a program at reducing recidivism. A 1994 study of recidivism in 15 states found that 67.5 percent of the approximately 300,000 offenders released were rearrested within in three years. Given the inability of individuals released from prison to maintain a life free of crime, detractors of work-release programs point out that it does not seem prudent to waste resources on developing programs for individuals who either refuse or are unable to change. To this end, work-release programs appear to be another example of failed programming in the attempt to address the revolving door of offender institutionalization and release.

Hidden Costs and the Economy

One of the arguments in favor of work-release programs is the cost savings. It is less expensive to house an offender in a work-release program than to house an offender in a traditional prison setting. However, in calculating the true cost, one must also take into consideration the cost when an individual recidivates, is processed by the criminal justice system again, and returns to prison. In this sense, individuals who fail on work release may be as expensive, if not more expensive, than housing offenders in the traditional prison setting.

In addition, the United States was still in the midst of an economic recession at the end of 2010. Companies declared bankruptcy, while others were forced to downsize. The recession left 15.3 million Americans without employment as of December 2009. Those who were fortunate enough to find employment often found they were underemployed and/or making a fraction of their former salary. In difficult economic times when jobs are scarce, it is unreasonable to expect employers to hire an offender participating in a work-release program over an equally qualified candidate who does not have a criminal record.

Public Sentiment

Following the publication of the *Martinson Report* in 1974, the public rejected rehabilitation and embraced retribution as the guiding philosophy of the correctional system. Through the 1980s and 1990s, the public has remained steadfast in their "get tough" approach to dealing with the offender population. The Willie Horton incident in 1987 horrified and bewildered the general public. The notion that a convicted murderer was released on furlough and harmed innocent members of the community was damning to the reputations of work-release programs nationwide. To this day, many people still reference the Willie Horton incident and are resistant to any correctional program, work release included, that places the general public in danger and/or is perceived to be too lenient on the offender. The temporary freedom and community mobility associated with work-release programs, coupled with the lasting memory of the Willie Horton incident, makes it difficult for many to embrace work-release programs as a promising approach to dealing with the offender population.

Need for Additional Research

The criminal justice system has finite personnel and economic resources, which must be allocated in a way that will provide the most return on its investment. To this end, policymakers must make difficult decisions regarding the funding of correctional programs. Program effectiveness—the ability of the program to reduce likelihood of recidivism—is the foundation for many of these funding decisions. Programs that are not empirically supported are in jeopardy of being cut or having funding reduced. A 2009 study by Leonidas Cheliotis, exploring extant literature on the effectiveness of work-release programs, reveals the lack of research in this area. Although work-release programs have been in existence in the United States since the 1920s, Cheliotis found only 23 studies that have examined effectiveness with adequate methodological rigor. Given the renewed interest in growing existing work-release programs and/or implementing new work-release programs, it is imperative that additional research is conducted to determine whether or not work-release programs are effective at reducing recidivism. To date, the research is somewhat limited, and without consistent empirical support, policymakers may want to pause before pursuing this type of programming.

Conclusion

Nearly 100 years of work-release programs in the United States have culminated in renewed interest in offender reentry, with both numerous benefits and drawbacks. Through the peaks and valleys in programming popularity, work-release programs have persisted as an integral part of the correctional continuum of care, and are poised to maintain this position in the foreseeable future.

See Also: 2. Clemency; 5. Early Release; 13. Preventive Detention; 14. Prison Labor; 15. Prison Overcrowding; 17. Punishment Versus Rehabilitation.

Further Readings

Andrews, Don, and James Bonta. *The Psychology of Criminal Conduct, Second Edition*. Cincinnati, OH: Anderson Publishing, 1998.

Braga, Anthony A., Anne M. Piehl, and David Hureau. "Controlling Violent Offenders Released to the Community: An Evaluation of the Boston Reentry Initiative." *Journal of Research in Crime and Delinquency*, v.46/4 (2009).

Bureau of Labor Statistics. "The Employment Situation—December 2009." http://www.bls.gov/news.release/pdf/empsit.pdf (Accessed January 2010).

Butzin, Clifford A., Steven S. Martin, and James A. Inciardi. "Evaluating Component Effects of a Prison-Based Treatment Continuum." *Journal of Substance Abuse Treatment*, v.22 (2002).

Cheliotis, Leonidas K. "Before the Next Storm: Some Evidence-Based Reminders About Temporary Release." *International Journal of Offender Therapy and Comparative Criminology*, v.54/4 (2009).

Clemmer, Donald. *The Prison Community*. New York: Rinehart, 1958.

Cullen, Francis T., and Paul Gendreau. "Assessing Correctional Rehabilitation: Policy, Practice, and Prospects." In *Criminal Justice 2000: Policies, Processes, and Decisions of the Criminal Justice System*, edited by Julie Horney. Washington, DC: U.S. Department of Justice, 2000.

Cullen, Francis T., and Karen Gilbert. *Reaffirming Rehabilitation*. Cincinnati, OH: Anderson Publishing, 1982.

Cullen, Francis T., John P. Wright, and Brandon K. Applegate. "Control in the Community: The Limits of Reform." In *Choosing Correctional Interventions That Work*, edited by Alan T. Harland. Thousan Oaks, CA: Sage, 1996.

Feeley, Malcolm M., and Jonathan Simon. "The New Penology: Notes on the Emerging Strategy of Corrections and Its Implications." *Criminology*, v.30 (1992).

Fox, Kathryn J. "Second Chances: A Comparison of Civic Engagement in Offender Reentry Programs." *Criminal Justice Review*, v.35/3 (2010).

Fulton, Betsy, Edward J. Latessa, Amy Stichman, and Lawrence F. Travis. "The State of ISP: Research and Policy Implications." *Federal Probation* v.61/4 (1997).

Glaze, Lauren E., and Thomas P. Bonczar. *Probation and Parole in the United States, 2005*. Washington, DC: U.S. Department of Justice, 2006.

Henderson, Martha, L. "Employment and Crime: What Is the Problem and What Can Be Done About It From the Inmate's Perspective?" *Corrections Management Quarterly*, v.5/4 (2001).

Immerwahr, John, and Jean Johnson. "The Revolving Door: Exploring Public Attitudes Toward Prisoner Reentry." http://www.urbaninstitute.org/UploadedPDF/410804_RevolvingDoor.pdf (Accessed January 2010).

Katz, Jonathan F., and Scott H. Decker. "An Analysis of Work Release: The Institutionalization of Unsubstantiated Reforms." *Criminal Justice and Behavior*, v.9/2 (1982).

Kurlychek, Megan, and Cynthia Kempinen. "Beyond Boot Camp: The Impact of Aftercare on Offender Reentry." *Criminology and Public Policy*, v.5/2 (2006).

Langan, Patrick A., and David J. Levin. *Recidivism of Prisoners Released in 1994*. Washington, DC: U.S. Department of Justice, 2002.

Latessa, Edward J., Francis T. Cullen, and Paul Gendreau. "Beyond Correctional Quackery—Professionalism and the Possibility of Effective Treatment." *Federal Probation*, v.66/2 (2002).

Lattimore, Pamela K., Danielle M. Steffey, and Christy A. Visher. "Prisoner Reentry in the First Decade of the Twenty-First Century." *Victims and Offenders,* v.5/3 (2010).

LeClair, Daniel P. "Home Furlough Program." *Criminal Justice and Behavior,* v.5/3 (1978).

LeClair, Daniel P., and Susan Guarino-Ghezzi. "Does Incapacitation Guarantee Public Safety? Lessons From the Massachusetts Furlough and Prerelease Programs." *Justice Quarterly,* v.8/1 (1991): 9–36.

Lyon, Jean-Marie, Scott Henggeler, and James A. Hall. "The Family Relations, Peer Relations, and Criminal Activities of Caucasian and Hispanic-American Gang Members." *Journal of Abnormal Child Psychology,* v.20/5 (1992).

MacKenzie, Doris Layton. *What Works In Corrections: Reducing the Criminal Activities of Offenders and Delinquents.* New York: Cambridge University Press, 2006.

Mann, Arthur. *The Progressive Era Liberal Renaissance or Liberal Failure?* New York: Holt, Rinehart and Winston, Inc., 1963.

Martinson, Robert. "What Works? Questions and Answers About Prison Reform." *Public Interest,* v.35 (Spring 1974).

Mumola, Christopher, J. *Incarcerated Parents and Their Children.* Washington, DC: U.S. Department of Justice, 2000.

Petersilia, Joan. "A Decade of Experimenting With Intermediate Sanctions: What Have We Learned?" *Federal Probation,* v.62/2 (1998).

Petersilia, Joan. *When Prisoners Come Home: Parole and Reentry.* New York: Oxford University Press, Inc., 2003.

Petersilia, Joan. *When Prisoners Return to the Community: Political, Economic, and Social Consequences.* Washington, DC: U.S. Department of Justice, 2000.

Rothman, David J. *Conscience and Convenience: The Asylum and Its Alternatives in Progressive America.* New York: Aldine de Gruyter, 1980.

Sabol, William J., and Heather Couture. *Prison Inmates at Midyear 2007.* Washington, DC: U.S. Department of Justice, 2008.

Seiter, Richard P., and Karen R. Kadela. "Prisoner Reentry: What Works, What Does Not, and What Is Promising, 2003." *Crime and Delinquency,* v.49/3 (2003).

Stephan, James J. *State Prison Expenditures, 2001.* Washington, DC: U.S. Department of Justice, 2004.

Travis, Jeremy. *But They All Come Back: Rethinking Prisoner Reentry.* Washington, DC: U.S. Department of Justice, 2000.

Turner, Susan, and Joan Petersilia. "Work Release in Washington: Effects on Recidivism and Corrections Costs." *The Prison Journal,* v.76 (1996).

Visher, Christy A. "Returning Home: Emerging Findings and Policy Lessons About Prisoner Reentry." *Federal Sentencing Reporter,* v.20/2 (2007).

West, Heather C., and William J. Sabol. *Prisoners in 2007.* Washington, DC: U.S. Department of Justice, 2008.

Zalman, Marvin. "Sentencing in a Free Society: The Failure of the President's Crime Commission to Influence Sentencing Policy." *Justice Quarterly,* v.4/4 (1987).

8

Gangs and Violence in Prisons

Kristine M. Levan
Plymouth State University

There are various definitions for prison gangs, but a generally accepted description is that a prison gang operates within the prison system as a criminally oriented entity that threatens, or is perceived to threaten, the orderly management of a prison. Inmates belonging to a prison gang will often have similar norms, values, and language and have a distinct code of conduct among its members. Many prison officials use the term *security threat group* (STG) to identify a gang. Prison gangs are usually informally organized along racial or ethnic lines, mimicking and often overlapping the organization of street gangs. Inmates often join gangs as either a means to secure personal protection from other inmates or for economic gain, often relying on gang members as surrogate family members.

Among prisoners, violence is often a means by which to gain status from other inmates, and gangs provide both a means to perpetuate this violence and protection from either unaffiliated prisoners or from rival gang members. Some forms of prison violence include assault, sexual assault, riots, and homicide. Much of the violence that occurs in prison remains unreported, making it difficult to address on an individual victim level. Correctional facilities often use various types of segregation techniques to reduce or punish different forms of violence. They may also rely on education on both gangs and violence in an effort to reduce their prevalence.

Types of Prison Gangs

Most prison gangs are based on an inmate's race and ethnicity. Some white gangs include the Aryan Brotherhood, Hell's Angels, and Dirty White Boys. African American gangs include members belonging to the Crips, the Bloods, the Vice Lords, the D.C. Blacks, and the Black Guerrilla Family. Some Hispanic and Latino gangs include the Mexican Mafia, La Nuestra Familia, and the Latin Kings. Although a few multiracial prison gangs exist, members belonging to gangs that are not organized primarily by race are often organized to engage almost exclusively in economic endeavors, such as drug cartels.

Many of the existing prison gangs began as street gangs that formed in the community. For example, the Hell's Angels, the Crips, and the Bloods have existed for decades in the free community. The United States began to use incarceration as its primary mechanism of punishment for gangs, and the gang population behind bars began to surge. As members of these street gangs became incarcerated, they began to form gangs using similar structures while they were incarcerated, importing many of their beliefs, values, and norms and assimilating them into their prison environments. As prisoners transfer between facilities, they may extend existing gang membership into new chapters. This not only increases membership, but also may create rivalries among the various chapters and gang affiliations. Depending on the security level of the facility, gang members may comprise as much as one-third of the total inmate population. Maximum-security facilities typically report the highest levels of gang membership, while minimum-security prisons have the lowest levels. The number of inmates involved in gangs also varies according to geographical location, with New Mexico, Texas, and California reporting the greatest number of gang members.

Gang Membership

Because prisons specifically prohibit gang membership, many members of prison gangs attempt to conceal their gang affiliation and activities. Many of the solutions to dealing with gang activities are punitive, such as placing known gang members in administrative segregation. As such, it is unclear as to the exact number of inmates who are affiliated with a gang. There are currently more than 100 known prison gangs throughout the United States.

Although many prison gangs engage in similar types of activities, each gang is unique and tries to differentiate itself from other rival gangs. They often have a unique motto, specific membership symbols, colors, and a constitution that dictates group behavior. Gangs often have a hierarchical structure, with a leader and a council of members who work directly under the appointed leader. The structure of a prison gang is often more stable and more organized than that of a typical street gang, in part because there tends to be less turnover of gang members in a prison gang than a street gang. Both require absolute loyalty to one's gang, as well as complete secrecy of affiliation with the gang.

Gang members often identify each other by tattoos of their particular gang affiliations. These tattoos may be made by either cutting into the skin, or by burning the skin with an iron. Each gang typically has specific tattoos that are associated with its members, and nonmembers who falsely self-identify as a gang member may have their tattoo forcibly removed by members of the gang. Most prisons expressly prohibit tattooing, in part because of gang affiliations, but also to curb transmission of diseases. However, inmates continue to tattoo themselves and each other and often hide the tattoos under their clothing. They may also carry scraps of paper with tattoo-like emblems that are specific to their gang for identification purposes.

Prison gangs often adhere to the "blood in–blood out" adage, and are more difficult to move in and out of than the average street gang. Violence is often required for gang membership, with many gangs requiring a violent act such as murder or assault to be performed against another inmate to gain admission. The "blood out" idea indicates the difficulty of leaving a gang. Exiting gang members are often injured and potentially even killed for what is perceived by other gang members as disloyalty to the gang. Common reasons for members to leave a gang include a loss of interest in gang activities, a general level of disagreement with the leadership of the gang, or a refusal to commit violence on a former member.

Prison gangs are almost exclusively a male phenomenon. Female inmates, though somewhat involved in violence (to a lesser extent than male inmates), are not reliant on gang membership. The primary group mechanisms used by female inmates are called *pseudofamilies*, which are small, family-like units comprised of female prisoners. Family members include typical roles, such as mother, father, and daughter, and very seldom result in interpersonal violence.

Participation in the Inmate Economy

Inmates may join a prison gang for economic purposes. Gangs often earn money by engaging in various illegal activities, such as selling drugs, extortion, theft, and prostitution. Gang members are often involved in theft of the property of their fellow inmates, sometimes invading another inmate's cell with other members of their gang to steal their valuables, only to sell them on the illegal black market within the prison. Members may also buy and sell their fellow inmates to other gang members for sexual purposes, or engage in other coercion or extortion tactics.

Anything not explicitly allowed by prison regulations is considered contraband, which has created a huge black market for gangs. The inmate economy thrives on illegal contraband, which may include drugs, alcohol, cell phones, cigarettes, condoms, and currency. Gang members residing outside the prison facilities are often instrumental in smuggling these items into the prison. Visitors may sneak items into the visiting area to give them to the inmate or toss them over the fence or wall and into the prison yard.

Furthermore, correctional officers may be coerced or blackmailed into bringing illegal items into the prison. If an inmate has knowledge of an officer breaking an institutional rule or engaging in illegal behavior, they may use this information as leverage against the correctional officer in an attempt to force them to help smuggle items into the facility. Other correctional officers may be willing to engage in illegal smuggling as a means to earn additional money.

Prison gangs are actively involved in all facets of the illegal inmate economy. However, their greatest level of participation is in the illegal drug market. In the 1980s, the amount of gang activity and gang membership began to increase. The War on Drugs increased the penalties for both drug use and drug trafficking. As such, the profit-making opportunities for drug sales both behind bars and in the community increased, coinciding with an increase in gang activity among inmates.

Participation in Violence

Although gangs often participate in the illegal prison economy, most inmates join gangs as a means of protection from potential violence at the hands of their fellow inmates, or as a way to gain status within the prison. Violence among prisoners, even those not involved in gangs, has become not only accepted, but also expected. Even drug and property offenders who did not commit violence pre-prison may be released as violent offenders as a result of their exposure to high levels of violence while incarcerated. Inmates must convey a tough and masculine appearance in order to thwart violent attacks at the hands of their fellow inmates.

Gang members may make up a relatively small number of the inmate population, but they are responsible for a disproportionately large number of violent activities occurring in prison. In addition to violent initiation ceremonies, violence may become part of everyday life for many gang members. Because they are often organized along racial lines, racial tensions among all prisoners, as well as between inmates and guards, may increase at a particular facility with the existence of gangs. Inmates rely on violence for purposes of intimidation and protection, thereby potentially increasing the level of violence at the institution. Gang members generally account for more assaults on other inmates and staff than inmates not affiliated with a gang. In addition to rival gang members, another common target of gang violence includes gang members who are suspected of disloyalty to the gang. This is especially prominent among members who are attempting to leave their current gang.

Just as with street gangs, turf wars may emerge over areas of the prison. Common areas, such as the cafeteria or recreation yard, are often the venue for these turf wars, in which rival gangs fight over specific, claimed territory they feel is being encroached upon by rival gang members. Unlike the turf wars among street gangs, there is no neutral or safe area for gang members to retreat to, often resulting in an eruption of violence among rival gang members.

Communication among gang members is essential to carry out organized violence within a facility. Some gangs use sophisticated code passed on slips of paper to communicate with other members, and others beat on cell walls or bars to convey messages across prison corridors. By communicating in this manner, gang members may be able to organize massive gang-related activities with less chance of recognition by correctional authorities.

Inmates go through a process termed *prisonization,* in which they adopt the norms, values, and beliefs that are endemic to the inmate subculture. Part of this prisonization process may involve joining a gang, initially for protection purposes. Many of the ideals encompassed by the inmate subculture counter those found in the general community, such as having no respect for authority and accepting involvement in crime and violence as normal. It is also believed that the longer an inmate remains in prison, the more ingrained these values become in the individual's personality. Because the inmate subculture values violence as a resolution to differences, inmates often become accustomed to violence as a way of life.

The deprivation theory can be paralleled with the primary ideals of prisonization. Deprivation theory suggests that the pains of imprisonment, such as a loss of liberty, heterosexual relationships, material goods and services, autonomy, and personal security account for the creation of the inmate subculture and, consequently, violent activities and acceptance of those activities as normal. In contrast, the importation theory suggests that inmates bring their criminogenic and antisocial norms, values, and beliefs with them from the community. According to this theory, violence is already a normal way of life prior to incarceration, not something that is learned within the correctional facility. If the tenets of this theory hold true, many of the inmates who engage in gang activity may have participated in similar activities prior to their incarceration.

Types of Gang Violence in Prison

Although homicide is among the most feared types of violence, it is also the least-frequently perpetuated type of violence among the inmate population. Prison homicides are most likely to result from either a particular gang activity, such as an initiation ceremony, or as the end result of an assault against another inmate. The prevalence of homicide among inmates has drastically decreased since 1980. Many believe this decrease can be partially attributed to the practice of segregating known gang members and other offenders who are frequent violators of violence-related rule infractions, preventing them from committing further acts of violence against other inmates.

Inmates may also use sexual violence in an attempt to control one another. All forms of sexual intercourse, including consensual sex, are prohibited by correctional policies. Although some sexual relations in prison are consensual, forced sexual contact is one way in which prisoners may exert their power and masculinity on other prisoners. Male prison society is almost completely devoid of females, many believe that males commit sexual violence against each other in an attempt to feminize their victims and act out power roles. Unlike sexual assault in the free community, the majority of sexual assaults that occur behind bars are interracial, and many are gang-related incidents occurring between rival gang members.

Male rival gang members may use both overt and covert sexual activities to exert dominance over one another. This phenomenon is less common among female inmates. Females are significantly less likely to become involved in gangs than their male counterparts. Additionally, female inmates are less likely to perpetrate sexual violence against their fellow inmates. Although sexual coercion may be relatively more common among female inmates than overt sexual violence, this coercion is seldom linked to gang involvement.

Many inmates adhere to the "convict code," which is an informal set of norms and values that are loosely followed. Some of the tenets of the convict code include "be a man" and "be tough," which may inadvertently encourage inmates to engage in violence against their fellow inmates to exert their masculinity and toughness. The code also endorses that inmates be loyal to other convicts and not attract attention to themselves, which may partially explain why many violent incidents ultimately go unreported to correctional authorities.

Levels of violence are at least partially correlated with overcrowding. As the number of inmates increases, the ability for correctional officers to continuously monitor inmates decreases. Double-celling inmates, or housing two inmates in a cell originally designed for one person, may also contribute to violence. This is especially illustrative when considering that a large number of violent physical and sexual acts occur among cellmates. Overcrowding also reduces the ability of authorities to segregate violent inmates or those who have been violently victimized into their own housing units to prevent future acts of violence. A higher prison population also results in fewer work opportunities, leaving idle those who may be the most likely to commit acts of violence against other inmates.

Gangs as a Correlate of Violence

Not all inmates are equally likely to participate in prison violence. An informally organized prison social system, known as the prison hierarchy, loosely dictates the likelihood of an inmate's involvement in violence, either as a perpetrator or as a victim. An inmate's place on the prison hierarchy is often determined by their individual characteristics. One of the major characteristics that determine whether an inmate will occupy a place on the prison hierarchy where they are less likely to be victimized is their involvement in a prison gang. Those who become prominent gang members will find themselves in the uppermost echelons of the prison hierarchy, which not only shields them from having violence perpetrated against them, but also makes it more likely that they will perpetrate violence against other inmates.

Some inmates engage in activities that make them more susceptible to violence. Involvement in the buying or selling of illegal contraband, such as drugs, alcohol, or cigarettes may place an inmate at particular risk. Gambling and especially owing gambling debts also places an inmate at risk, as inmates who are owed gambling winnings may resort to physical violence in an attempt to collect unpaid debts. These types of behaviors are considered high risk, and despite being cautioned against them, many inmates who are involved in prison gangs engage in these risky behaviors.

Reporting Issues

Issues related to prison violence are further exacerbated by the fact that many incidents go unreported. Inmates are reluctant to report victimization by other inmates, in part because of the informal social structure of prison. Inmates are encouraged to not fraternize or associate with correctional officers and staff, and to not "snitch" on their fellow inmates. The consequences for officially reporting these incidents may be revenge by their attackers or other inmates, as they may be viewed as weak. Although it would seem that inmates may be therefore more likely to report incidents perpetrated against them by correctional staff, they also may be reluctant to report these incidents. Some inmates believe that their reports of violence at the hands of correctional staff will not be taken seriously, and others fear the reprisal of reporting such incidents. This issue is particularly pertinent when the attacks are committed by gang members. Inmates who report victimization may be particularly fearful of not only their attacker, but of their attacker's fellow gang members seeking out revenge against them for reporting the incident to correctional officers.

Inmates are often hesitant to report sexual victimization to an even greater extent than other forms of physical victimization. Victims may fear that the perpetrator(s) may exact revenge for reporting the incident to correctional authorities, possibly leading to future acts of physical and sexual victimization. Victims may also feel embarrassed at their own perceived lack of masculinity. Because of the normative nature of violence among prisoners, inmates may not perceive that a crime has occurred. Especially among inmates who engage in risky behaviors, such as gambling and black-market involvement, sexual violence or sexual misconduct is often seen as a solution to indebtedness, and victims may believe they are deserving of this type of victimization.

Violence perpetrated by gangs poses particular problems with respect to reporting. Victims of gang violence may be especially likely to not report the violence to correctional authorities. Fear of reprisal by gang members is particularly feared by targets of violence. Furthermore, because a great deal of gang violence perpetrated behind bars is between rival gang members, it is likely that the target may not report it because they do not want their involvement in a gang to be revealed. The punishments and segregation methods in place at most facilities provide disincentives to reporting gang violence. Gang members are typically more likely to handle violence through vigilante justice, exacting revenge on their attackers either by themselves or with their fellow gang members.

Solutions to Gangs

Because correctional facilities prohibit gang membership among inmates, various official methods attempt to eliminate or reduce gang membership and gang violence within correctional facilities. These methods vary according to the state and the individual institution. Correctional policies try to account for the unique nature of prison gangs when determining appropriate solutions and responses to gang membership. The traditional method was to increase the length of a prison sentence for known gang members. However, because many gang members are already serving a life sentence, this solution provides little incentive for them to leave a gang. Prison policies also often consider the potential for punitive measures to increase the shroud of secrecy associated with gang membership.

Identification, Segregation, and Tracking

The first step to controlling gang activity is to successfully identify potential gang members. Upon intake, inmates are subject to a process of classification for housing purposes by classification specialists who are trained in identifying potential gang members. Some states require that inmates who are identified as gang members be placed in disciplinary segregation, which is meant as a form of separate housing from other inmates. In disciplinary segregation, inmates are given no privileges other than one hour of outdoor recreational time per day, which can be revoked at the discretion of correctional authorities. The rationale for disciplinary segregation is two-fold: it is meant as a punishment for gang membership, and prohibits interaction with other gang members in an attempt to reduce violence among inmates in the prison's general population.

Another scenario is that identified gang members may be sent to separate facilities. Again, the purpose of this segregation is to decrease interaction and violence among those housed in the general population. However, housing gang members together may allow for members to interact with other gang members, thereby increasing violence at the institutions exclusively housing gang members. Furthermore, after interstate transfers of high-ranking gang members, these members may simply open a new chapter in a new state.

Certain minimum-security institutions can also be deemed gang-free facilities. In order for inmates to be sent to a gang-free facility, they must have no existing or previous history of gang membership or association. These institutions are considered to be significantly less violent and safer than other types of institutions, and may prevent inmates who may have otherwise joined a prison gang from doing so.

Databases are now used by correctional agencies in an effort to track and monitor prison gangs and their activities. Not only can correctional agencies share information with each other on inmates who have been identified as gang members, but there is also the possibility of inter-agency information sharing, allowing police agencies to also be involved in the process. A major benefit to these databases is that photographs of the individual, as well as any identifying tattoos or scars, are associated with the individual's file. Database searches can be conducted simply based on these identifying marks.

Treatment, Rehabilitation, and Education

Some states have implemented gang treatment and rehabilitation strategies. In these venues, once a gang member has been identified by the classification staff and segregated, they are placed into a peer-led program. These programs are led by former gang members who instruct the newly arrived inmates on how to deal with and avoid violence within the facility without resorting to gang membership. Some facets of these programs include increasing an individual's problem-solving skills, utilizing role-playing strategies, and providing substance abuse treatment. Other alternatives may include programs for existing gang members who are committed to ceasing their membership status. Inmates who have been segregated for association or membership with a gang may show an interest in this type of program in order to be returned to the general correctional population.

Many prisons have programs that are meant to educate inmates on issues related to both physical and sexual violence. These programs center on educating inmates on what constitutes violence, providing them with alternatives to engaging in violence and the resources to deal with victimization.

They also encourage inmates to avoid high-risk behaviors that may place them at a greater risk of victimization, such as gambling and buying or selling goods on the illegal inmate market. These programs are often peer-led by other inmates who have firsthand experience as either the perpetrators or victims of prison violence.

Curbing Contraband

Prison administrators have long recognized the role that illegal contraband has in perpetuating violence among prisoners. Possession or trafficking of illegal drugs and alcohol are not allowed at any correctional institution, and cigarettes are banned at most institutions. Cigarettes are particularly problematic because they are both legal in the community and can be easily smuggled in by visitors or correctional officers. They are also often considered the primary currency among inmates, used in place of money for activities such as gambling and bartering for goods and services. Banning these various forms of contraband has become somewhat controversial. Although the prison administration fears possession of these items and the dangers associated with them, some believe that disallowing items in prison that would otherwise be considered legal, such as cigarettes, creates more violence by perpetuating the black market and allowing gang members and other entrepreneurial inmates the opportunity to extort and commit further acts of violence.

Connections With Loved Ones

In an effort to decrease the violence that occurs as an outcome of frustration or despair at the loss of contact with loved ones, many prisons allow for visits between prisoners and family members. By allowing inmates to visit with their families, especially their spouses and children, many believe they are better able to maintain a healthy, masculine self-image, reducing their need to commit violence against other inmates in an effort to exert male domination. Conjugal visits in particular may prevent sexual violence in that it allows inmates to maintain a healthy, nonviolent sexual relationship. All forms of visitation are believed to be helpful in preventing violent rule violations, as inmates view them as part of a reward system for good behavior. As such, allowing for visitation may prevent inmates from joining gangs by allowing them to continue their social contacts with the outside world.

Technology and Prison Structure

Some facilities are beginning to rely on various forms of technology to curb violence. Many facilities use some form of closed circuit television (CCTV) to monitor and record activities within the institution. Video cameras can be used to capture images and, if monitored, can prevent violence or prevent violent activities from escalating. There are also projects currently underway to use crime-mapping software to help determine whether a particular institution is at risk for particular violent incidents, such as attempted escapes, riots, sexual assaults, and assaults on staff members.

Others have recommended an overhaul in the structure of correctional administration on a large scale in order to address some of the issues related to gang violence. Because the inmate culture feeds on an "us versus them" mentality (the prisoners versus the correctional staff), breaking down the barriers between these two groups may be key to disentangling many of the issues associated with the convict code and inmate subculture. Some suggest that additional training of correctional officers to treat inmates more humanely may address some of the issues related to violence. Most notably, those associated with nonreporting of crimes and major violent incidents, such as riots, may be impacted by this upheaval of the existing correctional framework.

The negative aspects to having existing gangs within correctional facilities include potential increases in violence, gambling, and black market activity. However, some argue that the existence of gangs may actually be beneficial to correctional facilities and staff. Correctional staff may even look down upon inmates who cannot protect themselves against more aggressive, violent inmates.

Pro: Positive Aspects of Prison Gangs

Gang organizations may serve as a mechanism of informal social control. Prison is meant to be a total institution, one in which all aspects of inmates' lives are controlled. However, as the prison population continues to grow, it may become increasingly difficult for correctional officers to exercise the extent of formal social control necessary to consistently control the inmates. The number of incarcerated individuals continues to surge, often with few correctional officer hires, and there continues to be an increasing disparity between the ratio of inmates to officers. Gangs may therefore buttress the existing formal social order of the prison by providing norms and values to which inmates can adhere.

Moreover, gangs may actually help foster a sense of cohesion among group members. Although intergang violence is problematic, belonging to a gang may give inmates an informal social structure in which to survive the harsh realities of prison life. Gang affiliation may protect inmates against violence at the hands of other inmates, without physical violence to necessitate this protection. In other words, it may be the threat of potential retaliation by gang members, and not the actual retaliation, that isolates inmates within their gangs for protection.

Violence occurring among prisoners may also deflect some violence from correctional officers. If inmates view each other as being the enemy, they may be less likely to engage in violence against the correctional staff. Again, by providing a form of informal social control, the mechanisms of formal social control (in this case, the correctional staff), may become less of a threat to the existing social structure among the inmates.

Con: Drawbacks of Prison Gangs

There are many negative aspects to tolerating the existence of gangs within correctional settings. Gangs are likely responsible for a disproportionate amount of violence against other inmates, as well as against correctional officers and staff. They also smuggle drugs, cigarettes, and other contraband into the facility. Gangs are therefore responsible for creating a significant amount of criminogenic activities behind bars. Despite the deflection of violence against correctional officers and staff, it may be seen as more beneficial by the correctional administration to curb or even eliminate the existence of gangs from the facilities, and therefore reduce criminogenic activities.

See Also: 15. Prison Overcrowding; 19. Sex Offender Treatment.

Further Readings

Camp, G. M., and C. G. Camp. *Prison Gangs: Their Extent, Nature, and Impact on Prisons.* Washington, DC: U.S. Government Printing Office, 1985.

Cloward, Richard, Donald R. Cressey, George H. Grosser, Richard McCleary, Lloyd E. Ohlin, Gresham M. Sykes, and Sheldon Messinger.

Theoretical Studies in the Social Organization of the Prison. New York: Social Science Research Council, 1960.

Cressey, Donald R., and John Irwin. "Thieves, Convicts and the Inmate Culture." *Social Problems,* v.10/3 (1962).

Cunningham, Mark D., and Jon R. Sorenson. "Predictive Factors for Violence Misconduct in Protective Custody." *The Prison Journal,* v.87/2 (2007).

Decker, Scott, and B. VanWinkle. "Legitimizing Drug Use: A Note on the Impact of Gang Membership and Drug Sales on the Use of Illicit Drugs." *Justice Quarterly,* v.17/2 (2000).

Gaes, Gerald G., Susan Wallace, Evan Gilman, Jody Klein-Saffran, and Sharon Suppa. *The Influence of Prison Gang Affiliation on Violence and Other Prison Gang Misconduct.* Washington, DC: Bureau of Prisons, U.S. Department of Justice, 2001.

Gilligan, James. "How to Increase the Rate of Violence—and Why." In *Exploring Corrections: A Book of Readings,* edited by Tara Gray. Boston: Allyn and Bacon, 2002.

Hassine, Victor. *Life Without Parole: Living in Prison Today.* New York: Oxford University Press, 2008.

Kimmett, Edgar, Ian O'Donnell, and Carol Martin. *Prison Violence: The Dynamics of Conflict, Fear, and Power.* Devon, UK: Willan Publishing, 2002.

King, Kate, Benjamin Steiner, and Stephanie Ritchie Breach. "Violence in the Super-Max: A Self-Fulfilling Prophecy." *The Prison Journal,* v.88/1 (2008).

Kratcoski, P. "The Implications of Research Explaining Prison Violence and Disruption." *Federal Probation,* v.52 (1988).

Page, J. "Violence and Incarceration: A Personal Observation." In *Correctional Perspectives: Views From Academics, Practitioners, and Prisoners,* edited by L. Alarid and P. Cromwell. Los Angeles, CA: Roxbury Publishers, 2002.

Sykes, Gresham. *The Society of Captives.* Princeton, NJ: Princeton University Press, 1958.

9

Healthcare and Medical Assistance for Prisoners

Daryl Kosiak
University of North Dakota

In the first decade of the 21st century, the United States, with over 2.2 million persons incarcerated in prisons and jails, had an imprisonment rate of 756 per 100,000 persons. Other industrialized nations, such as New Zealand, incarcerate at a rate of 185 per 100,000, while England and Wales incarcerate at a rate of 153 per 100,000. As a 24/7 operation, prisons and jails are responsible for a number of services utilized by persons in custody, including food, shelter, and medical care. It is estimated that the United States spent over $70 billion on corrections in 2010. In 2001, the Bureau of Justice Statistics reported that U.S. state governments spent 12 percent of their correctional budgets on medical care, a sum of almost $3.3 billion. By 2008, two states alone—California and Texas—spent over $3 billion on inmate healthcare. If the 2001 proportion of correctional budgets spent on healthcare remains constant, governments will have spent an estimated $8.4 billion on prisoner healthcare in 2010.

Despite the massive amounts of government spending on healthcare for incarcerated persons, questions remain as to the quantity and quality of such healthcare. Inmate complaints, both administrative and in the courts, frequently allege receipt of poor medical care. Different media forums periodically report shocking stories of poor medical outcomes for prisoners. Correctional healthcare providers, like their private-sector counterparts, are subject to claims alleging medical malpractice, and pay settlements or judgments for injuries. Several states have had adverse court rulings finding constitutional violations related to the system-wide quality of prison healthcare.

To fully address the issue of correctional healthcare in the 21st century, it is necessary to examine the obligation of government to provide healthcare to prisoners, the costs of such healthcare, and issues related to the provision of healthcare to prisoners. While prisons and jails both detain prisoners, each component may have very different inmate needs. Of the 2.2 million persons detained by the United States in 2008, some 780,000 were held in jails as either pretrial detainees or convicted offenders sentenced to short sentences. Jails generally have more admissions and discharges than prisons, and hold each detainee for a shorter period of time—sometimes as little as 24 hours—but at other times, for over a year. Because of the transient population, jails deal with some issues more frequently than prisons, including substance withdrawal and injuries incurred during arrests. Because of the longer term of sentences, prisons deal with many chronic health issues.

History of the Legal Obligation for Prison Healthcare

The use of incarceration as a criminal sanction is a relatively modern development. Before 1800, prisoners were detained in jails only until trial, and then if convicted, were subject to fines and corporal or capital punishment. Detainees were expected to provide for the costs of their incarceration, and were charged fees for food, clothing, fuel for heat, and medical care.

With the rise of incarceration as a penal sanction, it became necessary for prisons to provide minimal healthcare to persons in custody. It was not until 1976 that the U.S. Supreme Court established that prisoners in the custody of the states had a constitutional entitlement to some medical care. In *Estelle v. Gamble,* a prisoner (Gamble) in Texas claimed that he was injured while working on the prison farm. Between the time of the injury in November 1973 and the time the litigation was initiated in February 1974, Gamble was seen by medical personnel about 17 times and provided various diagnostic tests and treatments. The prisoner was dissatisfied with the quality of care he received, and sued government officials, alleging that they had violated his Eighth Amendment right to be free from cruel and unusual punishment.

The Supreme Court analyzed Gamble's claim in light of previous cases by the Court. The original intent of the Eighth Amendment's Cruel and Unusual Punishment Clause was to prohibit torture and barbarous methods of punishment. As the country matured, its concept of what was "cruel and unusual" punishment also evolved. Because Gamble was incarcerated by the government involuntarily, duty was imposed on the state to treat the prisoner's medical needs. The failure to adequately treat a prisoner's medical need can result in unnecessary pain, suffering, and even death. The infliction of "unnecessary pain and suffering" is inconsistent with evolving standards of decency, and thus violates the Eighth Amendment.

The Court ruled that "deliberate indifference" to a serious medical need constitutes the unnecessary and wanton infliction of pain, and violates the Eighth Amendment. The Court did not define what a "serious medical need" was, nor did it explain how an individual government actor might be "deliberately indifferent" to such a serious medical need. However, under the facts of the case alleged by prisoner Gamble, being seen by medical staff 17 times in several months, and receiving various diagnostic tests and treatments, was evidence that the state actors were not deliberately indifferent.

Almost 20 years later, in a case that did not involve medical care, the Supreme Court did define "deliberate indifference." In the case of *Farmer v. Brennan,* inmate Farmer was a biological male who claimed to be gender dysphoric, and who exhibited some feminine physical characteristics. After being transferred from one prison to another, Farmer alleged that he was beaten and raped by other inmates at the new institution. The suit was dismissed by the trial court, as Farmer acknowledged never telling prison officials of subjective concerns for safety at the new prison. A federal court of appeals affirmed the dismissal, and review was sought in the U.S. Supreme Court. The issue for the Court was whether deliberate indifference requires acting with an intent to cause injury, simple negligence, or something in between. Because the lawsuit had been dismissed at the pleading stage, the Supreme Court assumed Farmer's factual allegations of being beaten and sexually assaulted were true and addressed the legal issue.

The Supreme Court determined that deliberate indifference was less than actual intent to cause injury, but was more than simple negligence. A government official acts with deliberate indifference when the official knows of and disregards an excessive risk to an inmate's health and safety. The Supreme Court sent the matter back to the lower court to apply the new standard set forth in its opinion. A federal jury, after hearing the testimony of inmate

Farmer and prison officials, determined that Farmer had not been assaulted, and judgment was entered in favor of the defendant prison officials.

While the deliberate indifference standard established by the Supreme Court is very high, prison officials constantly deal with how to meet it in terms of personnel and other resources. Although the deliberate indifference standard is best characterized as a minimum, it is not entirely clear how much medical care can be enough to meet even that minimal standard, or when a medical need is serious. Prisoners are not entitled to preferred or the best medical care. It is not deliberate indifference when a prisoner disagrees with a correctional healthcare provider over a diagnosis or course of treatment. While it may be desirable or even necessary to provide a community standard of care to prisoners, the issue then becomes whose community the standard is drawn from—that of the resourced (in terms of funds or insurance) with access to both quality and quantity healthcare, or that of the unresourced (no or limited funds or insurance) with little or no access to medical care.

Medical Needs of the Inmate Population

While the great majority of prisoners fall in the typically healthy age group of 18–45, prisoners may be sicker than their counterparts in the community. In the United States, 40 percent of the jail or prison population report having at least one chronic medical condition, a much higher rate than similarly aged Americans. Compared to unincarcerated Americans, prisoners are significantly more likely to have asthma, diabetes, and suffer from a heart attack. It is estimated that in a given year in the United States, 25 percent of all HIV-infected persons, 33 percent of persons with hepatitis C (HCV), and 40 percent of persons with active tuberculosis will spend time in a correctional facility, either a jail or prison. When dealing with HIV/AIDS, it is estimated that almost two percent of prison inmates are HIV positive, a rate four times higher than the general population.

Concerns over prison healthcare are not limited to the United States. Prisoners in England tend to be less healthy than nonprisoners in terms of mental illness, addiction, disease, and disability. To address perceived shortcomings in England's prisoner healthcare system, medical care for inmates was transitioned from a service provided by the prison system to "primary care trusts," which work with Britain's National Health Service to provide inmates with healthcare similar to persons in the community. The transition began in 2003 and was completed in 2006. A government report of the system reflects positive changes, including improved staff training and increased general standard of care. The same report noted problems with continuity of care after transfers, and lack of good dental care. Despite the transition, English inmates complain about long waits to see providers, being denied treatment, and a lack of privacy when discussing confidential healthcare matters.

The Aging Prison Population

As a person ages, the cost of health maintenance increases, and it costs more to provide healthcare to a typical 60-year-old than a typical 20-year-old. In 2006, the 293,000 United States inmates over 45 years of age represented 20 percent of the total prison population. In the United States, inmates over the age of 65 make up one percent of the prison population, but account for 15 percent of prisoner deaths. While U.S. prisoners in the age group 15–45 had a 19 percent lower death rate than counterparts in the community, prisoners in the age group 55–64 had a 56 percent higher mortality rate than those in the community. While some experts identify the age of 55 as a benchmark in human chronology that requires more healthcare, many prisoners consistently demonstrate at the age of 45 the signs and symptoms of an unincarcerated person at the age of 55. This premature aging may be caused by the stress and strain of imprisonment, or that prisoners tend to come from medically underserved segments of the community, which by and large have greater healthcare needs. Prisoners over the age of 55 totaled 76,500, or five percent of the estimated 1.4 million prison population. The over-50 inmate population in one representative state, Virginia, has grown from 900 in 1990 to over 5,000 in 20 years.

The United States is not alone in dealing with an aging inmate population. The fastest-growing age group of prisoners in Japan is the over-60 group. Prison officials in Japan estimate that 12 percent of its inmate population is elderly. While the percentage of Japanese over the age of 60 grew by 17 percent from 2000 to 2006, the prison population for that age group grew 87 percent. Like elderly prisoners in other countries, the older Japanese inmates deal with high blood pressure, diabetes, and incontinence.

Prisons in England and Wales are experiencing similar graying. In 2009, the United Kingdom housed 7,350 inmates over the age of 50, including 300 women. Of that number, 26 were older than 80. In 2007, 35 prisoners in the United Kingdom over the age of 60 died of natural causes. The number of elderly inmates increased by over 55 percent between 1995 and 2000. English prison officials note that elderly inmates, as a group, complain less; as a result, their needs are often forgotten or ignored. This passivity may be present in elderly prisoners in all cultures.

Increased Inmate Population and Healthcare Costs

Beginning in the 1980s, the United States declared a war on crime, increased law enforcement efforts with longer and more prison sentences, and eliminated parole and favorable good-conduct time systems to ensure "truth in sentencing." In 1980, there were just over 500,000 prisoners in U.S. jails and prisons. By 1990, that number had more than doubled to 1,167,511. The 1990 incarcerated population almost doubled again to 2.2 million in 2008. An increased number of prisoners will result in increased costs of correctional healthcare. But the increased population is only part of the issue; healthcare has also become more expensive.

Persons living in the United States have access to expensive treatments and technology unavailable in the 1970s, such as drugs and diagnostic procedures. As Americans have lived longer, the healthcare system has been compelled to address chronic diseases, which may account for as much as 75 percent of healthcare expenditures. Medical conditions like kidney failure, heart disease, and cancer have increased treatment options unknown in the 1970s. New interventions such as health-maintenance treatments for patients suffering from HIV/AIDS or hepatitis and the availability of treatment for mental illness has also increased the cost of healthcare.

Prisoners, like the general public, have access to more and better-trained healthcare professionals, including dentists; physicians; mid-level practitioners, such as physician's assistants and nurse practitioners; as well as nurses, lab technicians, and other support staff. Modern healthcare increasingly uses scarce and expensive diagnostic testing requiring complex and costly equipment to diagnose and treat patients. Like counterparts in the community, the administrative cost of healthcare in prison has grown as resources are spent on hiring and managing professional healthcare personnel, and upgrading systems such as medical records and diagnostic technologies. While developing a prison medical bureaucracy has benefits in terms of increased supervision and control of providers and support staff, the increased professional staffing requires administrative personnel such as healthcare administrators, directors of nursing, medical directors, supervisory pharmacists, medical records supervisors, quality assurance personnel, and other support staff who add to the cost of healthcare without directly providing patient services.

Defining the Cost of Prisoner Healthcare

In the United States in 2008, the per-person annual cost of healthcare was estimated at $7,681. Estimated total healthcare expenses exceeded $2.3 trillion in 2008, more than three times the $714 billion spent in 1990, and over eight times the $253 billion spent in 1980. In 1976, the year *Estelle v. Gamble* was decided, healthcare expenditure in the United States was just over $600 per person. The $7,681 annual healthcare expenditure needs to be placed in the context that some individuals, such as chronically or acutely ill persons with resources, receive a much greater amount of total healthcare dollars. And some persons, because of a lack of resources or simply little need for medical treatment, utilize fewer or no healthcare dollars.

One method of measuring the cost of prisoner healthcare is how much is spent per inmate. It is estimated that in 2008, per-prisoner medical costs were $11,600 a year in California, $2,920 in Texas, and $5,757 in New York. Florida, with one of the highest incarceration rates in the country, spent an estimated $421 million on inmate healthcare in 2008, a 37 percent increase over the $307.5 million spent in 2004. If the estimated $8.4 billion spent by all correctional systems for healthcare is divided by 2.2 million inmates, the per-capita expenditure is just over $3,800 per prisoner per year.

Critics have compared state figures like California and concluded that its prisoner healthcare costs are very high. However, it is important to ascertain what the dollar figure for healthcare includes. The modern correctional healthcare system is in many cases two-tiered. The first tier includes those services that can be provided in-house by employee or contract healthcare providers. The other tier includes those services that are provided in the community, usually specialty diagnostic and professional services, as well as hospitalization. In these instances, the prisoner needs to be escorted by staff. When an inmate is hospitalized in the community, the state must pay not only the cost of the hospital care, but also an additional cost to provide continuous supervision. For inmates who pose extreme escape or other safety risks, this supervision may require as much as three armed officers, 24 hours a day, for the duration of the hospital stay. When examining the state estimates on healthcare expenditures, it is unclear if these guard costs are included in the healthcare estimates.

Another method of determining the level of healthcare is to look at the frequency of contacts between prisoners and healthcare providers. Some surveys reflect that prisoners have more contacts than the unincarcerated, average person. For example, the average community citizen may see a healthcare provider 3.5 times per year, but an average prisoner may see a healthcare provider eight or nine times per year. While the same concern exists as to how any "average" person is determined, for example, resourced or unresourced prison issues may skew such results when only raw contacts are counted. Correctional concerns such as accountability and security dictate that prisoners do not have the same freedom of movement as persons in the community. Prisoners may need to see prison medical staff to obtain daily prescriptions of medication that a community counterpart might receive as a weekly or monthly supply. Such practices are necessary to minimize the risk of loss or abuse of medications, especially those with narcotic qualities. In other cases, inmates in controlled housing units are visited on a daily basis by prison healthcare personnel, as these inmates are unable to go to scheduled sick calls. In both cases, simple reliance on raw numbers can present misleading depictions of the cost of healthcare.

Since the 1970s, a number of factors have contributed to positive changes in prison healthcare. Various groups familiar with the complexities of correctional healthcare have studied the issues of prison healthcare and formulated standards and criteria for providing medical services to incarcerated persons. While not binding on any correctional entity, endeavoring to meet such standards provides uniform, articulated goals and a method of assessing what the system is doing and what it can do to improve. Despite increased spending, improved staffing, and larger medical bureaucracy, correctional healthcare systems continue to experience problems to the extent that one large correctional department's prison health system was ordered into receivership by a federal judge to remedy ongoing constitutional deficiencies. And administrative and legal complaints by inmates and inmate support groups about prison healthcare have not abated.

Substandard Care Providers

The level of public scrutiny aroused by high-profile correctional system litigation and media reports of inmate deaths caused by medical errors may warrant the conclusion that some correctional systems are staffed with unqualified healthcare practitioners who can't work anywhere else. Due to the low pay, low status, and perceived lower status of the prisoner patient population, providing health services in a correctional environmental is not a particularly desirable career. Unlike a traditional patient–provider relationship, correctional providers may be skeptical of their prisoner–patient's complaints as being an attempt to acquire some secondary gain such as time off of work, prescription painkillers, or more favorable prison conditions. There have been instances of prisoners feigning health emergencies, and then attempting to escape when taken to community resources for care. In at least one such instance, a correctional officer was killed during a shootout with the prisoner's accomplices. There are also examples of prisoners who malingered until the time of their deaths from untreated medical conditions.

Prisoners may be distrustful of correctional healthcare providers who are viewed as being just another part of the correctional system, or hold the perception that because the provider works for a correctional entity, the provider is incompetent. Some correctional systems are unable to hire the number of medical staff needed to provide all necessary care. Reports of correctional healthcare providers with one or more malpractice judgments or settlements, state licensing board actions, or limitations on licenses are usually accompanied by reports of medical care with bad or less than optimal outcomes. Some correctional medical systems have personnel with adverse licensing board actions at a rate higher than the national average of one in 40 (2.5 percent). Inmates, or their survivors, have won multimillion-dollar medical malpractice lawsuits or obtained settlements for negligent healthcare.

As noted in *Estelle v. Gamble*, medical malpractice and denial of constitutionally required medical care are not the same. Medical malpractice by a government healthcare provider does not become a constitutional violation just because of the government actor's status. Medical malpractice occurs when an injury to a patient occurs as a result of a negligent act or omission of a healthcare provider. In the community, the quality of healthcare is regulated by a number of factors, including requirements for medical licensing by state medical boards, authority to prescribe certain controlled substances by the DEA, medical malpractice litigation, and the ability of persons who believe they are receiving poor medical care to find another provider. Correctional healthcare is regulated by similar factors, except prisoners do not have the ability to choose healthcare providers, and instead must rely upon those provided by the state.

It is not known how many persons are injured in the United States annually as a result of medical errors. At one time it was estimated that as many as 98,000 deaths each year were caused by medical errors. Congress passed the Patient Safety Act in 2005 authorizing the U.S. Department of Health and Human Services (HHS) to begin collecting data on medical errors and the injuries caused by such errors. While not specifically addressing medical errors in correctional facilities, a systemized database may provide insight as to whether medical errors in correctional settings occur at higher rates than in the community.

Since 1990, the National Practitioner Data Bank (NPDB), operated by the HHS, has served as a repository for reports of professional negligence damage claims, actions by state licensing boards, and prescription and medicare limitations on healthcare practitioners. The most recent published data is for 2006, and it indicates that there were 15,843 malpractice payments and 7,044 licensing actions involving healthcare providers in that year. Of these reports, approximately 80 percent involved physicians; 10 percent involved dentists; and the remaining subjects were other personnel including nurses and physical therapists. The NPDB report does not indicate how many, if any, of these incidents involved a correctional healthcare provider. Since 1990, when the NPDB began operating, there have been almost 300,000 reported malpractice payment reports. Approximately one in every 100 physicians have a report of some type in the NPDB. Healthcare systems, including correctional systems, obtain malpractice and licensing data on healthcare providers from the NPDB prior to hiring or during periodic reviews to obtain information on healthcare providers.

Systemic Responses to Correctional Health Issues

While the lack of resources may not be the only cause of poor-quality prisoner healthcare, it is likely a significant cause. The estimate of medical-related deaths and reports to the NPDB would suggest that medical errors are not limited to providers of correctional healthcare. Even assuming that there are more medical errors in correctional environments than in the community, it is not clear if these are errors of individual providers or symptomatic of problems within a given correctional healthcare system.

Working under the assumption that resources for correctional health-care, as for corrections or any government program, are not without limits, are there alternatives for improving prisoner healthcare without increasing costs? The answer may be crucial, as prisoners are part of a small group of persons in the United States who have a constitutionally mandated right to healthcare, a right not available for those who are not in some type of government custody. And as with every other resource choice a government makes, adding a dollar to that budget takes a dollar away from another budgets such as education, defense, roads, or other worthy public projects.

Pro: Benefits of Methods to Reduce Healthcare Costs

Early Release for Sick or Elderly Prisoners

The burden of providing medical care for the chronically or acutely ill and elderly has created a burden on correctional healthcare systems. The Bureau of Justice Statistics reports that prisoners over the age of 45 account for more than two-thirds of all state prisoner deaths, and that deaths for prisoners over 55 are 11 times higher than for prisoners 35–44 years of age. In a 2004 study of recidivism conducted by the U.S. Sentencing Commission, offenders over the age of 50 recidivated at a rate of less than 10 percent, compared to 35 percent for offenders under the age of 20, and about 24 percent for offenders between 25 and 35. While most states do not keep a separate accounting of medical expenditures by prisoner age group, some states link increased correctional medical expenditures to a graying population and that group's greater medical needs. One state correctional system estimates that healthcare costs for prisoners over 55 is five times higher than for prisoners under 55 years of age.

Early release of sick or ill prisoners would ease the burden of providing healthcare on the correctional system for those who are very elderly or very sick. In the United States, there are already public resources for the sick and elderly in place and, but for the criminal offense committed, the prisoner would be entitled to utilize those resources. While these released prisoners may become wards of the state, it would be in a different capacity. Costs of care would be lower, as there would be no need for correctional supervision. It is inefficient and redundant to create and manage two government-operated systems, one in the community and one in a correctional system, to care for the very sick or the elderly.

The federal government and some states already have such systems. Federal courts may reduce the prison sentences of inmates over 70 years of age or for other compelling reasons, including terminal illness. Some states provide for medical parole of terminally ill prisoners. One state without medical parole estimates it spends almost $41 million per year for the care of just 21 severely disabled inmates, and is considering passing legislation to permit medical parole in appropriate circumstances.

Reducing the Time Served in Prison

Increased healthcare costs, and the increased societal burden of caring for the medical needs of incarcerated persons, are in part products of increased prisoner numbers. Prior to the "get tough on crime" era in the 1980s, state and federal correctional entities worked with favorable good-conduct time statutes and parole. As an example, a person convicted of a federal offense could reduce his sentence by up to one-half by compliance with institution rules, and such inmates were eligible for parole after serving one-third of their sentence. In real terms, a federal prisoner sentenced to 10 years in prison under the indeterminate regimen could serve as little as 3.3 years if paroled at the first eligibility, or released at five years if all institution rules were followed. That same federal prisoner today serves 85 percent of the sentence, or 8.5 years. Prisoners would be released under conditions that permit supervision by parole officers, require the parolee to comply with various rules and regulations, and impose a sanction of revocation and return to prison for serious noncompliance.

Reinstituting these measures would result in an almost immediate reduction in the prison population, with a concomitant reduction in the need for healthcare resources for the prisoners who are released early. Persons given such release would be responsible for their own healthcare. These early-release mechanisms also serve a useful prison management purpose in that prisoners who have demonstrated an ability to comply with prison rules would be provided an opportunity to get out of prison with good behavior and stay out of prison by compliance with laws and regulations. Reducing the current and future population would relieve population pressure on current prison space, may reduce the number of prison staff, and would likely reduce or eliminate the need for the construction of more prisons in the future.

Contracting Out Prison Healthcare

It is estimated that over half of the states contract out all or part of their correctional healthcare. Contracts can be assigned to a nonprofit or governmental entity, such as in Texas, which contracts its prison healthcare to the University of Texas Medical Branch (UTMB) and Texas Tech University. Other states have contracted with for-profit organizations such as Prison Health Services. Advantages of contracting include governments paying a set, negotiated amount for prisoner medical care, elimination or reduction in size of a public-sector bureaucracy (the state-operated prison healthcare system), utilization of private-sector contractors who can use managed care, and economy-of-scale techniques to provide efficient and less-costly service.

At least one limitation on the recruitment and retention of high-quality correctional healthcare providers are state spending limits on salary and benefits paid to an employee. Contract providers may not have these limitations, allowing for competitive salary and benefits to be offered to professional staff. Because these contractors are in the business of recruiting and retaining health professionals, a system is already in place to locate qualified persons.

As a result of contracting, Texas prisoner healthcare is estimated at less than $3,000 per inmate per year, far below the costs of California and New York. Since the U.S. Supreme Court's 1988 opinion in *West v. Atkins,* private healthcare professionals under contract to provide medical services within a prison can be liable under title 42 U.S.C. § 1983 for deliberate indifference to the serious medical needs of a prisoner. Contract providers are subject to medical malpractice and state licensing regulations, helping to ensure that high-quality staff are hired and retained. Correctional entities have utilized contract providers to control or reduce healthcare costs, and it has not been demonstrated that the lower cost has come with a lower quality of healthcare for prisoners.

An additional benefit of contracting healthcare is that under the law of agency, the contractor, rather than the government, would be liable for any damages to patient prisoners caused by the negligent acts or omissions of the contract healthcare providers. This would reduce the government's liability when negligence is established, and also eliminate the need to review frivolous claims and costs of litigation.

Con: Drawbacks of Methods to Reduce Healthcare Costs

Early Release for Sick or Elderly Prisoners

In the 1970s, a rationale for eliminating parole and decreasing good-conduct time awards was to keep dangerous offenders in prison and prevent commission of new offenses. Not all elderly or seriously ill inmates are harmless in terms of protection of the public. Elderly inmates have been incarcerated recently for violent crimes. In a 2006 analysis of state court felony sentences, persons over 50 years of age accounted for seven percent of homicide and aggravated assault offenses, eight percent of drug trafficking sentences, and 13 percent of sexual assault sentences.

Predicting who might be too sick, or too near death to be a threat to society, is difficult. Recently, a prisoner held in Scotland for blowing up an American airliner in the 1980s and killing almost 300 people was diagnosed with terminal colon cancer and released on medical parole. The bomber was still alive over one year after release. While many released prisoners would be harmless, there is the potential for those ill or elderly parolees who are still criminally dangerous to commit new offenses, including crimes against vulnerable residents of nursing homes or healthcare facilities.

Some inmates may have resources to provide for their own care and treatment, but given the statistics, it is likely that most released prisoners would become wards of the state in a nursing home or hospital. While correctional systems may save money, these savings may result in costs being shifted from one governmental entity to another.

It is unlikely that prisoners released under these programs would be taken to the jailhouse door and turned loose without planning and supervision. To protect the public, correctional systems would need to increase the size of their bureaucracy for deciding who should be released early, and how and by whom the released prisoners are monitored and supervised. Most governments have community monitoring programs staffed by probation and parole officers, but a new wave of early-released prisoners with complex medical issues would be infused into the system. This new wave of clients could require enormous amounts of help to locate housing and other services, requiring additional training and staffing. The additional costs of planning and supervision, coupled with a transfer of actual medical costs from prisons to the community, could seriously dissipate any savings recognized by early release.

Reducing the Time Served in Prison

Like efforts aimed at the sick and elderly, there would be hidden societal costs such as new or larger systems to supervise released prisoners, and increased crime by early-released prisoners. As with early releases for the seriously sick and elderly prisoner, in most cases, the financial burden would be shifted from corrections to another governmental source. The United States has experienced a decline in crime since the "get tough" policies of the 1980s were implemented, and returning to the sentencing and release days of that era will lead to more criminals in the community, committing more crimes, and incurring greater costs to society.

While a plan for early release of the seriously ill or elderly is focused on those offenders who may pose the least risk of committing new offenses, a general plan of reducing penalties for all offenders would place the less-dangerous elderly and sick in the same position as the more criminogenic healthy and younger prisoners. While there would be a reduced cost for corrections and correctional healthcare, society would likely see an increase in crime, which would necessitate increased costs in police and courts. While an effort at intensive supervision of the released offender may be implemented, opponents of this approach argue that it would not be as effective in controlling criminality as incarceration. While having fewer inmates in a correctional system would likely lead to less healthcare expenditure, there is no guarantee that the sickest or oldest prisoners would be released, effectively minimizing anticipated healthcare savings.

Contracting Out Prison Healthcare

It is not entirely clear that contracting out prisoner healthcare either saves public money or results in higher-quality healthcare. Prisoners complain about the quality of contract healthcare, and providers of contract medical services have been named as defendants in lawsuits alleging inadequate or unconstitutional healthcare. Contract healthcare providers have also been found liable for damages caused by professional negligence. There may be questions as to whether the decision to utilize contract healthcare considers quality of services, or is premised on a lower cost. As a private-sector business, profit motive becomes a factor in costs of operations. Contractors must not only pay for the salaries and benefits of healthcare providers, but also maintain other business overhead costs and earn a profit for shareholders. Private-sector managed care can reduce inefficiencies, but at some point, maintaining or maximizing profits may be achieved only by increasing reimbursement or by limiting service. Some states or political subdivisions have terminated relationships with private-sector vendors as a result of highly publicized patient outcomes and issues over what services are covered under the agreements. Utilizing contractors may not reduce either prisoner complaints or lawsuits concerning healthcare. States may incur additional costs for monitoring the contracts, further reducing any savings.

Recently, Texas medical contractors have sought additional funds due to increased costs. The UTMB proposed laying off almost one-tenth of its medical personnel providing healthcare to Texas prisoners. Media investigations have shown examples of private health-service providers utilizing medical professionals with more frequency than average state licensing board actions, raising questions as to the quality of these contract providers.

Recalling that medical malpractice is one method of regulating health-care practitioners, contracting can minimize a government entity's tort liability for professional negligence. However, this burden is passed on to the contractor, reducing if not eliminating the governmental entity's incentive in ensuring that timely, appropriate medical care is provided to prisoners. Most states and the federal government have an administrative claim process, through which an individual injured by the negligent act or omission of a government employee can have their claim reviewed and settled, if appropriate. The government's involvement at each step of this process, including payment of a settlement or judgment, provides an incentive to ensure appropriate medical care.

Conclusion

Since 1976, when *Estelle v. Gamble* was decided, medical care for prisoners has improved in terms of both number and qualifications of medical personnel. While prisoner healthcare is not a subject on the forefront of most members of the community, there are many individuals, including prisoners themselves, who have a real and ongoing interest as evidenced by activism, litigation, and other steps toward public awareness.

See Also: 1. Capital Punishment/Death Penalty; 3. Cruel and Unusual Punishment; 11. Life Sentence; 12. Mentally Ill and Mentally Challenged Inmates; 16. Prison Privatization and Contract Facilities.

Further Readings

Awofeso, N. "Making Prison Health Care More Efficient." *British Medical Journal*, v.331 (2005).
BBC News. "Prison Health 'Not Good Enough' Despite Overhaul." (May 28, 2010). http://www.bbc.co.uk/news/10171358 (Accessed November 2010).
Becker, J. "Many Prison Doctors Have Troubled Past." *St. Petersburg Times* (September 27, 1999).
Dabney, D., and M. Vaughn. "Incompetent Jail and Prison Doctors." *The Prison Journal*, v.80 (2000).

Estelle v. Gamble, 429 U.S. 97 (1976).

Faiola, A. "Errant Elders Find Amenities in Japan's Jails." *Washington Post* (April 17, 2006).

Farmer v. Brennan, 511 U.S. 825 (1994).

Fazel, S., T. Hope, I. O'Donnell, M. Piper, and R. Jacoby. "Health of Elderly Male Prisoners Worse Than the General Population, Worse Than Younger Prisoners." *Age and Aging,* v.30 (2001).

Jennison, K. "The Violent Older Offender: A Research Note." *Federal Probation,* v.50 (1986).

Kerle, K., S. Stojkovic, R. Kiekbusch, and J. Rowan. "A Rejoinder to Vaughn and Smith's 'Practicing Penal Harm Medicine in the United States:' Prisoners' Voices From Jail.'" *Justice Quarterly,* v.16/4 (1999).

Kiai, Jasmine L., and John D. Stobo. "Prison Health Care in California." *UC Health* (January 22, 2010). http://universityofcalifornia.edu/sites /uchealth/2010/01/22/prison-health-care-in-california (Accessed November 2010).

McCurry, J. "Pills and Porridge: Prisons in Crisis as Struggling Pensioners Turn to Crime." *The Guardian* (June 19, 2008).

McDonald, D. "Medical Care in Prison." *Crime and Justice,* v.26 (1999).

Onishi, N. "As Japan Ages, Prisons Adapt to Going Gray." *New York Times* (November 3, 2007).

Pear, R. "Health Spending Rises in 2008, but at Slower Rate." *New York Times* (January 4, 2010).

Pfeiffer, M. B. "Prison Is Riskiest for the Sick." *Poughkeepsie Journal* (January 5, 2003).

Prison Reform Trust. *Doing Time: The Experiences and Needs of Older Persons in Prison.* (2008). http://www.prisonreformtrust.org.uk/uploads /documents/Doing percent20Time.pdf (Accessed November 2010).

Smith, R. "History of the Prison Medical Services." *British Medical Journal,* v.287 (1983).

Triggle, N. "The Challenge of Providing NHS Care in Prison." *BBC News* (April 9, 2006). http://news.bbc.co.uk/2/hi/health/4876874.stm (Accessed November 2010).

U.S. Department of Health and Human Services. *National Practitioner Data Bank Annual Report.* (2006). http://www.npdb-hipdb.hrsa.gov /pubs/stats/2006_NPDB_Annual_Report.pdf (Accessed September 30, 2010).

10

Legal Assistance
for Prisoners

Christopher E. Smith
Michigan State University

People held in corrections institutions, whether convicted offenders in prisons or pretrial detainees in jail, have a right of access to the courts. This right is necessary so that they can communicate with courts in order to challenge the basis for their confinement, appeal their convictions, or seek protections for their constitutional rights. Although there is broad agreement about the existence of a constitutional right of access to the courts, there are many disagreements about what legal resources, if any, should be provided to prisoners so that they can make use of this right of access. Jailed pretrial detainees, who are criminal suspects charged with crimes and awaiting trial, are represented by attorneys under the right to counsel in the Bill of Rights; specifically, the Sixth Amendment of the U.S. Constitution. By contrast, convicted offenders serving sentences in prisons and jails do not have a general right to counsel for the pursuit of post-conviction legal actions. Thus, the U.S. Supreme Court and other courts have issued decisions defining what legal resources and assistance must be provided for prisoners as part of their right of access to the courts. These decisions have led to significant debates within the U.S. Supreme Court about the resources and assistance that are necessary in order to ensure that the right of access to the courts is fulfilled.

The Right of Access to the Courts

The words "right of access to the courts" do not appear anywhere in the U.S. Constitution, including the Bill of Rights. Prisoners' "right of access" developed through interpretations of the Constitution by the Supreme Court. When justices refer to a specific constitutional source for the right of access, they typically cite the Due Process Clauses of the Fifth and Fourteenth Amendments. Thus, the right of access is generally considered as a component of the right to due process.

The right of access to the courts is regarded as prisoners' most fundamental right. If there are errors in the process leading to a criminal conviction, or if prisoners' rights are being violated by officials inside a correctional institution, prisoners need to rely on decisions by judges to ensure that laws are properly followed and constitutional rights are protected. Without a right of access to the courts, prisoners would have no way to communicate with courts in order to raise claims about rights violations. Instead, there would be risks that prisons could operate as they did from the 19th century through the first decades of the 20th century, when prison officials were able to cut prisoners off from contact with the outside world and prevent any external scrutiny of conditions, practices, and procedures inside prisons.

The U.S. Supreme Court first acknowledged a right of access to the courts in its decision in *Ex parte Hull* (1941). Prisoners filed a legal challenge to Michigan's prison regulation that required all legal documents prepared by prisoners to be submitted to parole board investigators, who would decide whether the documents could actually be filed in court. Michigan claimed that the regulation performed a service for the courts by screening out documents that were not properly prepared, or that did not address appropriate legal issues. The Supreme Court, however, saw the regulation as raising the risk that prison officials could prevent prisoners from filing valid legal claims in court. The Court's opinion declared that judges must be able to see prisoners' legal filings for themselves in order to make their own determinations about whether or not prisoners are presenting valid claims.

The recognition of prisoners' right of access to the courts is universal among all justices on the contemporary Supreme Court. Justices Clarence Thomas and Antonin Scalia generally argue that the U.S. Constitution should be interpreted according to the original intent of those who wrote and ratified the document from 1789 to 1791. Because they do not see the nation's founders as intending to provide rights for convicted offenders after the announcement by the judge of the sentence to be imposed, they generally oppose the recognition of rights for prisoners, including Eighth Amendment rights against cruel and unusual punishments. However, the one right that these justices explicitly accept for prisoners is the right of access to the courts, presumably because of the right's function as providing the avenue for appeals of criminal convictions and other post-conviction legal actions. Justice Thomas, the Supreme Court's foremost opponent of the recognition of rights for prisoners, wrote in *Lewis v. Casey* (1996): "In the end, I agree that the Constitution affords prisoners what can be termed a right of access to the courts. That right, rooted in the Due Process Clause and the principle articulated in *Ex parte Hull*, is a right not to be arbitrarily prevented from lodging a claimed violation of a constitutional right in the federal court." Although a consensus among Supreme Court justices supports the recognition of the right of access, there are significant disagreements about what legal assistance, if any, prisoners should receive in order to make use of this right of access to the courts.

Prisoners' Legal Actions and the Right to Counsel

People confined to prisons and jails continue to face legal issues related to both the crimes for which they were charged and to the myriad legal matters that can affect all residents of the United States. People held in prisons and jails may be involved in various civil legal matters, including divorces, child custody disputes, lawsuits over leases and other contracts, and lawsuits concerning property ownership and property damage. The U.S. Constitution does not provide a right to counsel for any Americans involved in civil legal disputes, namely, lawsuits filed by individuals and organized entities, such as government agencies or businesses. The Sixth Amendment right to counsel in the Bill of Rights applies only to criminal cases, namely, those cases in which the government seeks to punish an individual for violating either federal or state criminal laws. Thus, questions emerge about the extent to which the Sixth Amendment applies, if at all, to people in prisons and jails.

In *Argersinger v. Hamlin* (1972), the U.S. Supreme Court interpreted the Sixth Amendment to guarantee a right to counsel for everyone facing criminal charges for which incarceration, including brief jail sentences as well as prison terms, may be the ultimate punishment upon conviction. The Court had previously decided in *Gideon v. Wainwright* (1963) that the Sixth Amendment right to counsel applies in state court criminal cases in the same manner that it applies in federal court cases. Criminal suspects who are too poor to hire their own attorneys must be provided with a defense attorney to represent them at government expense. Thus, pretrial detainees are supposed to have attorneys from whom they can seek advice and assistance about protecting their rights in the criminal justice process.

Appeals

With respect to criminal offenders who have been convicted and sentenced to prison, the Supreme Court decided in *Douglas v. California* (1963) that the Sixth Amendment right to counsel during trials also continues for the appeals process. However, in *Ross v. Moffitt* (1974), the Court clarified the scope of this entitlement by saying that it extends only to the first appeal of right. Appeals are legal actions filed in appellate courts that allege that uncorrected errors occurred in the investigation and trial court processing of the case that led to the criminal conviction. Appeals can be based on claims that the police improperly collected evidence or violated the offenders' constitutional rights concerning unreasonable searches or questioning. They can also assert that prosecutors made improper arguments or improperly presented evidence in court. In addition, there are often assertions that the trial judge acted improperly in admitting evidence at trial, failed to enforce court rules, or read improper instructions to the jury.

The goal of an appeal is to have a conviction reversed so that the offender can obtain a new trial. For most indigent offenders represented by government-provided defense attorneys, the limited scope of the right to counsel means that the attorney will represent them only in the first post-trial appeal that is presented to the state or federal court of appeals. The right does not continue for subsequent appeals to a state supreme court or the U.S. Supreme Court. Some states may choose to provide attorneys for subsequent appeals, but this is not required by the Supreme Court's interpretation of the Sixth Amendment. This means that convicted offenders who want to pursue challenges to their convictions beyond the initial appeal must rely on the legal resources and assistance provided in prisons as they attempt to carry their cases forward.

Writ of Habeas Corpus

People held in government custody are entitled to file a petition for what is termed a *writ of habeas corpus*, a traditional legal action carried over from Great Britain by the American colonists that is the vehicle for challenging the legality of one's detention. The entitlement to file a habeas corpus petition was so important to the nation's founders that they enshrined this legal protection in the main text of the U.S. Constitution before they even wrote and ratified the Bill of Rights. Most habeas corpus petitions filed by prisoners are submitted through a post-appellate procedure defined by federal and state laws. In other words, if prisoners convicted of state crimes lose their appeals in state appellate courts, they can use the habeas corpus process to pursue specific claims in federal courts. In this process, they cannot raise the full range of claims about errors in the investigation and trial processes of their cases. They can only use this habeas corpus process if they are claiming that specific rights in the U.S. Constitution were violated during the processing of their criminal cases. In particular, they may claim that they did not receive their full right to counsel through proper representation by a defense attorney at trial or that there were problems with their right to a speedy, fair jury trial. There is no constitutional right to counsel for filing habeas corpus petitions, so prisoners must rely on legal resources and assistance provided in prison to pursue this form of legal action.

1983 Actions

Many prisoners file federal civil lawsuits under Title 42, section 1983 of the U.S. Code. These lawsuits, typically referred to as *1983 actions,* use a federal statute to sue government officials for violating individuals' rights under the U.S. Constitution. Prisoners often sue corrections officers and administrators by alleging violations of many rights, including: the First Amendment entitlement to free exercise of religion; First Amendment speech rights, which can include opportunities to exchange letters with family members; Fourteenth Amendment due process rights in disciplinary proceedings; and the Eighth Amendment protection against cruel and unusual punishments, which covers limited entitlement to medical treatment as well as minimum levels of humane prison conditions concerning food, shelter, and sanitation facilities. If prisoners believe that their right of access to the courts has been violated, a lawsuit under section 1983 would be the vehicle to ask a federal judge to order prison officials to provide any required legal resources and assistance as well to prohibit actions that interfere with prisoners' communications with attorneys and courts. Because section 1983 actions are civil lawsuits, there is no right to counsel for the preparation, submission, and litigation of such cases. As with many other kinds of legal actions filed by prisoners, they must rely on the legal resources and assistance available in the prison for preparing and filing section 1983 actions.

There are other kinds of legal actions filed by prisoners. These include petitions for what is termed a *writ of mandamus,* a traditional legal action that seeks to have a judge order a governmental official take a certain action, and actions filed under specific federal or state statutes, such as the Americans with Disabilities Act, requiring certain accommodations and facilities for people with disabilities. However, these actions are much less numerous than appeals, habeas corpus petitions, and section 1983 actions. Nonetheless, there is also no entitlement to representation by counsel for these other noncriminal legal actions.

Except for those prisoners filing the first appeal of their convictions, prisoners do not have a right to counsel in filing subsequent appeals, habeas corpus petitions, and section 1983 actions. As a result, prisoners who cannot afford to hire an attorney—something that very few prisoners are able to do—must do their own legal research, prepare their own legal arguments, and create their own legal documents. When people represent themselves in court, they are called *pro se litigators,* and most prisoners, by necessity, must become pro se litigators if they wish to file legal claims. Being an effective pro se litigator is exceptionally difficult, especially for prisoners who typically do not have advanced education or familiarity with legal research. American attorneys have four years of college education followed by three years of advanced, post-graduate training in law before they are certified as sufficiently knowledgeable to prepare and present cases in court. By contrast, fewer than half of state prisoners are high school graduates, and only 11 percent of prisoners have taken any college classes. Fourteen percent of state prisoners dropped out before even reaching high school. The problems of limited educational attainment are compounded for the many prisoners who do not speak English fluently, who have below-normal intelligence, or who suffer from mental illness or developmental disabilities. Thus, from among the nearly two million people held in American prisons and jails in 2009, only a tiny number have sufficient formal education to readily prepare their own legal filings. The vast majority of prisoners must educate themselves, seek any available forms of legal assistance, or else surrender any hope of successful pro se litigation due to the many impediments to effective legal research and case preparation.

Prisoners Helping Other Prisoners

In *Johnson v. Avery* (1969), the U.S. Supreme Court addressed the issues of prisoners helping other prisoners to prepare pro se legal filings. A prisoner temporarily lost privileges for violating a Tennessee prison rule against prisoners providing legal assistance to each other. Prison officials asserted that the rule was intended to prevent having prisoners owe each other debts, and thus conflicts could be avoided if prisoners could not demand that other prisoners pay them for providing legal advice and assistance. The Court acknowledged that prisoner-to-prisoner assistance may pose some risks to discipline and order maintenance. However, the Court also emphasized that "it is fundamental that access of prisoners to the courts for the purpose of presenting their complaints may not be denied or obstructed." The Court also noted that "[j]ails and penitentiaries include among their inmates a high percentage of persons who are totally or functionally illiterate, whose educational attainments are slight, and whose intelligence is limited." Thus, the Court concluded that, "unless and until the State provides some reasonable alternative to assist prisoners in the preparation of petitions for post-conviction relief, it may not validly enforce a regulation ... barring inmates from furnishing assistance to other prisoners." In effect, the Court would not let prison officials stop prisoners from helping each other with legal matters unless the prison officials furnished some other form of legal assistance for those prisoners who need help in preparing legal documents.

In subsequent decades, prison officials provided legal resources for prisoners to assist them in the preparation of legal cases. Thus, prison officials were able to reimpose rules against prisoners providing legal assistance to each other. In *Shaw v. Murphy* (2001), the Supreme Court revisited the issue. This time, the case was presented as an assertion of a prisoner's First Amendment right to communicate with another prisoner by providing legal assistance. In other words, the claim was not based on the right of access for the prisoner seeking to file a case, but instead on the claimed free speech right of a prisoner who wished to provide legal assistance to another prisoner. The Supreme Court rejected the First Amendment claim and refused to endorse the idea that prisoners possess any freedom of speech right that would entitle them to communicate with other prisoners about legal research and law.

Providing Legal Resources

The key Supreme Court decision with the greatest impact on legal assistance for prisoners was *Bounds v. Smith* (1977). The case sought to clarify court decisions about what, if any, legal resources prison officials must provide in order to enable prisoners to exercise their right of access to the courts.

In *Bounds*, the Supreme Court mandated that officials provide prisoners with access to law libraries unless prisons chose, as an alternative, to provide law-trained workers to help with prisoners' cases. As stated by Justice Thurgood Marshall's majority opinion: "[T]he fundamental constitutional right of access to the courts requires prison authorities to assist inmates in the preparation and filing of meaningful legal papers by providing prisoners with adequate law libraries or adequate legal assistance from persons trained in the law."

Federal courts relied on the logic of this decision to create standard forms for habeas corpus petitions and section 1983 actions so that prisoners working on their own in a prison law library could follow the directions on the forms and fill them out as the means to initiate a legal case. Federal courts also have a process through which prisoners who are too poor to pay the required filing fees for initiating a case can request that the fees be waived. The forms made it easier for prisoners to initiate cases, but the forms did not necessarily lead to successful cases, because prisoners still needed to understand which kinds of claims could be filed through each form of action. Thus, most prisoners' cases are dismissed relatively quickly by the courts, because they do not properly state a legal claim that can be recognized by the courts, they are filed after a deadline established by law, or their forms are not properly prepared.

Moreover, the importance of filing proper claims increased after 1996 when Congress enacted the Prison Litigation Reform Act which, in its effort to reduce the number of section 1983 actions filed by prisoners in the federal courts, mandated that poor prisoners cannot request a waiver of court filing fees if they have previously had three cases dismissed for failing to properly present a claim. In theory, a prisoner experiencing a genuine constitutional rights violation in a correctional institution could be barred from filing a section 1983 action if he had previously made three unsuccessful attempts to file section 1983 lawsuits and he is too poor to pay the filing fees to initiate a subsequent federal lawsuit. The only exception to the prohibition on future no-fee filings for such poor prisoners is if the prisoner is raising a case about an imminent threat to his health or safety. However, many rights violations do not raise such issues, such as when a prisoner is deprived of free exercise of religion or access to the courts.

After the Supreme Court's decision in *Bounds*, prisons generally created law libraries within their institutions and permitted prisoners to prepare their own cases by using prison-supplied law books. According to the rule established in *Bounds*, the provision of prison law libraries, along with paper, pencils, and envelopes, fulfilled the officials' obligation to facilitate prisoners' right of access to the courts. However, it is apparent to many observers that relatively few prisoners can make effective use of law library materials as a means to prepare successful legal claims. Successful legal claims require a sufficient understanding of law to identify which specific rights may have been violated, the proper form of legal action, the proper documents to file, and the proper preparation of those documents.

Some judges in the lower federal courts noted the continuing difficulties experienced by prisoners who were forced to rely entirely on their own legal research and case-preparation efforts through the use of a prison law library. In *Falzerano v. Collier* (1982), a U.S. district judge in New Jersey expressed sharp criticisms of the Supreme Court's rule in *Bounds v. Smith*: "In this court's view, access to the fullest law library anywhere is a useless and meaningless gesture in terms of the great mass of prisoners...[Prisoners] are untrained laymen [who must] work with entirely unfamiliar books, whose content they cannot understand ... Access to full law libraries makes about as much sense as furnishing medical services through books like: *Brain Surgery Self-Taught*, or *How to Remove Your Own Appendix*." Yet, despite this sharp criticism of the *Bounds v. Smith* ruling, this district judge was obligated to follow the rule established by the Supreme Court and reject the prisoners' request for additional legal assistance beyond mere access to a prison law library.

Supreme Court Response to Lower Court Innovations

Several district court judges were presented with access to the courts claims from prisoners who had education or mental health issues that prevented them from effectively using prison libraries. They also had cases from prisoners who were isolated 23 hours per day in disciplinary or administrative segregation cells, and therefore could not go to the prison law library to prepare their cases. Typically, prisoners in solitary confinement can request that a limited number of law books be delivered periodically to their cells, but this is a very slow way to conduct legal research, especially for prisoners who are not knowledgeable enough to know exactly what law books to request. The judges in these cases believed that they could order additional forms of legal assistance for prisoners who could not make use of the law libraries, and that the Supreme Court would recognize that these other forms of assistance were essential for fulfillment of the right of access to the courts for these prisoners.

For example, in *Knop v. Johnson* (1988), a U.S. district judge in Michigan issued an order that: required the Michigan Department of Corrections to contract with a nonprofit corporation for providing paralegal assistance to prisoners; mandated the hiring of an attorney to function as program director; and established staffing requirements that included specified numbers of civilians with two-year paralegal degrees, prisoner paralegals, and/or inmate law clerks. When the state of Michigan appealed, the U.S. court of appeals reduced the extent of this mandated legal assistance, but accepted that something more than prison libraries was needed: "This means paralegals—not necessarily individuals who have completed two-year training courses ..., but intelligent laypeople who can write coherent English and who have had some modicum of exposure to legal research and to the rudiments of prisoner-rights law."

In 1996, however, the Supreme Court reviewed a similar case, *Lewis v. Casey*, in which a district judge had ordered the state of Arizona to provide legal assistance beyond access to a prison law library. The majority of justices, in an opinion by Justice Scalia, declared that the district judge went too far in ordering corrections officials to provide direct assistance from lawyers and paralegals and to provide qualified law librarians. The Court's decision emphasized that prisoners must first prove that they are not able to make use of a prison law library before a district court can order a specific remedy. It is not clear from the Court's opinion, however, how an illiterate or non-English-speaking prisoner who claims to need legal assistance in order to file a case in court would be able, on his own, to prove to the court that he cannot use a prison library prior to being give extra legal assistance.

To critics, the Supreme Court had created an impossibly difficult requirement of requiring prisoners who are incapable of filing a legal claim to actually file a claim in order to prove that they are incapable of filing a claim. As indicated by the language in Justice Scalia's opinion, a majority of justices believed that the lower courts had gone too far in ordering prison officials to provide various forms of legal assistance. The opinion emphasized that the right of access to the courts is simply a right to file claims, not a right to conduct extensive legal research. In addition, Justice Scalia emphasized that judges should show deference to prison officials in determining how to fulfill the right of access to the courts rather than give detailed orders to corrections officials about how to fulfill the right. Justice Scalia wrote, for example, "[W]e leave it to prison officials to determine how best to ensure that inmates with language problems have a reasonably adequate opportunity to file nonfrivolous legal claims challenging their convictions or conditions of confinement." As a result of the Supreme Court's decision in *Lewis v. Casey*, lower court federal judges were put on notice that they could order extra legal assistance only in special circumstances in which the prisoners' inability to make use of law libraries had been proven.

Pro: Benefits of Legal Assistance for Prisoners

Advocates of legal assistance for prisoners emphasize that the fulfillment of the right of access to the courts is exceptionally important because the protection of all other legal rights rests on prisoners' ability to present issues effectively to judges. Advocates argue that convicted offenders need advice and guidance from people trained in law, whether attorneys, paralegals, or advanced law students. Statutes and court decisions are written for a highly educated audience of lawyers and judges. It can be extremely difficult for people without legal training to understand the law, and thus it is significantly more difficult, if not impossible, for prisoners to make use of such materials on their own, especially since only half of prisoners are high school graduates and 14 percent dropped out prior to high school.

In order to prepare a legal action, an individual must have sufficient understanding of law to be able to identify what constitutional right or statutory entitlement may have been violated. Prisoners who have legitimate grievances about deprivations of medical care, impediments to religious practices, and violations of due process can easily have their cases dismissed because they have not described correctly what law governs their grievance. In addition, they must know which form of action to file, and many prisoners confuse the purposes and procedures of habeas corpus petitions and section 1983 actions. Moreover, each kind of legal action has its own technical rules for filing deadlines, supporting materials, and phrasing of allegations. It is common, for example, for prisoners to file section 1983 actions against a prison warden or state's governor for depriving them of a protected right, such as the opportunity to attend a religious service in the prison chapel. Unbeknownst to many prisoners, however, section 1983 lawsuits must be filed against the individual official who actually prevented them from receiving the benefit of a right, which would usually be a corrections officer or corrections supervisor who actually prevented them from attending the chapel service. Judges must immediately dismiss lawsuits filed against a governor or warden who was not directly involved in the alleged rights violations. Without guidance from someone with formal training in law, it is extremely difficult for prisoners to fulfill all of the technical requirements for filing proper legal actions.

For prisoners who are illiterate, not fluent in English, or mentally ill, it is virtually impossible to make use of a prison law library. Yet the Supreme Court emphasized strict requirements for proving an inability to make use of law library materials. The Court did not express any corresponding concern for the insurmountable difficulties facing these individuals who must attempt to present proof of their disabilities to a court on their own. These individuals would need a legal advocate in order to prove their disabilities, but the Supreme Court's decision in *Lewis v. Casey* implies that they must prove this issue on their own before a judge can consider giving them the legal assistance needed to file a claim.

Con: Drawbacks of Legal Assistance for Prisoners

Under the right of access to the courts, prisoners have a right, in the words of Justice Clarence Thomas, to "not be arbitrarily prevented from lodging a claimed violation of a constitutional right in federal court." To critics of providing additional legal assistance to prisoners, the right of access means that prison officials cannot interfere with prisoners' opportunity to file cases, but it does not require prison officials to assist them in preparing their cases. The provision of a law library under the doctrine of *Bounds v. Smith* makes sufficient resources available for prisoners to prepare their cases. However, according to Justice Thomas, "[w]hether to expend state resources to facilitate prisoner lawsuits is a question of policy and one that the Constitution leaves to the discretion of the States." Thus, it is not the proper role of judges to dictate precisely how corrections officials organize the distribution of institutional resources, including resources that might be used for legal assistance.

Legal assistance from trained professionals would be very expensive. States generally have limited budgets. Any additional money directed to prisoners' legal assistance means that less government money is spent for the benefit of law-abiding citizens through expenditures for schools, police protection, health, roads, and other necessary services. Law-abiding citizens in free society are not entitled to legal assistance for preparing civil lawsuits, so it would be unjust to give prisoners the extra, undeserved benefit of legal assistance for their section 1983 actions and habeas corpus petitions. In addition, studies have shown that approximately 97 percent of section 1983 actions and habeas corpus petitions are dismissed. In light of how rarely prisoner legal actions are successful, it seems wasteful to provide additional legal assistance that might facilitate the filing of numerous additional unsubstantiated cases that burden the court system and needlessly absorb the time of judges and their staffs.

See Also: 4. Due Process Rights of Prisoners; 6. Free Speech Rights of Prisoners; 9. Healthcare and Medical Assistance for Prisoners; 12. Mentally Ill and Mentally Challenged Inmates; 18. Religious Rights.

Further Readings

Branham, Lynn S. *The Law of Sentencing, Corrections, and Prisoners' Rights*. St. Paul, MN: West Group, 2002.

Fliter, John A. *Prisoners' Rights: The Supreme Court and Evolving Standards of Decency*. Westport, CT: Greenwood Press, 2001.

Mushlin, Michael. *Rights of Prisoners*. Colorado Springs, CO: Shepard's/ McGraw-Hill, 1993.

Palmer, John W. *Constitutional Rights of Prisoners*. Cincinnati, OH: Anderson Publishing, 2009.

Smith, Christopher E. *Law and Contemporary Corrections*. Belmont, CA: Wadsworth, 2000.

11

Life Sentence

Margaret E. Leigey
College of New Jersey

L ife sentences have always been utilized in the United States. They are the most severe prison sentences possible, and in the 15 U.S. states without the death penalty, a life sentence is the most severe punishment a convicted defendant can receive. Beginning in the 1970s, the number of inmates serving life sentences in the United States increased dramatically. The increased use of life sentences has been met with support by some, but also with contention by those who oppose their use.

Types of Life Sentences

There are two broad types of life sentences: life with the possibility of parole and life without the possibility of parole. The former means an inmate can be paroled at some point in the future. Typically, after serving a certain number of years or a specific portion of his or her sentence, the life-sentenced inmate will appear before the jurisdiction's parole board. The board will review the facts of the inmate's case and his or her progress in prison to determine evidence of rehabilitation. In particular, the board will examine the inmate's disciplinary record and participation in prison programs, including educational, vocational, and treatment programs. The parole board will then decide whether or not the inmate should be released. While release can occur with a life sentence with the possibility of parole, release is not guaranteed. If the inmate's parole application is denied, then a written explanation of the reason for the denial will be provided. He or she can appear before the parole board again at a later date.

Alternatively, a sentence of life without the possibility of parole means an inmate is ineligible for release on parole or through some other early release policy. However, the inmate can be released through executive clemency, which is the authority of the governor or president to amend a sentence or restore legal rights and privileges. An inmate serving a sentence of life without the possibility of parole can have his or her sentence reduced to life with the possibility of parole. While this option exists, executive clemency rarely occurs.

Historical Snapshot of Life Sentencing

Historically, life sentences were commonly prescribed within the indeterminate sentencing framework. Within this type of sentence, the judge, when sentencing the criminal defendant, would impose a wide range of time, such as a sentence of 10 years to life with the possibility of parole. After serving the minimum period of time, the inmate would be eligible for parole. Indeterminate sentencing schemes are closely intertwined with the sentencing objective of rehabilitation, which is the perception that offenders, if given the necessary treatment, can be reformed and become law-abiding citizens. The wide sentence lengths allowed each individual offender the necessary time to become rehabilitated, as it was believed that variance existed in the time it took for offenders to be reformed. Historically, most life-sentenced inmates were eventually released from prison, and consequently, there was only a small portion of inmates who spent a substantial part of their lives in prison and ultimately died there.

Beginning in the 1970s, indeterminate sentences and rehabilitation were increasingly criticized. Parole boards were criticized for releasing inmates serving indeterminate sentences prior to serving an appropriate amount of time. In addition, indeterminate sentences were challenged because of the concern of parole board bias, such as racial or gender bias, when making release decisions. As a result, federal and state legislatures implemented determinate sentences, which stipulate a fixed amount of time offenders must serve prior to release. Besides determinate sentences, other policies were developed to eliminate or reduce the authority of the parole board to determine which offenders should be granted parole. For instance, several states and the federal government no longer permit parole boards to determine which inmates should be granted early release. Additionally, some states do not permit their parole boards to make release decisions for life-sentenced inmates. These measures are designed to keep offenders incarcerated for longer periods of time. The sentence of life without the possibility of parole was also developed as a means to ensure that serious offenders would not be released.

Life Sentencing Today

According to the most recent estimates from the Sentencing Project, there are 140,610 individuals serving life sentences in the United States; of these, 41,095, approximately 29 percent, are serving sentences of life without the possibility of parole. The report also details the dramatic increase in the life-sentenced population in recent decades. For example, in 1984, there were 34,000 life-sentenced inmates in the United States. Twenty-five years later, the population had quadrupled.

There are a variety of explanations for the ballooning life-sentenced population. First, the increase reflects the more punitive sentencing practices in the United States in recent decades. There is less emphasis on the rehabilitation of offenders, and more on ensuring the protection of the public and punishing offenders for the harm they have caused. Second, life sentences, and in particular parole-ineligible life sentences, are used as an alternate to the death penalty. The increase in the life-sentenced population reflects the corresponding decline in the use of the death penalty nationally.

Every U.S. state, along with the federal criminal justice system, utilizes the sentence of life with the possibility of parole. Alaska is the only state that prohibits sentences of life without the possibility of parole. When New Mexico abolished the death penalty in 2009, it became the most recent state to implement parole-ineligible life sentences. In addition to the federal government, there are several states in which all life sentences are parole ineligible. These jurisdictions include Illinois, Iowa, Louisiana, Maine, Pennsylvania, and South Dakota. The report from the Sentencing Project further reveals that in five states (Alabama, California, Massachusetts, Nevada, and New York), the life-sentenced population accounts for at least 15 percent of the total prison population, while in nine states (Delaware, Florida, Iowa, Louisiana, Massachusetts, Michigan, Mississippi, Pennsylvania, and South Dakota), the life without the possibility of parole population exceeds five percent of the total prison population.

A life sentence can be imposed for a single crime or as a result of a history of offending, such as three-strikes laws. While most inmates who serve life sentences have been convicted of a violent offense, most often murder, property and drug offenses can also trigger the penalty, such as burglary, arson, and the possession or trafficking of drugs. In regard to demographics, the vast majority of life-sentenced inmates are male, although there is a small population of female life-sentenced inmates. Minorities comprise a disproportionate portion of life-sentenced inmates.

When life-sentenced inmates enter prison, they experience a wide range of emotions: denial that they could serve the remainder of their lives incarcerated; shock about the limitations of prison life, such as the loss of privacy and autonomy; and sadness because of the limited opportunities they will have to see their families and friends. Prior research indicates that it is difficult for life-sentenced inmates to sustain meaningful contact with their family and friends over the course of their confinements. Married, life-sentenced inmates often get divorced, and life-sentenced inmates infrequently receive visitations. In addition, parents or other relatives die or become ill, which makes visitations difficult. The distance to the institution or travel-related expenses, including gas, lodging, or the loss of work, also deters regular visitations.

Juveniles Sentenced to Life

Because juveniles can be tried and convicted in adult criminal court and thus are eligible to receive life sentences, there is a group of life-sentenced inmates who have been sentenced to both types of life sentences prior to the age of 18. For example, Lionel Tate was one of the youngest offenders to ever receive a sentence of life without the possibility of parole in the United States. At the time of the offense, in 1999, 12-year-old Tate performed a series of wresting moves on his six-year-old playmate, Tiffany Eunick. The girl later died of the injuries she sustained, including bruises, lacerations, a ruptured spleen, and contusions to and swelling of the brain. In a Florida criminal court, Tate was tried and convicted of first-degree murder, and at the age of 14, received a life sentence. However, Tate's conviction was later overturned because he did not receive a mental competency hearing, and he was released. After his release, Tate was arrested two times, most recently for violation of probation, armed burglary, and armed robbery stemming from an incident in which he allegedly attempted to rob a pizza delivery employee. At the age of 19, Tate received a sentenced of 30 years and was returned to prison.

Life Sentences and the U.S. Supreme Court

The U.S. Supreme Court has affirmed the use of both life with and without the possibility of parole sentences and has consistently ruled that they do not violate the prohibition against cruel and unusual punishment contained in the Eighth Amendment of the Bill of Rights. In *Schick v. Reed* (1974), the Court determined that a commutation, or reduction, of a death sentence to life imprisonment made by President Eisenhower was constitutional. The commutation explicitly stated that the defendant would serve a parole-ineligible life sentence. While the life sentence as an alternate to the death sentence has been determined to be constitutionally permissible, the Court has heard a series of cases outlining the use of life with and without the possibility of parole for habitual offenders.

In *Rummel v. Estelle* (1980), the Court agreed that a sentence of life with the possibility of parole was constitutionally acceptable. The defendant, who was previously convicted of two property offenses, received a life sentence when he was convicted of a new charge of felony theft. More recently, the Court has upheld California's three-strikes legislation in *Ewing v. California* (2003) and *Lockyer v. Andrade* (2003). In these two cases, the majority of the Court determined that the sentences of 25 years to life for the two habitual offenders, whose most recent convictions were for shoplifting golf clubs and videotapes, respectively, were constitutionally permissible. One of the few exceptions to the Court's history of upholding life sentences is *Solem v. Helm* (1983). In this case, the Court considered the sentence of life without the possibility of parole for Helm, who had seven prior nonviolent convictions. They determined that the South Dakota statute violated the Eighth Amendment prohibition against cruel and unusual punishment.

The Court has also addressed the legality of life sentences for two other types of offenders: defendants convicted of drug offenses, and defendants under the age of 18. In *Harmelin v. Michigan* (1991), the Court upheld the constitutionality of a mandatory sentence of life without the possibility of parole for the adult defendant, Harmelin, who was convicted of the possession of approximately 700 grams of cocaine. In the fall 2009 term, the Supreme Court heard oral arguments to determine the constitutionality of life without parole sentences for juvenile offenders who have been tried and convicted in the adult system for nonhomicide offenses, such as armed robbery and rape. In the *Graham v. Florida* decision in May 2010, the Court deemed as unconstitutional these life without parole sentences for juveniles convicted of nonhomicide offenses.

Pro: Arguments in Support of Life Sentences

Life sentences are supported by death penalty abolitionists, who maintain that life sentences should replace capital punishment as the most severe sentence possible in the United States. Supporters argue that the abolition of the death penalty would be cost effective, as life sentences are cheaper than capital punishment. In addition, the fact that the sentence can be reversed also makes it more attractive as compared to the finality of the death penalty. For example, a life-sentenced inmate can be released from prison if DNA or other discovered evidence exonerates them at a later date. However, no recourse exists for the offender who was erroneously put to death, although the offender's family can seek legal remedy. For these reasons, life sentences are thought to be more respectful of human life and considered to be less morally offensive than the death penalty.

When reviewing public opinion polls regarding the death penalty and its alternatives, there appears to be widespread public support for life without the possibility of parole. Previous research consistently demonstrates that there is a decline in citizen support of the death penalty when alternatives, such as life without the possibility of parole or the sentence plus restitution, which are payments made to the victim or victim's family, are introduced. Depending on the poll, public support for alternatives to the death penalty, such as life without the possibility of parole, is equal to or greater than support for the death penalty.

Reducing Recidivism

In addition, death penalty abolitionists argue that life sentences are as effective as or more effective than capital punishment in preventing future offending. One sentencing objective and reason for punishment is to make an example of an offender, also known as *general deterrence*. According to the general deterrence perspective, society uses punishment as a means to reinforce laws and discourage others from committing crime. One method to determine the existence of a general deterrent effect for capital punishment is to compare the murder rate, violent crime rate, or overall crime rate in a jurisdiction before and after the abolition of the death penalty.

If a general deterrent effect exists, it is hypothesized that there would be a decline in the crime rate after the abolition of capital punishment. Another method is to compare states with and without the death penalty, with the hypothesis that states with the death penalty would have lower crime rates than states without it. Regardless of the method used, it appears that life sentences are just as effective as the death penalty in acting as a deterrent. In other words, capital punishment does not produce the expected general deterrent effect; in fact, in some studies, states with the death penalty have higher crime rates than non-death penalty states. As such, death penalty abolitionists contend that life sentences are an effective, cost-effective, and publicly supported alternative to capital punishment.

Opponents have also expressed concern that inmates sentenced to life without the possibility of parole would have little incentive to behave in prison, as the likelihood of release through executive clemency is low. However, research on the disciplinary conduct of life-sentenced inmates overwhelmingly demonstrates that life-sentenced inmates, including those who are parole ineligible, are less likely to commit rule violations than inmates serving shorter or parole-eligible sentences. When first incarcerated, life-sentenced inmates are more likely to be disruptive; however, in time, they abide by the rules of the institution. Life-sentenced inmates have even been characterized by some correctional administrators as model inmates.

Tough on Crime and Victims' Rights

Other than death penalty abolitionists, groups that endorse life sentences include supporters of tough-on-crime policies and victims' rights groups. While life-sentenced inmates at one time had a greater chance of being released, presently the likelihood of release is low, and for those sentenced to life without the possibility of parole, the chance of release is almost nonexistent. These groups support life sentences because they allege that prolonged prison sentences remove dangerous offenders from the community. Life-sentenced inmates have been convicted of violent offenses or a series of offenses, and are thought to pose a continued threat to public safety. Especially in cases of sentences involving life without the possibility of parole, life sentences ensure that an offender will serve a lengthy sentence prior to release, if it ever occurs. Moreover, supporters of life sentences maintain that the severity of the offense committed justifies the severity of the sentence. For example, a serious crime, such as murder, deserves a serious punishment, and these groups object when offenders are released from prison or released prior to serving a sufficient amount of time.

Con: Arguments Opposing Life Sentences

Those who object to life sentences can be divided into two groups: those who believe the sentence is too lenient, and those who believe the sentence is too severe.

Life Sentences as Too Lenient

In the first group, opponents of the life sentence take issue when it is used as an alternative to the death penalty because it does not have the same assurances of protecting public safety as capital punishment. They maintain that the public can still be victimized by life-sentenced inmates and cite instances in which these inmates have attacked other prisoners, correctional officers, or medical staff at the institutions in which they were incarcerated. In addition, while evidence indicates that the actual risk is low, opponents of life sentences are concerned that life-sentenced inmates could escape. Thus, justice would not be attained if escaped inmates did not serve the time to which they were sentenced, and would continue to pose a threat to the public. Proponents of capital punishment argue that serious offenders need to be executed in order to neutralize the danger of future offending.

Historically, the chances of release for life-sentenced inmates used to be higher; but in recent decades, the release of life-sentenced inmates has declined, and the likelihood of release for parole-ineligible offenders is even lower. Nevertheless, opponents of the life sentence argue that the possibility exists for life-sentenced inmates to be released from prison, and maintain that a life sentence is intended to exist for the duration of the offender's life, or "life means life." In addition, since many life-sentenced inmates have been convicted of murder, opponents of life sentences object to the fact that the offender remains alive while his or her victim is dead. Opponents' notion of justice is violated when an offender does not receive a severe sentence, and especially if the offender is released from prison.

Life Sentences as Too Severe

Others disapprove of life sentences because they believe them to be too severe. In general, they maintain that individuals can become law abiding in the future and believe in the promise of rehabilitation for most offenders. This point is especially true for advocates of the abolition of life without parole sentences for convicted juvenile offenders, or those offenders who were below the age of 18 when the offense occurred. This cadre of opponents object to the notion that these offenders cannot be reformed and that children should be incarcerated for the remainder of their lives.

Critics of life sentences also contend that the sentence is too severe for some offenses that can trigger a life sentence, such as nonviolent offenses. Under some states' three-strikes legislation, such as California, the third strike—even a nonviolent offense such as burglary or drug possession—can trigger a sentence of 25 years to life. In this view, the punishment is too severe for the crime. In addition, critics object to life sentences for women who have killed their abusers.

Opponents of life sentences point out that murderers and older inmates have the lowest recidivism (reoffending) rates of inmates who are released from prison. In other words, the probability of a released offender convicted of murder or an older offender committing another serious offense is extremely low. One study highlighting the minimal threat posed to public safety by life-sentenced inmates was conducted by James Marquart and Jonathan Sorensen, who tracked the criminality of 47 commuted inmates in Texas from 1973 to 1986. These inmates had originally been sentenced to death, but because of the Supreme Court decision in *Furman v. Georgia* (1972), in which the administration of the death penalty in the United States was declared unconstitutional, their death sentences were automatically commuted to life sentences. The researchers found that in general, the majority of the inmates were well behaved in prison, as they did not receive any disciplinary writeups for serious rule infractions, such as violence against a correctional staff member or another inmate or escape. Eventually, 31 of the inmates were released from prison and reentered society. Three of the men violated the conditions of their parole, for example, with the use of drugs or alcohol; and four committed new offenses, such as burglary, rape, and murder. One released inmate killed his girlfriend and then committed suicide. Despite this extreme act of violence, however, the recidivism of the group and the comparison group of life-sentenced inmates was low.

Overall, the authors maintain that death-sentenced and life-sentenced inmates do not pose a major risk to the public. Opponents of life sentences use this study as evidence that most life-sentenced, and even death-sentenced inmates, do not recidivate. Thus, opponents of life sentences rely on evidence of the good conduct of life-sentenced inmates and their low likelihood of recidivating as proof that a true life sentence, for the remainder for his or her natural life, is not necessary because the offenders no longer pose a threat to the public.

Life sentences, including life without parole sentences, should be reserved for only the most serious offenders, recommend opponents; instead, they urge the use of long prison terms in a similar fashion as other nations. First, certain countries, including Brazil, Croatia, Columbia, El Salvador, Mexico, Nicaragua, Norway, Portugal, Slovenia, Spain, and Venezuela prohibit the use of life sentences. Second, even countries that permit life sentences use them differently than the United States, which applies them at a much higher rate than other nations. In addition, other countries assume that eventually, life-sentenced inmates will be released; however, a similar assumption is not made in the United States. In other countries, inmates sentenced to life are expected to be released after serving a certain number of years of parole ineligibility, usually 25. However, released inmates could remain on parole, or some other form of surveillance, for the remainder of their lives; if they were to re-offend in the future, they could be returned to prison.

Critics of life sentences allege that the fact that inmates do not know if they will ever be released from prison, also referred to as *indeterminacy*, constitutes cruel and unusual punishment. Using previous research, they contend that the uncertainty of whether life-sentenced inmates will ever be released is detrimental to the their mental health.

Questions of Fairness

Opponents of life sentences object to the fact that inmates sentenced to life with or without the possibility of parole do not receive any additional measure of review by courts. In death penalty cases, the appellate courts carefully review cases to ensure that the offender's constitutional rights were not violated at trial, such as prohibition against self-incrimination, the admittance of illegally seized evidence at trial, ineffective assistance of counsel, double jeopardy, and the unlawful selection and/or composition of jury members. However, the same scrutiny given to capital cases is not afforded to life-sentence cases, even though the inmate could remain incarcerated for the remainder of his or her life. Opponents of life sentences argue that life sentences, and especially life without the possibility of parole sentences, closely resemble death sentences, and as a result should receive the same measure of scrutiny that appellate courts provide to capital cases.

Another issue raised by opponents of life-sentences is the limited programming available for this population in prison. As a group, life-sentenced inmates may be given lower priority to participate in vocational and educational classes than inmates serving shorter sentences, given the reduced likelihood of their using the acquired skills in future employment. However, opponents contend that it is important for life-sentenced inmates to participate in programs because they provide purpose and structure in their lives. Thus, one recommendation offered by this group is to have programs specifically designed for life-sentenced inmates and the challenges they face, such as reduced contact with family or dying within the institution.

The High Cost of Incarceration

The cost of confining life-sentenced inmates is extremely high. According to the Sentencing Project, the cost of incarcerating an inmate for a life sentence, on average about 29 years, is $1 million per inmate. As inmates age, they have greater healthcare needs and require more expensive healthcare. Correctional administrators must contend with providing medical care for an aging population, including complications such as heart disease, cancer, stroke, emphysema, diabetes, arthritis, loss of sight and hearing, and mental health issues such as dementia and Alzheimer's disease. In part because of the higher healthcare expense, the cost of caring for older inmates is approximately three times higher than the cost of incarcerating younger inmates. Due to the high cost of incarcerating life-sentenced inmates, combined with their low likelihood of release, critics contend that most inmates should be eligible for parole after serving 25 years, with a life without parole sentence reserved for only the worst inmates. If the vast majority of life-without-parole inmates become parole-eligible after serving 25 years, they would be incapacitated during the crime-prone segment of their life course. Furthermore, correctional departments would no longer have to care for their cost of incarceration in their geriatric years. Opponents contend that the money spent on the incarceration of older inmates, of which a significant number are serving life sentences, could be better spent on treatment and rehabilitation programs for inmates.

The Political Game

Opponents also object to the fact that politicians endorse tough-on-crime policies, such as life sentences without parole, as a means to acquire votes and influence elections. For example, during the 1988 U.S. presidential race, the Republican candidate, George H.W. Bush, criticized Democratic candidate Michael Dukakis for being too lenient in inmate management during his tenure as governor of Massachusetts. Bush, who was later elected president, cited a specific incident involving an inmate named Willie Horton.

Sentenced to life in Massachusetts without the possibility of parole, Horton was eligible for a weekend furlough program, which is a temporary release from the institution. Horton did not return to prison after one of his furloughs. While free, Horton committed several violent offenses, including robbery, rape, and assault. The Horton incident was used by the Bush campaign to highlight his opponent's leniency with offenders. This incident also served to increase the reluctance of politicians to grant executive clemency to life-sentenced inmates. For example, if a governor commutes an offender's sentence, and the offender later commits a serious punishment, the governor may face public criticism for his or her clemency decisions.

See Also: 1. Capital Punishment/Death Penalty; 3. Cruel and Unusual Punishment; 17. Punishment Versus Rehabilitation.

Further Readings

Abramsky, Sasha. "Lifers." http://www.legalaffairs.org/issues/March-April -2004/feature_abramsky_marpar04.msp (Accessed January 2010).

Aday, Ronald H. *Aging Prisoners: Crisis in American Corrections.* Westport, CT: Praeger, 2003.

Amnesty International and Human Rights Watch. *The Rest of Their Lives: Life Without Parole for Child Offenders in the United States.* New York: Human Rights Watch, 2005.

Appleton, Catherine, and Bent Grøver. "The Pros and Cons of Life Without Parole." *British Journal of Criminology*, v.47/4 (2007).

Bohm, Robert M. "American Death Penalty Opinions: Past, Present, and Future." In *America's Experiment With Capital Punishment*, edited by James R. Acker, Robert M. Bohm, and Charles S. Lanier. Durham, NC: Carolina Academic Press, 2003.

Cain, Burl, and Cathy Fontenot. "Angola's Long-Term Inmates." *Corrections Today*, v.63/5 (2001).

Cheatwood, Derral. "The Life-Without-Parole Sanction: Its Current Status and a Research Agenda." *Crime and Delinquency*, v.34/1 (1988).

Cunningham, Mark D., and Jon R. Sorensen. "Nothing to Lose? A Comparative Examination of Prison Misconduct Rates Among Life-Without-Parole and Other Long-Term High-Security Inmates." *Criminal Justice and Behavior*, v.33/6 (2006).

Flanagan, Timothy J. "Lifers and Long-Termers: Doing Big Time." In *The Pains of Imprisonment*, edited by Robert Johnson and Hans Toch. Beverly Hills, CA: Sage, 1982.

Graham v. Florida, 560 U.S. ___ (2010).

Harvard Law Review. "A Matter of Life and Death: The Effect of Life-Without-Parole Statutes on Capital Punishment." Note. *Harvard Law Review*, v.119/6 (2006).

Hassine, Victor. *Life Without Parole: Living in Prison Today*. New York: Oxford University Press, 2009.

Johnson, Robert, and Ania Dobrzanska. "Mature Coping Among Life-Sentenced Inmates: An Exploratory Study of Adjustment Dynamics." *Corrections Compendium*, v.30/6 (2005).

Johnson, Robert, and Sandra McGunigall-Smith. "Life Without Parole, America's Other Death Penalty: Notes on Life Under Sentence of Death by Incarceration." *The Prison Journal*, v.88/2 (2008).

Krajick, Kevin. "Growing Old in Prison." *Corrections*, v.5/1 (1979).

Marquart, James W., and Jonathan R. Sorensen. "Institutional and Postrelease Behavior of *Furman*-Commuted Inmates in Texas." *Criminology*, v.26/4 (1988).

Mauer, Marc, Ryan S. King, and Malcolm C. Young. *The Meaning of "Life": Long Prison Sentences in Context*. Washington, DC: The Sentencing Project, 2004.

Morton, Joann B. "An Administrative Overview of the Older Inmate." (1992). http://www.nicic.org/pubs/1992/010937.pdf (Accessed January 2010).

Nellis, Ashley, and Ryan S. King. *No Exit: The Expanding Use of Life Sentences in America*. Washington, DC: The Sentencing Project, 2009.

Ornduff, Jason S. "Releasing the Elderly Inmate: A Solution to Prison Overcrowding." *The Elder Law Journal*, v.4/1 (1996).

Rothman, M. B., B. D. Dunlop, and P. Entzel. *Elders, Crime, and the Criminal Justice System: Myth, Perceptions, and Reality in the 21st Century*. New York: Springer, 2000.

Sheleff, Leon S. *Ultimate Penalties: Capital Punishment, Life Imprisonment, Physical Torture*. Columbus, OH: The Ohio State University Press, 1987.

Sorensen, Jon, and Robert D. Wrinkle. "No Hope for Parole: Disciplinary Infractions Among Death-Sentenced and Life-Without-Parole Inmates." *Criminal Justice and Behavior*, v.23/4 (1996).

Stewart, Jim, and Paul Lieberman. "What Is This New Sentence That Takes Away Parole?" *Student Lawyer*, v.11 (1982).

Sundby, Scott E. *A Life and Death Decision: A Jury Weighs the Death Penalty*. New York: Palgrave Macmillan, 2005.

van Zyl Smit, Dirk. *Taking Life Imprisonment Seriously in National and International Law*. New York: Kluwer Law International, 2002.

Villaume, Alfred C. "'Life Without Parole' and 'Virtual Life Sentences': Death Sentences by Any Other Name." *Contemporary Justice Review*, v.8/3 (2005).

Welch, Randy. "Can This Be Life? The Implications of Life Without Parole." *Corrections Compendium*, v.11/8 (1987).

Wikberg, Ronald, and Burk Foster. "The Long-Termers: Louisiana's Longest Serving Inmates and Why They Have Stayed So Long." *The Prison Journal*, v.80/1 (1990).

Wright, Julian H., Jr. "Life-Without-Parole: An Alternative to Death or Not Much of a Life at All?" *Vanderbilt Law Review*, v.43/2 (1990).

12

Mentally Ill and Mentally Challenged Inmates

Noelle E. Fearn
Saint Louis University

Challenges regarding how to respond to the increased number of criminal offenders and inmates with mental illnesses (and also those suffering from mental retardation/developmental disability) have confronted criminal justice and corrections officials since the widespread deinstitutionalization of mentally ill individuals in the 1960s. Attributed both to the public outcry against the dismal and inhumane conditions of state mental hospitals and the advancement of medications to respond to various mental illnesses, the 1960s witnessed a mass exodus of the mentally ill from these mental health facilities into U.S. communities. Unfortunately, without the structure and professional/medical oversight of the mental institution and its staff, many of these mentally ill individuals were confronted with, among other serious issues, a lack of housing and employment options have led to an increasingly large homeless population. Homeless individuals, especially those with mental illnesses, typically have much more to worry about than keeping track of medications that manage mental illnesses. This complex situation has resulted in a significant mentally-ill homeless population that has become primarily the responsibility of the criminal justice system when these individuals act out in deviant or criminal ways. This is due, at least in part, to the fact that their mental health disorders are not being dealt with medically, since many individuals no longer know where to get and/or can no longer afford to purchase their medications.

Estimates of the prevalence of mentally ill offenders and inmates vary widely; however, a recent report published by the Bureau of Justice Statistics (BJS) indicates that mental health issues are likely widespread among both jail and prison inmates. More specifically, BJS concludes that mental health problems—defined in a variety of ways—are suffered by approximately 45 percent of federal prison inmates, 56 percent of state prison inmates, and 64 percent of jail inmates. These numbers suggest that mental health problems are quite common among correctional institutional populations, perhaps more common (and challenging) than thought before now. An equally important concern, however, is whether correctional staff can and/or should be responsible for evaluating, diagnosing, and treating inmates with mental health issues (or those who are mentally challenged) who reside within correctional institutions.

There are myriad issues that arise from the incarceration of mentally ill and mentally challenged persons in America's correctional institutions. There is also debate regarding the benefits and drawbacks of incarcerating mentally ill and mentally challenged individuals. In the United States, being mentally ill is not generally considered an acceptable defense to criminal punishment. As such, mentally ill individuals who may opt to plead insanity as their defense to criminal responsibility are likely be found guilty—despite their mental illness—especially since most U.S. jurisdictions adhere to the stringent criteria for legal insanity set forth in the M'Naghton Rule.

A Brief History of Mentally Ill Inmates in Corrections

Correctional facilities such as prisons and jails have long been places where criminal offenders of all types are contained. Several hundred years ago, there were specific penal institutions, such as jails, relied on to house individuals who were seriously mentally ill (without the stigma of being labeled as criminals). In the 1800s, the United States conducted many reforms to this system, due primarily to the poor conditions and inhumane treatment of the individuals in these jails. These sweeping reforms primarily resulted in the removal of these mentally ill individuals from jails and their placement in new state-run mental health hospitals and institutions. This lasted for about 150 years, until the same accusations of inhumane treatment and poor conditions were leveled at the state mental health hospitals in the 1960s and 1970s. About this same time, significant medical (and medication) advances had been made, so it was thought that mentally ill individuals would benefit from their removal from these hospitals and placement in the community. The premise was that mentally ill individuals (some institutionalized for most, if not all, of their lives) would be able to live and function in society with the assistance of mental health treatment, especially medications such as the newly developed psychotropic drugs. The definition of a psychotropic drug is typically any drug used to modify or change a person's feelings, thoughts, and/or behaviors. Essentially, these drugs are used to alter the behaviors of mentally ill individuals, and generally include antianxiety/sedatives, antidepressants, antipsychotics, and mood stabilizers.

Today, many more mentally ill individuals are swept up into the criminal justice and corrections systems than are in state or private mental health hospitals and institutions. More specifically, in the 1990s, it was estimated that less than 100,000 mentally ill persons were housed in mental health facilities, whereas a recent (mid-2000s) BJS report estimates that more than one million inmates in state and federal prisons and local jails had (or have) a mental health problem. Although today's correctional facilities were not originally designed or created to house and treat mentally ill persons, this has become one of their main responsibilities, as increasing numbers of mentally ill persons—often off their medication or unable to access needed mental health treatment, and thus engaging in criminal behavior—are brought into the correctional system. National reports indicate that well over half of the inmates in both state prisons and local jails, and just under half of federal prison inmates, have suffered or currently suffer from a mental illness. These estimates likely underestimate the problems of mental illness in correctional populations, as some inmates either are unaware of their mental illnesses or fail to report them.

A Snapshot of Mentally Ill Inmates in Local Jails

U.S. jails have become the nation's dumping ground (at least temporarily) for a variety of problematic individuals, including those with mental illnesses. The majority of jail inmates are held for very short periods of time, ranging from one or two days to several months or more. A higher proportion of individuals come into contact, in one way or another, with the more than 3,500 U.S. jails than with any other correctional facility. This is simply because jails are the nation's gatekeeper into corrections. More specifically, it is extremely rare for an individual to come into contact with the correctional system without having first been detained in a local public or private jail of some kind.

Transient and Highly Varied Population of the Mentally Ill

Even more challenging to jail staff (and mental health professionals) than the continuous population turnover in the nation's jails is that jail populations are not homogenous, but instead are made up of various kinds of individuals with a range of issues or problems, housed there for many different reasons: held over for trial or sentencing; held for transfer to the federal or other state authorities; convicted and sentenced but awaiting transport to or an open bed at a state-run or private prison; held as a juvenile for transfer to a youth court, agency, or facility; held on alleged probation or parole violations; held for transfer to a mental health facility; and convicted of one or more crimes and sentenced for a term of up to one year in jail. In a 12-month period ending in June 2009, BJS estimated that 12.8 million individuals were admitted to local jails. This extremely large and quickly rotated population poses significant challenges for jail staff and administrators with regard to identifying and responding to the mental health problems of detainees and inmates. The transient nature of jail populations tends to relegate the recognition and treatment of mental illness to the bottom of the "to do" list, while maintaining a safe and secure institution tends to be the primary (and often only) goal of jail staff, given the lack of financial, medical, and mental health resources.

Various kinds of mental illnesses and disorders have been recognized in almost two-thirds (64 percent) of the nation's jail population. Nationwide data collection efforts on mental illnesses tend to focus on two ways to identify mentally ill inmates: (1) a recent history of mental illness, defined by a clinical diagnosis or some kind of prior treatment by a mental health professional; or (2) current symptoms of a mental illness, which are typically identified using the criteria in the seminal psychiatric text, *Diagnostic and Statistical Manual of Mental Disorders,* fourth edition (DSM-IV). According to the most recent BJS report, the most common kinds of mental illnesses and disorders found among jail inmates include mania, major depression, and psychotic disorders. Mania and major depression, reported by more than half of all inmates, are identified by inmate symptoms such as insomnia (or hypersomnia), persistent anger or irritability, persistent sadness, or loss of interest in activities. Psychotic disorders are evidenced by hallucinations or delusions. Almost a quarter of all jail inmates report one or more symptoms of a psychotic disorder, such as hearing or seeing things that others do not. Overall, jail inmates tend to have the highest rates of mental illness or mental disorder symptoms when compared to state or federal prison inmates.

Demographics of Mentally Ill Inmates

A 2006 BJS report indicates that female jail inmates report higher rates of mental health problems than male jail inmates. Approximately three-quarters of females in jail reported a mental health illness or disorder as compared to 63 percent of males. Also, more female jail inmates (23 percent) reported a prior diagnosis of a mental illness by a mental health professional in the prior year than males (approximately eight percent). Additionally, reports of mental illness by jail inmates varied by race and ethnicity as well as age, with significantly more whites (than blacks or Hispanics) and more young persons (up to 24 years of age) reporting some kind of mental health problem. Further, almost half of all jail inmates (49 percent) were identified as having a dual diagnosis of both a mental illness and substance dependency or abuse. Far fewer jail inmates had only one or the other problem, lending support to the notion that dual diagnoses of mental illnesses and substance abuse problems are increasingly common in the jail population. Jail inmates with mental illnesses were significantly more likely than jail inmates without a mental illness to have been victimized in the past by physical or sexual abuse.

Although brief stays in jail are common (and not altogether conducive to effective mental health treatment), and safety and security tends to be the primary concern of jail staff and administrators, recent focus on inmate health has resulted in attempts to provide at least a minimum of mental health resources and treatment to those in jail. In spite of the various challenges posed by the jail environment and lack of financial and medical resources, a concerted effort has been made to provide basic mental health services to inmates held in local jails. However, not all jails provide the same kind, quantity, or quality of mental health services. These services primarily include: mental health screening procedures, professional mental health counseling and/or therapies, and administering psychotropic medications to inmates with mental illnesses. More extensive treatment responses are not common, although jail inmates may be transported to a hospital for a brief (or extended) stay in certain kinds of more serious situations. BJS reported that 17 percent of all mentally ill inmates received mental health treatment of some kind during their stay in jail. Although several treatment protocols may be provided in combination, the use of psychotropic medications was the most common treatment of mentally ill inmates in jails (15 percent), followed by counseling or therapy with a mental health professional (seven percent), and an overnight (or longer) stay in a hospital (two percent).

Institutional problems associated with (especially untreated) mentally ill inmates incarcerated in jails include higher numbers of rule violations, greater prevalence of fights and assaults (on both staff and other inmates), and more injuries from fighting and assault behaviors than are recorded for inmates without mental health problems. These are problematic safety and security concerns for jail staff and administrators, but they also reflect the additional physical and mental threats posed to mentally ill inmates housed in local jail facilities.

Mentally Ill Inmates in State and Federal Prisons

Although both state and federal prisons see much lower population turn-over than local jails, many of the same issues are confronted when housing and responding to the needs of mentally ill prison inmates. Prison populations tend to be much more homogenous than jail populations, as individuals housed in state or federal prisons have been convicted of a crime or technical violation while on probation or parole, rather than being held awaiting trial, sentencing, or transfer to another facility. Also, prisons tend to have specific intake and release days, and times that regulate the entry and exit of inmates through the prison, resulting in a more systematic and organized schedule for both staff and inmates. Further, prisons are typically larger and tend to have more time, opportunity, and resources to assess and classify inmates in order to separate particular problematic and/or vulnerable groups of prisoners from one another, as well as to identify potential problems and challenges during inmates' initial entry into the facility.

Lower Incidence Than Jail but More Treatment

National reports indicate that mentally ill inmates represent lower proportions of the prison population than the jail population, and receive greater levels of treatment. The identification of mentally ill inmates in state and federal prisons occurs via the same mechanisms as for jail inmates (e.g., recent history and recognition of symptoms). Just over half (56 percent) of state inmates and a bit less than half (45 percent) of federal inmates have been identified as mentally ill. Again, similar to the identification of mentally ill jail inmates, mentally ill state prison inmates were classified as exhibiting symptoms of mania (43 percent), major depression (23 percent), or psychotic disorders (15 percent). The specific breakdown of mental illnesses has not been reported for federal prison inmates. Similar to the process found in jails, state and federal prisons also utilize the criteria specified in the DSM-IV in order to identify, evaluate, and respond to mentally ill inmates. State prison inmates were more likely than either jail or federal prison inmates to report any recent history of mental illness (24 percent versus 21 percent and 14 percent, respectively) at the time of intake.

Similar to the prevalence of mental illness among jail inmates, mental illness among state and federal prison inmates is more commonly reported among female inmates than male inmates (state, 73 percent of females versus 55 percent of males; federal, 61 percent of females versus 44 percent of males). Mental illness also appears more commonly suffered by white than minority prison inmates, and by younger than older prison inmates, reflecting the same kinds of demographic patterns as found in the national report on local jails. Additionally, state prisoners who reported past abuse (physical, sexual, or both) were more than two times more likely to report a mental health problem (27 versus 10 percent). Comparable to jail inmate statistics, both state and federal prison inmates also tend to have dual diagnoses of mental illness and substance abuse/dependency problems (state, 42 percent; federal, 29 percent). State inmates suffering from some kind of mental illness were more likely to be serving time for a violent offense (49 percent) than non-mentally ill state inmates (47 percent), and significantly more likely than all federal (29 percent) and all jail inmates (with mental illness, 27 percent; without mental illness, 24 percent). Finally, state prisoners with mental illnesses served longer incarceration sentences than those without—about four months longer, on average.

In sum, state and federal prison inmates identified more access to mental health treatment and resources than those reportedly found in local jails. Overall, approximately one-third of all state prisoners with mental illnesses reported some kind of mental health treatment since their intake (as compared to 24 percent of federal prisoners and 17 percent of jail inmates). Similar to mental health treatment in jails, however, the most common type of treatment for state and federal prison inmates was the prescription of a psychotropic medication (state, 27 percent; federal, 20 percent) followed by professional counseling or therapy (state, 23 percent; federal, 15 percent), and hospitalization (state, five percent; federal, two percent).

A variety of complex problems and safety issues are reportedly more commonly found among state and federal inmates with mental illnesses, including: increased rule violations and infractions (58 percent of state inmates with mental illnesses versus 43 percent without; 40 percent of federal inmates with mental illness versus 28 percent without); fighting and assaultive behavior toward staff and/or other inmates (24 percent of state inmates with mental illnesses versus 14 percent without; 15 percent of federal inmates with mental illnesses versus seven percent without); and injuries sustained due to involvement in fights and assaults (20 percent of state inmates with mental illness versus 10 percent without; 11 percent of state inmates with mental illness versus six percent without). These kinds of problems that are found more often to involve mentally ill inmates are troublesome safety and security concerns for prison staff and administrators, but also further highlight the physical and mental threats posed when housing mentally ill individuals in state and federal prisons.

Mentally Challenged Inmates in Correctional Facilities

Very little is currently known about the prevalence and experiences of mentally challenged (developmentally disabled) inmates in U.S. correctional facilities. At the national level, the most controversial and visible point of this issue has been whether the execution of mentally challenged/developmentally disabled offenders is constitutional, or whether it constitutes cruel and unusual punishment. A landmark 2002 Supreme Court decision (*Atkins v. Virginia*) ruled that the execution of mentally challenged offenders constituted cruel and unusual punishment, effectively abolishing the use of the death penalty for mentally challenged individuals.

National data indicate that approximately two to three percent of the nation's population is mentally challenged/developmentally disabled, while mentally challenged/developmentally disabled persons represent between four and 10 percent of the prison population (and likely higher proportions in jails). Mental retardation/developmental disability has been defined by the American Association on Mental Retardation (AAMR) using the following standards: (1) I.Q. is 75 or below; (2) significant limitations in two or more skill areas (e.g., education, work, communications, etc.); and (3) problems present from childhood/adolescence (18 or younger, although they are more commonly present at birth).

The lack of comprehensive and national data on the prevalence of mental retardation/developmental disability among jail and prison populations makes it difficult to draw definitive conclusions about the treatment of and particular safety, security, health, or other problems posed by incarcerating individuals with this condition. However, several statements are warranted by the limited literature in this area. First, it appears that U.S. correctional facilities house disproportionately high numbers of mentally challenged individuals as compared to their representation in society. This indicates that the criminal justice and corrections systems have likely become more common societal responses to the behaviors of mentally challenged individuals than in the past, which may be partially due to the fact that these persons are less able to understand and exercise their rights, such as the right to a lawyer or to remain silent, thus placing them in more vulnerable positions when prosecuted and on trial for (or pleading guilty to) a charge of criminal behavior.

Second, the behavior of mentally challenged/developmentally disabled inmates seems to be especially problematic, as they tend to react much differently (and more physically) than others to extreme situations and environments. This tends to be associated with increased rule violations and misbehavior or acting out during incarceration terms. Third, due to a lack of understanding and inability to effectively function in prison or jail, mentally challenged/developmentally disabled inmates often fail to acclimate normally to the environment, which tends to increase their poor (or neglectful) treatment. This includes (1) the inability to effectively negotiate and access appropriate and needed rehabilitation, vocational/educational, and early release programs; (2) taking up significant amounts of staff attention; and (3) the failure to earn good-time credits or other resources that either enhance the effectiveness of their incarceration or speed up their time to release.

Overall, it appears that the criminal justice and correctional systems have been tasked with the enormous responsibility to identify; keep safe; and effectively rehabilitate, treat, and contain mentally challenged/developmentally disabled inmates without sufficient training, education, and resources to meet the challenge. Additional attention to the issue of mentally challenged/developmentally disabled inmates in jails and state and federal prisons is sorely needed in order to more fully understand and respond to the issues of safely and securely incarcerating these special populations.

Pro: Benefits of Incarcerating the Mentally Challenged

Although the literature on the incarceration of mentally ill and/or mentally challenged inmates indicates the significant and complex issues posed by these populations, there are some bright spots. First, incarcerating these special populations allows for the identification, evaluation, and response to mental illness (and mental retardation) in a secure, residential setting where these individuals literally make up a captive audience. The recent attention given to effective mental health treatment and the increasing numbers of mental health professionals employed in and/or contracted to provide services in correctional facilities enables access to treatment options that these individuals may not have in the community. In fact, in certain instances, inmates may not even have been aware of any mental illness, and it is only upon incarceration that these individuals are screened for and diagnosed with a mental illness that may be effectively treated by a professional.

Another benefit of incarcerating mentally ill and/or mentally challenged/ developmentally disabled offenders is public safety. National statistics indicate that mentally ill offenders were incarcerated (slightly) more often for violent offenses than offenders who were not mentally ill, especially in state prisons (as compared to federal prisons or local jails). Thus, it is possible that a small reduction in violent crime may be realized when mentally ill or disordered offenders are taken off the street and placed in a custodial institution.

Additionally, significantly more attention is currently being given to the rights of mentally ill (and other) inmates, as well as highlighting the responsibility and accountability of prison and jail staff and administrators for providing effective responses in a custodial environment. Moreover, the Supreme Court's abolishment of the death penalty for both mentally ill (*Ford v. Wainwright*, 1986) and mentally challenged (*Atkins v. Virginia*, 2002) offenders has helped to guarantee, or at least allow for, the securing of these inmates in facilities that are tasked with their care. Finally, scholars and practitioners have become more aware of and more committed to their responsibility regarding mentally ill and/or mentally challenged/developmentally disabled individuals in order to more effectively identify and treat them.

Con: Drawbacks of Incarcerating the Mentally Challenged

According to much of the literature on jail and prison facilities, these are exactly the wrong kinds of environments for assessing, evaluating, diagnosing, and treating mentally ill and mentally challenged/developmentally disabled persons. One of the problems discussed in the relevant research on this issue concerns the lack of resources in the criminal justice system generally, and in the correctional system specifically, needed to effectively house, protect, monitor, and rehabilitate inmates with mental or behavioral problems. Some critics argue that mental health facilities or hospitals, not correctional facilities, are the more appropriate institutions for responding to mentally ill and mentally challenged/developmentally disabled individuals, whether they have violated the criminal law or not.

Correctional institutions, with their historical and current focus on incapacitating and securing criminal offenders, tend not to be attractive environments for mental health professionals searching for potential employment. The pay, work environment, lack of financial and medical resources, and lack of institutional and collegial/peer support (on the part of correctional or security staff members) for the goals of mental health treatment tend to minimize the benefits of professional employment in correctional facilities. Therefore, well-trained mental health professionals do not often apply for or accept employment in U.S. jails or state and federal prisons. As such, most correctional facilities lack the trained mental health staff necessary for high-quality, effective mental health treatment. Additionally, because most correctional budgets are reserved mainly for staff and inmate safety and security, there remains a significant lack of financial resources in corrections to effectively respond to needs of mentally ill and mentally challenged/developmentally disabled inmates.

Additionally, correctional staff generally exhibit a lack of concern or feeling of responsibility in regard to mentally ill and mentally challenged/developmentally disabled inmates. These line staff (correctional staff that engage in the day-to-day monitoring and supervision of inmates) are typically not trained in recognizing and responding to issues resulting from mental health problems. Most correctional training focuses on teaching skills that enhance and ensure the safe and secure operation of the jail or prison, rather than dealing with the problems and situations that develop due to incarcerating offenders with mental health and behavioral issues.

Finally, even with the recent advances made in recognizing and ensuring the constitutional and human rights of jail and prison inmates (especially with regard to protecting due-process rights and defending against cruel and unusual punishment), too often inmates who suffer from mental illness or mental retardation/developmental disabilities do not fully understand or have the resources to respond to problem situations or to request the professional assistance necessary for them to navigate (or even survive) in the correctional institution. Thus, it is even more crucial that criminal justice officials, correctional officials, and mental health professionals recognize their responsibility in ensuring and protecting the rights and treatment of mentally ill and mentally challenged/developmentally disabled offenders who may not be able to do this on their own. This added responsibility (not thought to be necessary for inmates not suffering from mental illness or mental retardation/developmental disabilities) takes additional time, effort, and funds, and likely takes these correctional and mental health professionals away from their duties.

Future Issues for Mentally Challenged Inmates

As greater numbers of individuals with mental illnesses or those suffering from mental retardation/developmental disabilities come into contact with the criminal justice system and are subject to incarceration, the need for mental health professionals, access to mental health treatment, and increased financial and health resources will also increase. Approximately 90 percent (or slightly more) of prison inmates will eventually return to free society. Thus, funds spent on identifying and treating mental health issues, to the extent that the correctional system can, will likely earn dividends if these inmates are able to successfully return to their communities having dealt with their problems instead of suffering in silence during their incarceration term.

A potentially promising alternative to incarcerating mentally ill and mentally challenged/developmentally disabled individuals, regardless of increased custodial treatment programs, may be the increased use of a particular kind of specialty court called mental health courts, which were first established in Florida in the late 1990s. Typically, these courts are collaborative partnerships between criminal justice agencies and community service providers (including hospitals) with the goal to divert mentally ill offenders out of corrections without increasing the risk to public safety. Essentially, members of the collaboration respond quickly to identify and remove mentally ill persons from local jails (before a lengthy involvement with the criminal justice system) and place them in a mental health treatment facility in the community. The potential benefits of the use of mental health courts are not yet well known, nor are these courts used extensively throughout the United States, but it seems likely that with increasing prison and jail populations, along with increased costs, these alternative courts may well become much more important responses to dealing with mentally ill (and perhaps mentally challenged/developmentally disabled) offenders.

See Also: 1. Capital Punishment/Death Penalty; 3. Cruel and Unusual Punishment; 4. Due Process Rights of Prisoners; 9. Healthcare and Medical Assistance for Prisoners.

Further Readings

American Psychiatric Association. *Diagnostic and Statistical Manual of Mental Disorders, Fourth Edition (DSM-IV)*. Washington, DC: American Psychiatric Association, 1994.

Beck, Allen J., and Laura M. Maruschak. *Mental Health Treatment in State Prisons, 2000*. Washington, DC: U.S. Department of Justice, Office of Justice Programs, Bureau of Justice Statistics, 2001.

Bureau of Justice Statistics. "Jail Population Counts." http://bjs.ojp.usdoj .gov/index.cfm?ty=tp&tid=121 (Accessed March 2011).

Cox, Judith F., Pamela C. Morschauser, Steven Banks, and James L. Stone. "A Five-Year Population Study of Persons Involved in the Mental Health and Local Correctional Systems: Implication for Service Planning." *The Journal of Behavioral Health Services and Research*, v.282 (2001).

Ditton, Paula M. *Mental Health and Treatment of Inmates and Probationers*. Washington, DC: U.S. Department of Justice, Office of Justice Programs, Bureau of Justice Statistics, 1999.

Floyd, Jami. "The Administration of Psychotropic Drugs to Prisoners: State of the Law and Beyond." *California Law Review*, v.78/5 (1990).

Gido, Rosemary L., and Lanette Dalley, eds. *Women's Mental Health Issues Across the Criminal Justice System*. Upper Saddle River, NJ: Pearson Prentice Hall, 2009.

Greenberg, Greg A., and Robert A. Rosenheck. "Jail Incarceration, Homelessness, and Mental Health: A National Study." *Psychiatric Services*, v.59/2 (2008).

James, Doris J., and Lauren E. Glaze. *Mental Health Problems of Prisons and Jails*. Washington, DC: U.S. Department of Justice, Office of Justice Programs, Bureau of Justice Statistics, 2006.

Mitka, Mike. "Innovative Program for Mentally Ill Inmates." *JAMA*, v.285/21 (2001).

Muraskin, Roslyn, ed. *Key Issues in Correctional Issues*. Upper Saddle River, NJ: Pearson Prentice Hall, 2010.

Petersilia, Joan. *Doing Justice? Criminal Offenders With Developmental Disabilities*. Berkeley, CA: California Policy Research Center, 2000.

Ross, Jeffrey Ian. *Special Problems in Corrections*. Upper Saddle River, NJ: Pearson Prentice Hall, 2008.

Wilper, Andrew P., Steffie Woolhandler, J. Wesley Boyd, Karen E. Lasser, Danny McCormick, David H. Bor, and David U. Himmelstein. "The Health and Health Care of U.S. Prisoners: A National Study." *American Journal of Public Health*, v.99/4 (2009).

13

Preventive Detention

Meghan Sacks
Fairleigh Dickinson University

Alissa R. Ackerman
University of Washington, Tacoma

Although the original purpose of bail was to ensure the appearance of accused individuals in court, the Bail Reform Act of 1984 resulted in an expansion of the use of bail, explicitly allowing the use of preventive detention in cases involving defendants who were presumed dangerous by the court. Preventive detention is the temporary incarceration of an individual who has not been convicted of a crime. Provisions of the Bail Reform Act state that a defendant should not be released in the community if the release would not ensure his return to court or if his release would place members of the community in danger. This position was clarified in *United States v. Salerno* (1987), when the U.S. Supreme Court held that, under the Bail Reform Act of 1984, "dangerousness" was a constitutional and formal criterion for making bail determinations.

While the use of preventive detention first surfaced in bail proceedings, the practice has spread to various other arenas. The evolution of preventive detention can be traced from its beginning in pretrial decisions to its use in cases involving sexual predators, illegal aliens, and enemy combatants. The topic of preventive discussion also requires a discussion of the use of

predictions of dangerousness. While preventive detention is commonly justified on grounds that it protects the community from harm, the practice is
also criticized for violating various constitutional and due process rights.
Regardless of the argument, preventive detention is currently practiced in
the U.S. legal system.

Right to Bail

The Eighth Amendment of the Constitution provides that "excessive bail
shall not be required." Early researchers of bail practices—most notably
Caleb Foote—interpreted this as a constitutional guarantee to bail, a right
more clearly delineated in the Federal Rules of Criminal Procedure, which
states that any person arrested for an offense not punishable by death must
be granted bail. The right to bail was further clarified with the Supreme
Court's decision in *Stack v. Boyle* (1951), where the Supreme Court stated
that bail is a traditional right to freedom and permits a defendant to fully
participate in his defense. In addition, the Court explained that bail protects
individuals from punishment before a conviction, and that the purpose of
bail was to ensure a defendant's appearance in court. This standard was
subsequently questioned with research that exposed inequitable practices
of a cash bail system. More specifically, in 1954, Caleb Foote conducted a
prominent study of bail practices and found the following: release decisions
were based primarily on the offense, with little consideration given to factors related to appearance in court; cash bail was being used to detain and
punish the poor; and defendants who were incarcerated pretrial received
harsher sentences.

Bail Reform Acts of 1966 and 1984

Bail Reform Act of 1966

Bail reform efforts flourished in the 1960s in response to the criticisms
of the cash bail system. Most notably, the Vera Foundation formed the
Manhattan Bail Project in 1961, which led to a significant increase in the
use of release on recognizance (ROR), which is a nonfinancial release,
subject to the defendant's assurance of return to all court proceedings.
The Bail Reform Act of 1966 strengthened the use of ROR and offered an
alternative to the cash bail system that had governed for the prior decades.
The 1966 act provided that an individual charged with a noncapital crime

was to be released on personal recognizance or an unsecured personal bond unless the release would not sufficiently assure the return of the defendant to future court proceedings. If needed, additional conditions could be imposed by the court to safeguard the accused's presence at court proceedings. This act was designed to safeguard the original intent of bail, which was to guarantee that defendants would show up for court appearances. Preventive detention was only authorized for individuals charged with capital offenses.

The increased use of ROR and the provisions for conditional release fueled the development of pretrial service agencies in the 1960s. Since the first bail reform movement of the 1960s, hundreds of pretrial agencies have been established nationwide. Pretrial agencies have become commonplace in both the state and federal criminal justice systems. These agencies, although sharing similar goals, range in their services, which include some of the following: collecting criminal history information, providing information about community ties, making release recommendations to the court, and supervising offenders who receive conditional release.

Just as the use of ROR was on the rise, a change in the purpose of bail was also becoming apparent. The traditional goal of assuring a defendant's appearance in court had been replaced with the goal of protecting the community. This change was not necessarily surprising, as the criminal justice system as a whole was also undergoing a significant transformation. Rehabilitation had been the prevailing philosophy of the criminal justice system for several decades; however, this model of justice came under attack in the 1970s, when studies showed that rehabilitation was not effective at reducing crime. In addition to the criticism of rehabilitation, evidence of sentencing disparities surfaced in the 1970s and 1980s. Civil rights activists expressed concern that sentencing disparities found in the criminal justice system were the result of racial and class biases.

Bail Reform Act of 1984

These concerns were further compounded with evidence of rising crime rates, which led to a public campaign for harsher sentencing legislation. At approximately the same time, a jail overcrowding crisis placed the bail reform movement in a tenuous position. The conflict was made moot with the passage of the Bail Reform Act of 1984, which only authorized preventive detention when a defendant was charged with a capital offense. However, the new Bail Reform Act authorized preventive detention in cases where release would not ensure the appearance of the defendant and when the individual posed a danger to the community, not just a risk of flight. Protecting the public from "dangerous" individuals outweighed other concerns and became a new objective of bail. The use of preventive detention was given the blessing of legislators with the priority of identifying potentially dangerous offenders. Ironically, as pointed out by many death penalty researchers, the most dangerous offenders, mainly murderers, have lower rates of recidivism than other serious offenders. Other notable research on bail practices supports the argument made by death penalty researchers, concluding that pretrial misconduct rates are lowest for offenders arrested for murder or rape, and much higher for defendants charged with drug crimes and motor vehicle thefts. However, from the passage of the Bail Reform Act of 1984, identifying dangerous individuals had become a central priority of bail proceedings, and preventive detention has become the preferred form of protection.

The Eighth Amendment states that all citizens have the right to not have excessive bail set by the court. The traditional right to bail was further clarified in the landmark case *Stack v. Boyle* (1951). Research in the early to mid-1900s exposed several inequities in a system dominated by the use of monetary bail. The first bail reform movement of the 1960s resulted in an increase in the use of ROR and the development of several pretrial agencies nationwide. In the 1980s, a second bail reform movement occurred, which focused primarily on potentially dangerous offenders. The result of the second bail reform movement was an expansion of the original goal of bail to include protecting the community from "dangerous" individuals through the use of preventive detention.

Predictions of Danger

Preventive detention rests on the idea that certain individuals pose a threat of danger if released into the community. The use of preventive detention requires judges to make predictions about the future dangerousness of defendants. Some scholars argue that the use of predictions of danger is subject to criticism, as judges may not be suited to make predictions about future behavior. Other critics point out that judges often have insufficient information during bail determinations, resulting in unreliable decisions and overprediction of danger. Preventive detention laws, however, have been used by most states since the 1980s to detain defendants whom judges determine to be dangerous.

Clinical and Actuarial Methods of Risk Assessment

Mental health specialists are typically relied upon for opinions about future dangerousness, also known as violence risk assessments. These professionals often rely on actuarial methods to assess dangerousness, commonly thought of as an objective approach that relies on statistical probabilities of outcomes based on specific factors to determine future conduct. A second type of assessment, known as the clinical assessment, is a more subjective approach involving discussion and a recommendation ultimately based on a clinician's experience and interpretation. However, mental health specialists are not the only ones required to make predictions of future dangerousness. With the advent of preventive detention, judges are also required to make these determinations. To do so, judges use a combination of both actuarial and clinical methods when making risk assessments about defendants.

The debate over the superiority of clinical methods versus actuarial decision making is a long-standing one, originating from an article written in 1954 by Paul Meehl positing the superiority of statistical, formalistic decision making. Since then, the topic of how to assess the risk of recidivism among individuals has been researched, critiqued, and debated among top scholars and practitioners. Concern over the growing importance of risk of recidivism and dangerousness during the 1980s led to research aimed at improving risk-prediction methods. The research showed that clinical risk assessments were effective under certain conditions and with specific populations. However, this research also prompted a focus on creating actuarial instruments to help improve risk assessments.

Actuarial instruments identify risk factors of populations and utilize a mathematical approach to risk prediction, rather than the explanatory approach used by clinicians. There has been a great deal written about the advantages and proper uses of actuarial decision making. In addition, several studies have demonstrated the value of using actuarial methods for the purpose of recidivism prediction. A debate currently exists over whether actuarial methods of predicting risk should be adjusted by clinical judgments, or whether the system of clinical decision making should be completely replaced by more formulaic methods of risk prediction. While mental health professionals debate the use of these methods, judges use both to assist in their determinations. The critical difference is that mental health professionals often have sufficient time and information to make these decisions, while judges must make quick assessments of defendants based on little information.

Do These Methods Work?

In addition to the debate over the use of actuarial or clinical danger assessments, there is another significant issue presented by the reliance on violence risk assessments: Do they work? The failure of risk assessments to predict future dangerousness has been widely debated, with some of the most well-recognized studies positing that predictions of danger by mental health specialists are wrong two out of three times. However, these conclusions are refuted by those who claim that they are unsupported and interpreted inaccurately. In addition, it has also been argued that most studies discrediting risk assessments are unverifiable. Some studies have found that mental health specialists make correct predictions of dangerousness more often than chance would allow. Nevertheless, some experts caution that assessments of future danger are difficult to make.

The difficulties presented by predictions of danger are even more critical for judges making decisions about preventive detention. There is evidence that individuals released pretrial are rarely rearrested, and that accurate predictions of pretrial criminal behavior are generally poor. Others criticize the criteria for preventive detention decisions as being unreliable for predictions of future criminal behavior. Nevertheless, since the advent of preventive detention, judges are expected to make predictions of dangerousness during bail hearings.

Dangerousness and the Federal Courts

The use of assessments of danger gained significant attention with the Supreme Court's decision in *Barefoot v. Estelle* (1983). In this case, the petitioner was found guilty of capital murder of a police officer and was sentenced to death. The petitioner appealed the decision of the appellate court, arguing that the appellate court had improperly denied the petitioner's request for a stay of execution. The petitioner argued that testimony provided at the sentencing hearing by a psychiatrist was improper, as the psychiatrist made predictions about the petitioner's future dangerous behavior.

The Supreme Court in *Barefoot* upheld the decision of the appellate court, concluding that it was permissible to have a psychiatrist testify as to the future danger posed by a defendant. The majority, in a 6–3 decision, found that the testimony of psychiatrists was not unconstitutional, since it could not be shown that the testimony was entirely unreliable, and since the fact finder could recognize and take account of any shortcomings presented by the testimony. While the Court acknowledged that predictions of future behavior are often wrong and prejudicial, it also made clear that this is an issue for the fact finder to decide. In addition, the decision in *Barefoot* opened the door for predictions of future behavior in other facets of the legal system, such as bail.

Shortly after the decision in *Barefoot*, the Supreme Court again tackled the issue of predictions of future dangerousness in the case of *Schall v. Martin* (1984). In *Schall*, the Juvenile Justice Department of New York City appealed the decision of the appellate court, which affirmed the lower court's decision that a statute authorizing the preventive detention of juveniles was used as punishment, and was therefore unconstitutional. The statute, also known as the New York Family Court Act, contains a provision authorizing the pretrial detention of juveniles who are found to pose a risk for criminal activity during the pretrial phase. However, both the lower and appellate courts found this provision unconstitutional, as it was administered as punishment without a finding of guilt.

The Supreme Court in *Schall* reversed the decision of the appellate court, concluding that sufficient procedural safeguards exist and that the preventive detention served a regulatory rather than punitive process and therefore did not violate the due process rights of the juveniles. Moreover, the Court rejected the appellees arguments with which the lower courts agreed—that it is difficult to accurately predict future criminal behavior. The Supreme Court responded to this argument, declaring that there is nothing inherently unattainable about a prediction of future criminal behavior from a legal point of view.

1987 Salerno *Court Upholds Preventive Detention*

The Court's decision in *United States v. Salerno* (1987) took preventive detention and predictions of future criminal behavior from the juvenile legal system to the adult legal system. In *Salerno*, the government appealed the decision of the appellate court, which found the preventive detention standard under the Bail Reform Act unconstitutional. In accordance with its finding, the appellate court reversed the decision of the lower court, which had denied the defendants bail after their arrest in connection with numerous racketeering charges. The Supreme Court disagreed with the decision of the appellate court, holding constitutional the provision of the Bail Reform Act authorizing preventive detention. The Court concluded that this provision did not violate the Due Process

Clause contained in the Fifth Amendment or the Excessive Bail Clause found in the Eighth Amendment.

With its decision, The *Salerno* Court upheld the Bail Reform Act of 1984, legitimizing the purpose of bail for preventive detention. The Court, relying on its earlier decision in *Schall,* found that preventive detention served a regulatory rather than punitive purpose. In accordance with this view, the Court affirmed the decision of the lower court, stating that it agreed with the position of the Court of Appeals, that pretrial detention under the Bail Reform Act was regulatory and not penal in nature. The Court articulated the following conditions, under the Bail Reform Act, for which preventive detention is sanctioned: cases involving violence, crimes for which the penalty is either a life sentence or death, significant drug offenses, and specific repeat offenders. The category of specific repeat offenders is more clearly defined under the Bail Reform Act itself, which classifies these offenses to include a felony conviction for two or more of the above-listed offenses, two or more similar state or local offenses, or a combination of these offenses. Under this categorization, the Court gave primacy to the seriousness of the current offense and the defendant's prior criminal history.

Preventive Detention and the Mentally Ill

Several cases since *Salerno* have limited the use of preventive detention, while a few have expanded its use. In 1992, the Supreme Court tackled the issue of detention to prevent dangerousness among the mentally ill. In *Foucha v. Louisiana* (1992), the petitioner was found not guilty by reason of insanity of aggravated burglary, and was subsequently committed to a state mental hospital. The petitioner later applied for release from the hospital, and although he was no longer mentally ill, the hospital found that he still posed a danger to society and denied his release. Both the lower court and the Supreme Court of Louisiana found that the Louisiana statute allowing for indefinite preventive detention for insanity acquitees who were no longer mentally ill, but who may still be dangerous, did not violate due process. However, in *Foucha,* the U.S. Supreme Court reversed the decision of the lower court, stating that preventive detention of a person who was no longer mentally ill and who was acquitted of criminal conduct served as punishment and therefore violated the Due Process Clause. The Court, relying on its decision in *Salerno,* explained the circumstances under which the preventive detention of potentially dangerous persons is authorized. In *Salerno,* the detention was imposed for a limited time for the most serious crimes, and the accused were granted the proper procedural protections.

In contrast, the Supreme Court expanded the use of preventive detention with its decision in *Kansas v. Hendricks* (1997). The petitioner in *Hendricks* was diagnosed with pedophilia, which qualifies as a mental abnormality under Kansas's Sexually Violent Predator Act. In accordance, the petitioner was ordered by the trial court to be civilly committed. The Kansas Supreme Court reversed the decision of the trial court, holding that the petitioner's due process rights were violated, as "mental abnormality" does not have the same meaning as "mental illness" with regards to the requirements for civil commitment. The U.S. Supreme Court reversed the decision of the Kansas Supreme Court, holding that due-process requirements are satisfied by proof of mental illness or abnormality and proof of dangerousness. The Court, relying on its decision in *Salerno*, explained that detention does not always mean punishment. The *Hendricks* Court articulated that detention for the purpose of protecting the community from potentially dangerous and mentally ill persons is not considered punitive detention. With its decision, the *Hendricks* Court broadened the conditions under which preventive detention is allowed. Specifically, the Court provided that indefinite detention could be used for sexual predators who are both dangerous and unable to control their behavior.

Preventive Detention and Illegal Immigrants

The issue was again brought to the attention of the Supreme Court a few years later in a case involving indefinite, preventive detention of undesirable aliens in *Zadvydas v. Davis* (2001). In this case, the petitioners were subject to deportation; however, the government could not find countries willing to accept them. Therefore, the U.S. Immigration and Naturalization Service (INS) concluded that it was permissible to detain the petitioners until a country would accept them. Both petitioners challenged their detention after the 90-day removal period had passed, and in both cases, the district courts ordered the illegal immigrants to be released under supervision. In one of the cases, the appellate court reversed the decision of the district court, concluding that the noncitizen's detention did not violate the U.S. Constitution; however, in the second case, the appellate court affirmed the decision of the district court, stating that the foreigner's continued detention was not authorized. The Supreme Court consolidated the cases for review, and while the *Zadvydas* Court upheld the deportation statute, it also explained that the statute did not allow indefinite detention, as this would violate due-process rights. The Court referenced its holding in *Salerno,* where it stated that preventive detention is permissible for the most serious crimes when there are proper procedural safeguards and "stringent time limitations."

The U.S. Supreme Court addressed the issue of the detention of noncitizens in *Demore v. Kim* (2003). In this case, the INS took into custody and detained without bail a deportable permanent resident pending a removal hearing. The petitioner challenged the detention as a violation of his due-process rights. The district court granted the petitioner's habeas corpus action, finding that his detention was a violation of due process, as the INS had made no showing that the noncitizen was a flight risk or posed a danger to society. The appellate court affirmed the lower court's decision, finding that the alien's detention was in violation of his due process rights. On certiorari, the U.S. Supreme Court reversed the finding of the appellate court, holding that the mandatory detention of the petitioner was not a violation of due process. The Court stated that Congress could detain for a brief period of time a deportable alien, and that the detention in this case was not indefinite. However, critics of this position argue that mandatory detention under 236(c) of the Immigration and Nationality Act (authorizing detention pending removal proceedings of noncitizens convicted of specified crimes under the act) is unconstitutional under *Salerno.* According to some commentators, 236(c) authorizes detention for individuals who do not pose a flight risk and who pose no danger. In addition, it has been claimed that 236(c) does not provide adequate procedural protections and detention is often prolonged, making detention under 236(c) unconstitutional in accordance with the *Salerno* Court's decision.

Preventive Detention and Enemy Combatants

In *Hamdi v. Rumsfeld* (2004), the Court tackled the issue of the detention of unlawful enemy combatants. In this case, the petitioner, born in the United States, was classified as an enemy combatant after being detained in Afghanistan and subsequently transferred back to the United States, where he was also detained. The petitioner challenged the detention as unlawful and a violation of his due-process rights. The Court of Appeals dismissed the petitioner's claim, holding that the petitioner's detention was legally authorized under the Authorization for Use of Military Force (AUMF), which allows the president to use "all necessary and appropriate force" against "nations, organizations, or persons" associated with the September 11, 2001, terrorist attacks. The Supreme Court found that the petitioner was entitled to a hearing to refute his classification as an enemy combatant. In addition, the Court held that enemy combatants could be detained for the duration of the war in Afghanistan, but not for the length of the war on terror. The Court cited its decision in *Salerno*, explaining that "[w]e have repeatedly held that Government's regulatory interest in the community safety can, in appropriate circumstances, outweigh an individual's liberty interest. For example, in times of war or insurrection, when society's interest is at its peak, the Government may detain individuals whom the Government deems to be dangerous." Interestingly, however, as pointed out by some commentators, the *Hamdi* Court did not address to what extent Congress can sanction indefinite detention for individuals not convicted of a crime.

Ever Since Salerno

Several cases have addressed the use of preventive detention to detain potentially dangerous individuals, but it was *Salerno* that first gave preventive detention legitimacy. Since *Salerno*, a string of significant cases have addressed the use of preventive detention in different forums, including the detention of sex offenders, noncitizens, and enemy combatants. In all of these cases, the Court has discussed the relevance of its holding in *Salerno*. The 1984 Bail Reform Act and the *Salerno* decision, in allowing dangerousness to be a central concern in bail proceedings, have institutionalized the practice of preventive detention. Furthermore, by stating that judges could consider "community protection" even in nonserious cases, the 1984 act invited the judiciary to become stricter even when release was granted, imposing various conditions, including financial sureties, even in cases where own-recognizance release would previously have been expected.

Pro: Arguments in Support of Preventive Detention

The Supreme Court has consistently articulated that preventive detention is only appropriate in very specific cases involving very serious crimes. The strongest argument in favor of preventive detention is that it is used for the protection of society. Although the Court acknowledges that liberty is a fundamental right, it also acknowledges that at certain times one's right to liberty must be temporarily suspended for the greater good of society. Preventive detention is used to detain individuals who are deemed to endanger the safety of members of the community, and it is the state's responsibility to prevent harm of its citizens. The use of preventive detention with sexual predators protects community members from harm by a predator. The use of preventive detention in cases involving enemy combatants protects the nation from possible further attack from the combatant. In certain cases, preventive detention is used for the protection of a community; however, on a larger scale, preventive detention can help safeguard national security.

To date, the Court has not authorized the indefinite preventive detention of individuals, with one exception. In *Hendricks,* the Court authorized the indefinite detention of sexual predators who are dangerous and who cannot control their behavior. However, the Court was careful to state that detention in this type of case is not punitive in nature, and is still subject to sufficient due-process safeguards. Preventing danger to society has been recognized by the law as a legitimate regulatory goal and not as a form of punishment. In *Salerno,* the Court articulated that preventive detention can only be used for a limited time and when proper procedural safeguards are in place. The Speedy Trial Act requires that prosecution of a case occur in a timely fashion, thereby ensuring that any term of pretrial detention period cannot be excessive.

Con: Arguments in Opposition to Preventive Detention

Preventive detention is often criticized on grounds that it is punishment without a conviction. Although the Supreme Court has held that preventive detention is not a form of punishment, critics argue that it is a deprivation of liberty of individuals who are innocent in the eyes of the law. In the United States, all persons are presumed innocent until proven guilty in a court of law. While preventive detention proceedings provide certain procedural due-process rights, such as counsel and a hearing, they do not provide all due-process rights found in the U.S. Constitution. Specifically, a hearing is not the same as a trial; a trial is required before a guilty verdict and before any punishment can occur. However, without a trial, preventive detention hearings can result in the detainment of individuals who have not been convicted. Many see this detention as a violation of due-process rights.

Research has also shown that pretrial detention can impact the course of an entire case. More specifically, defendants who are detained are not able to participate fully in their defense; even more troubling are findings that pretrial detention increases both the likelihood of conviction and a sentence of incarceration. Additionally, even when it is not used for pretrial detention, preventive detention is a form of incarceration, and the range of negative effects associated with incarceration is well-documented. Some of the impacts of incarceration on offenders and family members include employment barriers, financial hardship, physical and psychological conditions, and weakened familial relations. Some or all of these adverse events may be experienced by individuals who are subject to preventive detention.

Predictions of Dangerousness

A third concern has been raised with the discussion of predictions of dangerousness. Predictions of dangerousness provide a foundation for preventive detention decisions, and are necessary to attempt to predict future dangerousness. This is a widely debated topic, with many who argue that actuarial methods are able to predict future danger better than clinical methods, and others who claim that clinical methods are superior to actuarial methods. Aside from the technical argument is the larger question: Do predictions of dangerousness actually work? The results are mixed, with the best conclusions suggesting that mental health specialists predict future dangerousness more accurately than chance. These conclusions are not very promising, and these results apply to mental health specialists who have extensive education, training, and experience using these methods. However, the reality in preventive detention hearings is that the judge must make the decision, which probably lessens the odds of accurate predictions. Either way, these predictions should be used with extreme caution, as should the practice of preventive detention.

See Also: 3. Cruel and Unusual Punishment; 4. Due Process Rights of Prisoners; 10. Legal Assistance for Prisoners; 12. Mentally Ill and Mentally Challenged Inmates; 19. Sex Offender Treatment.

Further Readings

Bail Reform Act of 1984. 18 U.S.C. 3142.
Barefoot v. Estelle, 463 U.S. 880 (1983).
Beeley, Arthur. *The Bail System in Chicago.* Chicago: University of Chicago Press, 1927.
Cohen, Thomas H., and Brian A. Reaves. *State Court Processing Statistics, 1990–2004: Pretrial Release of Felony Defendants in State Courts.* Bureau of Justice Statistics. Washington, DC: U.S. Department of Justice, 2007.

Corrado, M. L. "Sex Offenders, Unlawful Combatants, and Preventive Detention." *North Carolina Law Review,* v.84, (2005).

Demore v. Kim, 538 U.S. 510 (2003).

Doherty, Fiona, and Deborah Pearlstein. *Assessing the New Normal: Liberty and Security Post-September 11.* New York: United States Lawyers Committee for Human Rights, 2004.

Fagan, Jeffrey, and Martin Guggenheim. "Preventive Detention and the Judicial Prediction of Dangerousness for Juveniles: A Natural Experiment." *Journal of Criminal Law and Criminology,* v.86 (1996).

Feeley, Malcolm M. *Court Reform on Trial.* New York: Basic Books, 1983.

Foote, Caleb. "Compelling Appearance in Court: Administration of Bail in Philadelphia." *University of Pennsylvania Law Review,* v.102 (1954).

Foucha v. Louisiana, 504 U.S. 71 (1992).

Goldkamp, John. "Danger and Detention: A Second Generation of Bail Reform." *Journal of Criminal Law and Criminology,* v.76 (1985).

Goldkamp, John. *Two Classes of Accused: A Study of Bail and Detention of American Justice.* Cambridge, MA: Ballinger, 1979.

Grove, William M., David H. Zald, Boyd S. Lebow, Beth E. Snitz, and Chad Nelson. "Clinical Versus Mechanical Prediction: A Meta-Analysis." *Psychological Assessment,* v.12 (2000).

Hamdi v. Rumsfeld, 542 U.S. 507 (2004).

Jackson, Patrick. "The Impact of Pretrial Preventive Detention." *The Justice System Journal,* v.12 (1987).

Kansas v. Hendricks, 521 U.S. 346 (1997).

Litwack, Thomas R., Patricia A. Zapf, Jennifer L. Groscup, and Stephen D. Hart. "Violence Risk Assessment: Research, Legal, and Clinical Considerations." In *Handbook of Forensic Psychology,* edited by Irving B. Weiner and Allen K. Hess. New York: John Wiley and Sons, 2006.

Meehl, Patrick. *Clinical Versus Statistical Prediction: A Theoretical Analysis and a Review of the Evidence.* Minneapolis: University of Minnesota Press, 1954.

Schall v. Martin, 467 U.S. 253 (1984).

Skolnick, Jerome H., Malcolm M. Feeley, and Candace McCoy. *Criminal Justice: Introductory Cases and Materials.* New York: Foundation Press, 2004.

Stack v. Boyle, 342 U.S. 1 (1951).

United States v. Salerno, 481 U.S. 739 (1987).

Zadvydas v. Davis, 533 U.S. 678 (2001).

14

Prison Labor

Christine Martin
University of Illinois at Chicago

The use of prison labor in the United States has existed for centuries. Regular use of inmate labor began in 1790. Eventually, those who opposed the use of inmate labor, which was largely comprised of organized free laborers, protested enough to have laws passed restricting the use of prison labor by private companies. However, since the early 1980s, there has been a revival in the private use of inmate labor with the passage of the 1979 Prison Industry Enhancement Certification Program. Incarceration has become big business in today's economy, and inmate labor is a significant aspect of this business, which has come to be known as the prison industrial complex.

The History of Prison Labor

Regular use of inmate labor in U.S. prisons began in 1790 in the Walnut Street Jail of Philadelphia, which was designated as the first state prison in the United States. Prisoners were contracted out to private business for profitable production, and made nails, sawed marble, made shoes, carded wool, and chipped wood used to make dyes. Women prisoners made clothing. All inmates were paid a small amount per item.

By 1885, there were six systems of prison labor: the contract, piece price, lease, state-account, state-use, and public works and ways. With the contract system, private contractors supplied the machinery and raw material for the prison workers and supervised their work inside the prison under the surveillance of the state prison guards. The piece-price system of inmate labor was a variation of the contract system. Contractors provided raw materials and paid the state for each piece produced by its prisoners. The lease system was widely adopted in 1825 in the south as a substitute for African slavery in agricultural production. Under this system, inmate labor was sold to the highest bidder for a fixed period. The private entrepreneur assumed control of prisoners, including labor, food, clothing, shelter, and discipline. Under the state-account and state-use systems, the state assumed the role of entrepreneur by operating and managing the production and labor of the inmates as well as assuming all financial risks and gains. The state-account system sold products on the open market, while the state-use system sold products only to their own institutions or other state agencies. The public works and ways system of inmate labor used inmates in construction projects on roads, railways, public buildings, and prisons.

Industrial and Nonindustrial Work in the Prison Industry

Currently, 80 percent of federal and state prisoners work during their time in prison, within two general categories of work: nonindustrial, which includes institutional maintenance and agriculture; and industrial, which involves profitable production. The majority of federal, state, and local inmates work to maintain the operation of their institutions (nonindustrial work). They engage in janitorial duties, food preparation, medical service, laundry, library, office help, recreation, and barber or beauty shop services. Very few inmates work on prison farms, but those who do perform such tasks as gardening, farming, forestry, ranching, and other agricultural activities. Federal and state inmates work an average of six hours per day and receive $1.03 to $4.38 per day for their nonindustrial work.

Industrial work, which drives the prison industry, is the most controversial form of prison labor because inmates are employed for profitable production and services. There are three systems of prison industry: the federal and state government-operated prison industry, the Prison Industry Enhancement Certification Program (PIECP), and the prison industry operated by private prisons. The federal government and every state government own and operate prison industries. The inmate-made products in these industries can only be sold to governmental agencies, public organizations, tax-supported entities, or markets in other countries. The PIECP system of prison industry allows private corporations to enter into joint ventures with state prisoners for profitable production. Inmate-made products in the PIECP system are sold on the open market.

Federal Prison Industries, Inc. (FPI) is the largest government prison industry in the United States, and operates under the trade name UNICOR. Established by Congress in 1934, it is a government-owned corporation within the U.S. Department of Justice. FPI operated 103 factories in 2000 within the federal prison system and offered 150 diverse products and services. It generated $546 million in net sales and $17 million in profit, and employed 18 percent of federal inmates. The inmates work in textiles, furniture, electronics, metals, graphics, and services. In 1999, FPI paid seven percent of its budget to inmate wages. FPI workers work an average of 7.5 hours per day and receive daily wages that range from $1.73 to $8.63. Fifty percent of the inmates' wages are garnished for court fines, child support, and victim restitution. Post-garnished inmate wages are miniscule.

Every state prison operates its own prison industry. Inmate-made products in state government-operated prison industries include wood/furniture, metal, paper/printing, vehicle-related products and garment/textile products. In 1999, state prison industries employed seven percent of the state prison population and generated $3 billion in sales and $67 million in profits. Inmates worked seven hours per day and earned daily wages that ranged from $2.26 to $6.52. The gross wages paid to inmates totaled $80 million, and the net wages totaled $24 million. States garnished 70 percent of inmate wages for victim restitution, child support, and the cost of incarceration. The Texas Correction Industry (TCI), established in 1963, is the largest state prison industry. TCI factories produce signage, mattresses, shoes, garments, brooms, license plates, printed matter, detergents, furniture, textiles, and steel products. In 2000, it used 7,000 inmates, generated $83 million in sales, and made a $350,000 profit. TCI does not pay the inmate workers wages.

Models of Partnership

The PIECP operates under one of three models of partnership: the employer, customer, or manpower model of partnership. Most inmate workers in the PIECP system operate under the employer model, in which the state prison provides the space and qualified pool of inmates, while the private corporation employs, supervises, and trains inmate workers. Under the customer model of PIECP partnership, the company contracts with prisons or jails to provide finished products at an agreed-upon price. The prison owns and operates the business that employs, supervises, and trains inmates. The manpower model is similar to temporary labor agencies, where companies lease rather than employ prison workers. PIECP partnerships require participating businesses to pay workers the prevailing wage, provide benefits similar to government employees, meet the national Environmental Protection Act requirements, consult with local organized labor and businesses, and not replace free workers. Worker participation is voluntary, and inmate workers must contribute five to 20 percent of their gross wages toward victim restitution programs. The total deduction from inmates' wages cannot exceed 80 percent.

These PIECP restrictions do not apply to service jobs and private correctional facilities. In 2000, 80 percent of PIECP prison industry workers manufactured apparel, metal, electronic equipment, furniture, and wood products. Ten percent were employed to provide business and automobile services, and very few worked in agriculture and construction. PIECP workers work an average of seven hours per day and receive daily average wages that range from $27.04 to $43.23. In 1999, gross wages from inmate labor totaled $25 million, the net wage totaled $9 million, and 64 percent of inmate wages were garnished for taxes, room and board, and family support.

Private prisons use the majority of their inmates' labor for institutional maintenance. Six percent is used for prison industry and 12 percent is used for prison farm work. Inmates work longer hours and receive lower wages than inmates in the public prison industry. Inmates in private prisons work an average of eight hours per day and receive daily wages that range from $0.96 to $3.20. Private prisons pay inmates at a lower rate for institutional maintenance (nonindustrial work) than public prisons.

Prison Privatization and the Prison Industrial Complex

The practice of using prisoners to provide services and make products that are sold for profit is called *prison industry*. Over time, this practice has evolved into a sophisticated industrial system called the *prison industrial complex* (PIC), which is characterized as an alliance of government and business groups that comprehend incarceration as a profit opportunity. There are two major components of the PIC: prison privatization and prison industrialization.

Prison Privatization

Prison privatization is a trend that consists of private corporations that manage and sometimes build and own prisons. In the western United States, when areas were still territories, either the territory or the federal government constructed prisons. During the late 1970s and early 1980s, after a four-decade cease in private-sector use of prison labor, elected officials began to pass laws allowing privatization of prisons. Prison privatization takes place when a firm builds and owns their prison facility, and with a contract from a governmental agency, houses inmates on a per-diem or monthly fee basis; or a firm manages, operates, or purchases new or existing federal, state, or local facilities. The first modern-day, privately owned facility for adult felons was opened in Kentucky in 1986.

Prison privatization requires collaboration among business leaders, elected state officials, political party elites, and correctional experts. Corporations attract elected officials by promising to absorb soaring incarceration rates and save taxpayers money. In 2002, 28 states had statutory authority for private prisons. The Corrections Corporation of America (CCA) was the first correctional corporation, holding over 50 percent of the U.S. market in 2000, as well as international operations. CCA was founded in 1983 and is based in Nashville, Tennessee. The CCA's cofounder was the former chairman of the Tennessee State Republican Party. The former head of the American Correctional Association and commissioner of the corrections departments in Virginia and Arkansas provided technical expertise for the company, and several high-ranking state officials owned CCA stock. In 1989, CCA contracted 3,448 beds. By 2000, they had 15,000 employees and managed 75 facilities with 77,500 beds in 21 states. They owned 50 facilities in the United States, Puerto Rico, England, France, and Australia. CCA became a publicly traded company in 1986, with an annual growth rate of 70 percent from 1992 through 1997, ranking as one of the five top performers on the New York Stock Exchange.

The Prison Industrial Complex

The modern-day PIC developed from a series of events that began in the 1980s, when politicians used national campaigns to bolster and leverage public concern in order to garner public support for a conservative criminal justice agenda. This "get tough on crime" agenda was ultimately supported by Republicans and Democrats alike, and included such policies as abolishing parole, replacing judicial discretion in the courtroom with mandatory minimum sentencing, three-strike laws that mandated life sentences for a wide range of violent and nonviolent offenses, generating very long prison sentences for drug offenders, and building more prisons. Tactics to stir up public concern were successfully used to win public support of the agenda. This situation created a swell in the prison population, overcrowded prisons, and increased spending on state prisons. In just four years, the total spending on state prisons increased by 74 percent between 1980 and 1984, from $4.5 billion to $7.7 billion, and in 1996, $29 billion was spent in corrections by state government.

What also occurred during the evolution of the current PIC was an arrangement between the federal government and states that rewarded states for passing legislation requiring inmates to serve at least 85 percent of their sentence, with grant dollars for prison construction. In Illinois in 2004, this program was referred to as the Violent Offender Incarceration and Truth-in-Sentencing (VOI-TIS) grant program. It was described as providing funding to states to build or expand correctional and juvenile detention facilities. To receive funding, states were required to comply with specific conditions, which included implementing laws mandating 85 percent completion of imposed sentences for prisoners who were convicted of the most violent offenses.

By 2008, the language describing the VOI-TIS program in Illinois was expanded to include not only the building and expansion of correctional and juvenile detention facilities, but also to support community-based correctional options such as halfway houses, day reporting centers, community-based substance abuse centers, and aftercare services. The conditions to qualify for these grant dollars remained the same in 2008, which was to implement laws requiring those convicted of violent offenses to serve 85 percent of their sentences. VOI-TIS grants allow 15 percent of the money to be used for local jails and juvenile detention centers. In federal fiscal year 2008, $16.4 million in VOI-TIS funding was distributed to 30 programs in Illinois.

There are several groups that comprise the alliance that makes up the PIC. These groups include those who sell their services to state corrections departments such as for-profit prison and prison healthcare corporations, prison transport services, and the construction industry. Additional groups that comprise PIC include lobbyists for privatization of criminal justice and prison construction, Wall Street firms that underwrite prison construction bonds, prison guard unions, and companies and government agencies that hire prison labor. As major players in the PIC, states have a stake in the generation of jobs that come from imprisonment, as well as low-cost labor.

Opposition to Prison Labor

One unintended and historical effect of the use of prison labor has been opposition from unionized laborers, who view prison labor as competition for jobs. Organized labor and manufacturers' associations view prison labor as unfair competition and have been protesting against it since its inception. During the 1880s, The National Labor Union denounced inmate labor at its first conventions; and the Federation of Organized Trades and Labor Unions petitioned state legislatures, lobbied state and federal politicians, and condemned manufacturers and purchasers of inmate-made products at rallies.

The combination of the economic slump from the Great Depression, as well as strong political protest from organized labor, small businesses, and humanist organizations influenced Congress to pass a series of laws that restricted prison labor. As a result, the 1940 Sumners-Ashurst Act was passed that outlawed private-sector use of prison labor and interstate sales of prison-made products. During the next four decades, only the state-use system was in operation. In 1979, Congress created the Prison Industry Enhancement Certification Program (PIECP), which once again allowed certified businesses to employ inmates and sell prisoner-made goods in interstate commerce.

Across the nation, organized labor groups and businesses are actively opposing the use of prison labor. Their complaints range from accusations of prison laborers stealing union jobs to accusations that inmates are being used for skilled tasks. For example, a state employees' union filed a lawsuit against the Minnesota governor, who allegedly planned to use prisoners to clean up highways. The complainants believed that the use of prison labor in this way would supplant union workers. The lawsuit charged that the state must demonstrate that state workers could not do the work before turning to prison labor to handle it. In response, the governor's office distributed a state statute written in 1935 that says the Corrections Department can put inmates to work on land over which the state has jurisdiction. Prior to this lawsuit, the union sued when the state wanted to outsource printing and signage jobs. That lawsuit was settled out of court.

In another example, the Missouri Department of Corrections states that it will not use inmates in a way that adversely affects any statewide economic growth or industry, nor result in the displacement of civilian workers. The inmates are also prevented from working in skilled employment positions or performing work that requires certification or licensing. However, in summer 2002, inmates worked on the construction of baseball fields where they allegedly helped install plumbing, which is a licensed practice.

Business groups and labor unions challenged the Washington State Department of Corrections' prison industries program in court. A lawsuit, filed in 1999 by seven companies in the Washington Water Jet Workers Association, accused the prison industry program of causing free-population laborers to be laid off so that convicts could work. The private company paying inmates to do work inside the state prison was able to underbid companies that hired conventional workers by about one-third because they did not have to provide healthcare and other benefits to the inmate workers, and because prison officials supplied them with 11,000 square feet of workspace, which included utilities at no cost. The Washington State Supreme Court ruled in 2004 that private companies could not set up shop in state prisons or hire inmates to do work that competed with the private sector. This ruling struck down part of the laws enacted in the late 1970s early 1980s that lifted the four-decade ban on private-sector use of prison labor. The justices concluded that private use of prison labor conflicted with a provision of Washington State's constitution on the use of prison labor.

Impact of Fiscal Crisis on the Prison Industry

Prison labor is a vital component of the PIC, and private sector companies such as Dell, Victoria's Secret, and Starbucks have used inmate labor. However, as states across the nation experienced a deepening economic and budget crisis, brought on by the global recession of 2008, it became a catalyst for the increase in the use of prison labor. Prison labor has legitimated and sustained mass incarceration by allowing states to save money in costly yet essential areas such as sanitation and laundry services. For example, the South Carolina Department of Corrections, in an attempt to offset a $28 million deficit, raised rates for the use of prison labor from $4 to $6 per day to $10. The prisoner work crews are contracted to 49 city, county, and state agencies to perform tasks that would have been completed by minimum-wage workers. According to one state's correctional department, inmate labor saved state, city, and county agencies $3.5 million.

Small rural communities have come to depend on prison labor to provide basic services, and some state legislators have encouraged corrections departments to make better use of prison labor. Mike Fair, South Carolina state senator and chairman of the Corrections and Penology Committee, stated that "in effect, we have a Third World [nation] in there ... and we probably should take advantage of that."

Future Directions of Prison Labor and the Prison Industry

Some theorists have recognized prison labor and the prison industry as part of a transformation of the penal system. This transformation occurs in prison discourse, techniques, and management objectives. The discourse concerning the penal system and its prisoners is changing from a management of surplus populations to the commodification of these surplus populations. In other words, prisoners are becoming commodities. Penal objectives are changing from the containment of unruly groups to a focus on weighing the costs and social benefits of using prisoners as a labor pool. The techniques used for selective incapacitation, which is an accusation leveled against the criminal justice system as evidenced by the disproportion of African American, urban, and poor young men in the system, is being transformed into efforts to integrate prisoner-workers into the global labor market. Management concepts are changing from "iron hand" or tough-on-crime policies to an emphasis on wage incentives. However, this transformation of prisoners into wage earners does not equate to a new acceptance of the prisoner; instead, it reinforces their persistent exclusion from genuine citizenship.

Pro: Arguments in Support of Prison Labor

Proponents of prison labor characterize jobs that are particularly suited to prison industry to typically be labor-intensive, low-pay, and low-skilled. In their opinion, these are the kinds of jobs that have been relocated to foreign countries. Based on this viewpoint, prison labor poses more of a threat to labor forces in foreign countries than it does to the domestic labor force.

Proponents also contend that even though a large percentage of prisoners' wages are garnished, many workers still have enough remaining to purchase amenities that the state does not provide, or accumulate savings to access once they are released.

Proponents of prison industries argue that work programs provide inmates with marketable skills and training, and subsequently reduce recidivism rates. For example, a study conducted by the National Institute of Justice compared a group of post-release inmates who worked in PIECP systems with inmates from traditional industries and "other-than-work" activities. They found that those participating in PIECP found jobs more quickly and held them longer than their counterparts. They also found that PIECP releasees had lower rates of rearrest, conviction, and incarceration than offenders who were in the other groups. On the other hand, studies have shown that even though participants of work programs return to crime at a lower rate than nonparticipants, this lower recidivism rate may result from background differences. It was discovered in some research that inmates who participated in work programs had legitimate jobs before entering prison.

Those in favor of prison labor suggest that its most important benefit is a reduction in prisoner idleness, which is considered by legislators and prison officials to be associated with prisoner-against-prisoner violence and other behavioral problems. Also, prison labor provides incentive to inmates to practice good behavior, which is required for them to have access to opportunities to earn wages; it also builds a track record of employment.

Proponents of prison labor not only suggest that recidivism can be decreased because of prison labor and that studies report this decrease, but also contribute this reduction specifically to job skills and training that inmates receive as prisoners. They believe that the job skills learned in the prison industry can be transferred to the free community. Additionally, prison labor generates tax savings to the public in that inmates pay taxes on the income they earn and money is deducted from inmates' salaries, often covering room and board, which results in less cost to run prisons.

Con: Arguments Against Prison Labor

Organized labor groups and opponents to private and public prison industries believe that there is an adverse impact of prison labor on free workers' job security, wages, and working conditions. Economists calculate that even if all inmates worked, prison labor would add only 0.2 to 0.4 percent of the total U.S. Gross Domestic Product. They maintain that the current prison workforce is relatively small compared to the civilian labor force.

Some economists warn that a significant increase in prison labor may displace the lowest unskilled strata of the work force and depress their wages. This displacement can turn workers in this stratum toward illegitimate means for economic survival, which will make the social costs of displacement greater than the initial economic benefits.

Another problem associated with prison labor is the potential for deprivation of prisoners' work rights, benefits, and working conditions. Many inmate workers are deprived of rights to collective bargaining, minimum wage, unemployment compensation, worker's compensation, and workplace safety, except those employed in PIECP arrangements. Most prison industries offer only low-skilled and labor-intensive jobs, which are unlikely to provide inmates with marketable skills, training, or experience suitable for post-release work.

Scholars have also suggested that the use of prison labor is influenced by race; that PIC is a system that has removed unwanted competition from the free-population labor market and has facilitated the extraction of the surplus value of inmates by state prison and corporations. They contend that changes in drug laws during the 1980s "get tough" policy trends activated a judicial mechanism that justified the incarceration of a significant portion of what is now the inmate population. This judicial mechanism, in the form of policy and passed laws, amounted to the removal and relocation of men, disproportionately African American, from the free-population labor pool to a captive labor pool that is highly exploitable.

One study has shown racial disparity in prison job assignments with whites being more likely to get assigned to skilled jobs earning higher hourly wages than blacks. As a result, blacks were more likely to engage in illegitimate economic activities, such as drug selling, prostitution, and theft in prison to supplement their income. This increased their misconduct reports, loss of good time and privileges, and increased their remaining time in prison.

See Also: 7. Furlough and Work-Release Programs; 8. Gangs and Violence in Prison; 16. Prison Privatization and Contract Facilities; 17. Punishment Versus Rehabilitation.

Further Readings

Blumberg, Joe. "Inmate Labor Creates Headaches for City." *St. Joseph News-Press* (November 2006).

Chang, Tracy F. H., and Douglas E. Thompkins. "Corporations Go to Prisons: The Expansion of Corporate Power in the Correctional Industry." *Labor Studies Journal,* v.27/1 (2002).

Falk, Julie. "Fiscal Lockdown." *Dollars and Sense,* v.248 (July/August 2003).

Illinois Criminal Justice Information Authority. *2004 Annual Report.* Chicago: Illinois Criminal Justice Information Authority, 2004.

Johnston, Norman. "Evolving Function: Early Use of Imprisonment as Punishment." *The Prison Journal*, v.89/1 (March 2009).

Misrahi, James J. "Factories With Fences: An Analysis of the Prison Industry Enhancement Certification Program in Historical Perspective." *American Criminal Law Review*, v.33/2 (Winter 1996).

Moses, Marilyn C., and Cindy J. Smith. "Factories Behind Fences: Do Prison 'Real Work' Programs Work?" *National Institute of Justice Journal*, v.257 (2007).

Smith, Earl, and Angela J. Hattery. "Incarceration: A Tool for Racial Segregation and Labor Exploitation." *Race, Gender and Class*, v.15 (2008).

Stassen-Berger, Rachel E. "State Workers' Union Sues Over Prisoner's Road Cleanup." *Saint Paul Pioneer Press* (April 2005).

Turner, Joseph. "Washington State Supreme Court Restricts Inmate Labor." *The News Tribune* (May 2004).

Weiss, Robert P. "Repatriating Low-Wage Work: The Political Economy of Prison Labor Reprivatization in the Postindustrial United States." *Criminology*, v.39/2 (2001).

15

Prison Overcrowding

Alan Harland
Temple University

A s extensively noted in popular, professional, and academic sources, there is widespread concern that the United States has been experiencing severe prison overcrowding for some time. However, there are significant differences of opinion as to what actually constitutes overcrowding, what role it plays in causing or exacerbating prison management and inmate-related problems, or what steps should be taken to deal with it.

Prisons Versus Jails

Discussions of overcrowding frequently merge concerns about state and federal prisons together with municipal and county jails, which in states such as Pennsylvania, are confusingly referred to as county prisons. With the exception of Alaska, Hawaii, and a small number of northeastern states that operate integrated jail/prison systems, state and federal prisons or penitentiaries house exclusively sentenced felons, usually committed for a minimum of one year. Jails typically hold varying proportions of felons and misdemeanants sentenced to less than one year. However, they also house pretrial detainees who have not yet been convicted but are held pending prosecution and disposition of their cases, usually because they have not been able to secure pretrial release by posting bail. Because the extent of crowding, along with the reasons, consequences, and potential remedies can vary considerably depending upon whether the focus is on prisons versus jails, it is important to separate the two. In this discussion, focus will be primarily on the issue as it involves state and federal prisons.

Overcrowding Versus Overimprisonment

Much of the literature on prison crowding focuses on the overall size and growth of inmate populations and correctional facilities as indicators that the United States builds prisons and incarcerates at far higher rates than most other countries. Data on prisons and prison populations to support such conclusions are usually drawn from two general sources. The most complete picture is found in the annual reports and on the Websites of the Federal Bureau of Prisons and many individual state departments of corrections. On a national level, data are provided by the U.S. Department of Justice, Bureau of Justice Statistics (BJS), from two of its many criminal justice system survey programs. First, through its national prisoner statistics program, BJS produces annual and semiannual data on prisoners in state and federal prison facilities. Second, BJS conducts a census of state and federal correctional facilities approximately every five years, which collects more detailed information such as facility type, size, security level, capacity, court orders, and use of private contractors.

The most recent complete BJS census, in 2005, identified 1,821 correctional facilities operating primarily at state and federal levels. More facilities operated at the state (1,719) rather than federal (102) level, and 415, or almost 23 percent, were privately operated under contract to federal or state authorities. Institutions most typically counted as prisons or penitentiaries, including prison camps and farms, are classified as confinement facilities, and accounted for 1,292 (71 percent) of the total. The remaining 529 (29 percent) were community-based facilities such as halfway houses, residential treatment centers, restitution centers, and pre-release centers. As of the 2008 National Prisoner Statistics (NPS) annual survey, BJS reported that the number of prisoners under the jurisdiction of federal and state correctional authorities reached an all-time, year-end high of 1,610,446. Excluding prisoners housed in local jails and places such as privately contracted and community corrections facilities, 162,252 inmates were in custody in federal prisons, and 1,320,145 in state prisons.

A recent Pew Center report estimates that the number of state inmates alone increased over the last four decades by more than 700 percent, rising from 174,379 in 1972 to over 1.4 million by the end of 2009. If inmates of federal prisons are included, the latter figure climbs over the 1.6 million mark, and this does not include the more than 100,000 persons estimated to be held in prisons in the U.S. territories, U.S. Immigration and Customs Enforcement facilities, and in separate residential facilities for juvenile offenders. Such growth has been accompanied by a sizeable investment nationwide in building new prisons and adding beds to existing institutions. The California Department of Corrections, for example, added 21 new prisons from June 1980 to September 1997, and added beds to several of the 12 existing prisons. Most of the new prisons house in excess of 4,000 inmates each. A 2004 study by the Urban Institute reports that the number of state prisons increased from 592 in 1974 to 1,023 in 2000—a 73 percent increase. Between 1979 and 2000, in 10 states in which the greatest increases were recorded, the number of additional new prisons ranged from 19 in Missouri to 120 in Texas, which translates into an average of over five new prisons every year over the entire 21-year period.

As noteworthy as the foregoing boom in prisoners and prisons may be in its own right, and although it prompts heated debate over whether the United States is imprisoning too many offenders or imprisoning them for too long, it says nothing directly about whether or not prisons are overcrowded. In other words, overuse of imprisonment and overcrowded prisons are related but distinguishable problems. Because judgments of what constitutes overcrowding and how to respond to it can depend upon a variety of normative values and empirical standards, applied by researchers, administrators and, ultimately, legislative and judicial decision makers in different federal and state jurisdictions, is a very unsettled and contentious topic.

Measuring Overcrowding

Most discussions of overcrowding define it in relation to the number of prisoners compared to the accommodation capacity of the institution. Even this seemingly obvious ratio calculation, however, leads to still further confusion and disagreement over the correct yardstick to use for making capacity determinations.

Typically, capacity is defined as a function of prison population density based upon either design capacity, rated capacity, or operational capacity. For the purposes of the BJS census, for example, design capacity is the number of inmates that planners or architects intended for the facility; rated capacity is the number of beds or inmates assigned by a rating official to institutions within the jurisdiction; and operational capacity is the number of inmates who can be accommodated, based on a facility's staff, existing programs, and services. Although prisons are most commonly considered to be overcrowded when the population exceeds 100 percent of capacity, laws and policies often apply a lower figure, such as 90 percent, in order to allow for sudden spikes in the number of new admissions, or unforeseen reductions in available space, as may occur, for example, if cells or whole sections of a facility need to be temporarily taken offline for renovations or repairs.

Applying even the most generous capacity figures provided by state and federal authorities, the resulting picture is one of numerous jurisdictions operating in excess of their self-defined upper limits. The most recent data from the 2008 NPS survey for the 49 states and the District of Columbia reporting capacity data (Connecticut state law prohibits doing so) show that Texas and California topped the charts at over 160,000 each, both outstripping the total capacity of 122,479 for all federal prisons combined. At the opposite end of the spectrum, capacity figures for North Dakota, Vermont, and Montana were 1,044, 1,470, and 1,739, respectively. Converting population and capacity figures at the end of 2008 into an overcrowding index—inmate total as a percent of highest capacity reported by each jurisdiction—reveals that federal facilities were operating at 135 percent of capacity; 18 states were operating at or above 100 percent capacity; 18 were operating between 90–100 percent capacity; and 13 reported occupancy levels below 90 percent of capacity. State overcrowding index figures ranged from highs of 140 percent and 133 percent in Massachusetts and Illinois, to lows of 64 and 48 percent in Iowa and New Mexico, respectively.

For a more nuanced sense of the capacity picture, and to emphasize how the choice of metric can determine crowding determinations, it is helpful to examine the situation in individual states. In California, for example, measured against the highest operational-capacity standard, the state's prisons in the 2008 NPS report were at 106 percent of their limit. If the more conservative design-capacity yardstick is used, however, the overcrowding index almost doubles to 204 percent. Adding further to the ambiguity of overcrowding estimates is the fact that, regardless of the measure of capacity used, different conclusions can be reached depending upon the unit of analysis. For example, although particular prison systems or institutions might not be overcrowded in terms of absolute numbers, they may experience severe space problems with respect to subpopulations such as female inmates or prisoners with special mental health, medical, disciplinary, or vulnerability issues requiring segregation or separate housing arrangements.

Likewise, systemwide estimates often mask much more severe problems within specific institutions. In Alabama, for example, state prison facilities were operating at 98 percent of operational capacity at the end of 2008, and that figure increases to 188 percent if the more conservative design capacity measure is used. More critically, a handful of facilities operated at well over 200 percent capacity, including one maximum-security prison that was reported to be at 322 percent of design capacity in the Department of Corrections 2008 annual report. Used as the reception and classification center for all incoming male inmates in Alabama, the prison in question was built in 1969 with an intended population of 440 inmates, but has been reconfigured over time to accommodate 1,459 beds.

Consequences of Overcrowding: What's the Problem?

Recognizing that the number of prison inmates in many jurisdictions exceeds even the highest capacity ratings under which facilities are supposed to operate does not explain what specifically makes crowding a problem. From a number of perspectives, crowding is viewed as acceptable and, within limits, even beneficial. From a purely fiscal perspective, for example, squeezing more inmates into a facility adds relatively little to the fixed operating costs if it is achieved without major expenditures for physical restructuring or increases in staffing and service resources. As such, covering larger populations without significant budget increases takes on positive connotations as a way of reducing the average cost per prisoner. Similarly, for "get tough" politicians and like-minded, law-and-order advocates, overcrowding concerns are frequently offset by arguments that prison is supposed to be unpleasant, and that we should worry less about coddling criminals in prisons and be more interested in making sure offenders are kept off the streets and victims get the satisfaction they deserve.

Inmate-rights groups, correctional personnel, and other critics offer a different perspective, pointing to a wide variety of problems associated with operating overcrowded prisons. Such problems arise when the inmate population outstrips the prison's ability to assure adequate health, safety, and management standards. For example, to accommodate more prisoners in crowded facilities, beds or even just mattresses are often set up in spaces originally designed as gymnasiums, dayrooms, and storage, and temporary program trailers are converted into dormitories. Sometimes referred to as nonconventional housing areas, such options for expanding bed space are met with approval by some as inventive ways of dealing with large inmate populations. They are condemned by others as creating substandard and unsafe living conditions; reducing direct supervision and inmate monitoring capabilities; and taking away space originally designed for educational, work, treatment, and other program activities designed to reduce recidivism and/or institutional tensions. The practice is common in jurisdictions across the country. In California, for example, according to their Department of Corrections 2009 annual report, 8,900 nontraditional or "bad beds" were in use as of August 2009, down from a high of 19,618 in August 2007.

Specific Problems From Overcrowding

The catalog of specific problems attributed by critics to overcrowding is extensive, ranging from overburdening such basic resources as toilets, showers, and food services, to making it difficult or impossible to provide critical mental health or medical care, or adequate protection from physical and sexual violence. For example, when supervision and programming capabilities that are stretched too thin due to overcrowding result in control practices such as extended periods of lockdown and inactivity, the potential increases for frustration-related conflicts between inmates and staff. If such conflicts occur, overcrowding can also reduce the ability of correctional officials to separate offenders or otherwise deal with the problem—a particular challenge in institutions in which inmate populations include sizeable numbers of rival violent gang members. Similar problems may arise if inmate numbers surpass the ability of intake, evaluation, and classification procedures to flag prisoners likely to present special health and safety risks and treatment needs, or the ability to provide adequate treatment programs to those who are identified. Prison populations notoriously include, for example, large numbers of offenders who suffer from severe substance abuse as well as cognitive, emotional, or psychological problems. To the extent that overcrowding plays a role in the failure to identify them and/or match them with appropriate housing, supervision, counseling, and treatment arrangements due to overtaxed diagnostic and program resources, problems can ensue both for management of disruptive institutional conduct and for efforts to reduce recidivism after prisoners are released.

In short, overcrowding has been widely assailed as causing or exacerbating adverse prison conditions, resulting in a range of grave consequences such as assaults, suicides, killings, rapes, the spread of communicable diseases, deaths due to failure to provide timely medical treatment, and prison disturbances—including, in the extreme, hostage taking and riots.

Responding to Overcrowding

Pressure on both federal and state governments to do something about prison overcrowding takes two different forms. First, the need to take action to address crowding as a political and public policy issue is urged by lobbyists ranging from prisoners' and human rights groups to corrections department heads and employee organizations. Second, and more forcefully, in response to extensive litigation by inmates, federal and state courts have ordered the alleviation of overcrowding as a legal/constitutional issue, to remedy prison conditions found to violate, for example, constitutional standards of cruel and unusual punishment and/or due process. Whether responding to demands to address overcrowding as a policy problem or a legal problem, legislators and correctional officials have essentially two options—reduce the size of inmate populations, and/or increase prison capacity. Each response reflects a different view of the issue, with the former seeing it as a problem of too many prisoners, and the latter as one of too little capacity.

The federal government and many state officials in recent years have struggled with massive budget deficits and pressure to cut public expenditures in areas such as education, healthcare, and a variety of social services. Therefore, the high cost of incarceration and prison construction has been seized upon by proponents of the "too many prisoners" point of view as a powerful incentive to question the wisdom and feasibility of continuing to expand capacity, arguing that we simply cannot afford to "build our way out of overcrowding." At the same time, one of the most contentious questions in the debate over what to do about overcrowding remains whether prison populations can be reduced significantly without posing an undue risk of jeopardizing public safety or failing to punish offenders as severely as they deserve. Because of its prominent position in overcrowding discussions, it is important to review the pros and cons of the population-reduction strategy as a preferred method of tackling the problem.

Pro: Arguments for Population Reduction Strategies

Proponents of the "too many prisoners" position contend that overcrowding can best be addressed by reducing the number of offenders admitted to prison and the amount of time they are incarcerated. These arguments, that reductions can be achieved without sacrificing central criminal justice goals such as public safety or retribution, hinge on a number of overlapping factors. First, many of the inmates in federal and state prisons are serving sentences for nonviolent offenses for which shorter terms of incarceration or community-based sanctions might be substituted. According to most recent U.S. Justice Department statistics, for example, approximately 50 percent of sentenced prisoners in state prisons are incarcerated for either property or drug offenses or other crimes not categorized as crimes of violence. About a third of all prison admissions fall into the drug crime category. Second, fears about releasing dangerous offenders to the community are mitigated by evidence that the volume and seriousness of recidivism among released prisoners is much less than it may at first appear. While as many as two-thirds of prisoners admitted to state prison are incarcerated for failing to comply with their terms of probation or parole, about half of probation or parole violators are not committed on new offense convictions. Rather, they are imprisoned for technical violations such as failing a drug test, nonpayment of financial sanctions, failure to appear for scheduled treatment or supervision appointments, or for new misdemeanor or felony arrests that frequently involve less serious drug and property offenses not normally resulting in incarceration.

Proponents of reducing overcrowding by reducing prison admissions and length of stay further point to very mixed findings of research on the effect on crime rates as a result of the massive increases in incarceration over the last several decades. Although some researchers have reached opposite conclusions, an equal or greater number have failed to find any consistent relationship between rates of crime and imprisonment. Moreover, even under estimates most favorable to the "more prisons–less crime" point of view, studies suggest that external forces other than incarceration play a significant and difficult-to-separate role in the rise and fall of crime rates. Such factors include changes in the economy, percent of the population in younger "criminogenic" age groups, and improved policing prevention strategies.

Arguing along similar lines, comparison with other nations such as Canada, Britain, France, and Sweden shows that U.S. offenders receive sentences that are many times as long as prisoners in most other Western countries, but their rates of violent crime are lower. In California, the passage of three-strikes legislation has resulted in offenders receiving very long sentences, up to life imprisonment in some cases, for nothing more than multiple petty offenses. Several studies have been conducted to evaluate the impact of such laws and, while finding that they have been a major contributor to growth in state prison populations, almost all conclude that the impact on crime reduction has been marginal at best. Among multiple possible explanations for this are that most offenders "age out of crime" as they get older, so that extended imprisonment beyond their highest crime-prone years has less and less crime reduction payoff. Similarly, long-term incarceration of one offender, especially for crimes such as selling drugs, may simply create an opening for another to step into the role, thus increasing rather than reducing the total size of the offender pool.

Community Programs Versus Prison Programs

A related line of argument in support of population reduction strategies points to a growing body of research on the effectiveness of programs to reduce recidivism. Community-based alternatives are at least as likely to be successful as their prison-based counterparts, especially where the latter operate under resource and inmate-access constraints due to overcrowding. Prison programs such as Scared Straight and rigorously punishment-oriented Boot Camps have been widely touted, but evaluation studies have shown little or no evidence that they reduce recidivism, and that they may even increase it. Consequently, population reduction advocates reason that decreases are achievable in rates of both imprisonment and recidivism if funds necessary to increase capacity are invested instead in supporting and improving generally less costly sentencing and reentry options. Frequently mentioned candidates include a variety of treatment and supervision programs such as drug courts, home detention, day reporting centers, and community-based residential facilities. Claims that such options can serve as cost-effective and safe alternatives to incarceration are further bolstered by advances in technological mechanisms that enhance supervision capability, such as global positioning systems and other electronic devices to monitor offenders' whereabouts or to instantly detect drug or alcohol use. Comparable advances in empirically developed and validated risk/needs assessment tools are likewise invoked as evidence of the improved ability of criminal justice decision makers to differentiate offenders who pose high, medium, or low risk of reoffending, and to match them with programs and case-management plans most likely to maximize chances of success.

Finally, advocates for tackling overcrowding by reducing prison admissions and length of stay point to support for their position and acceptance of their arguments by a number of critical audiences. Perhaps most dramatically, in 2009, a federal court in California ordered the state to cut its prison population within two years by over 40,000 inmates, or an approximately 30 percent reduction. The court's decision was based on its identification of overcrowding as the primary cause of longstanding failure to remedy constitutional violations in the provision of medical and mental healthcare. Pointing to evidence of avoidable inmate deaths, spread of contagious disease, and unmanageable facilities, the court drew an inextricable link between overcrowding and what it called "criminogenic conditions" in the prisons. Based on testimony and evidence from an array of correctional experts, the court ruled that continuation of overcrowding jeopardizes public safety by exacerbating recidivism rates by former prisoners. The court further concluded that through the adoption of enhanced reentry programs and other safeguards, the state should readily be able to comply with the order to reduce the number of prisoners while realizing a simultaneous increase in public safety over current practices.

A different source of support for a decarceration approach to overcrowding emerges from recent public opinion research studies, which show that when respondents are given details about the facts of particular offenses and the criminals involved, there is substantial support for alternative sanctions, especially in cases of nonviolent offenders. Likewise, legislators and correctional authorities in a number of states have already adopted recent policy and legal reforms, resulting in sizeable reductions in prison populations. Michigan, for example, has experienced a drop of over 6,000 prisoners in less than three years since the population peaked at a historic high of 51,554 in 2007, following changes such as releasing more inmates upon completion of their minimum sentence, fewer parole revocations, and enhancements to reentry planning and supervision. Texas, Mississippi, and a growing number of other states have also achieved significant population reductions or reversed projected increases through a combination of similar reforms such as rolling back mandatory sentencing laws, expanding residential and community-based treatment programs, increased good-time incentives, and other earlier parole release strategies.

Con: Arguments Against Population Reduction Strategies

Opposition to attempts to address overcrowding primarily via a strategy of making cuts in prison admissions and length of stay stems from several basic objections. One common response from conservative critics, for example, even in extreme circumstances such as the California case, has been to reject the very legitimacy of overcrowding complaints as being the product of unrealistic assumptions about appropriate capacity limits and prison conditions by inmate litigants, prison reform advocates, correctional unions, and especially by "activist" courts. Population reduction strategies further meet with resistance on grounds that they cannot be pursued in most cases without allowing offenders to get off with a less severe sanction than critics feel is warranted by retributive notions of punishment. Protests of this type resonate especially among law and order and victims' advocacy groups, and are difficult to counter because they stem from unfalsifiable but strongly held moral or personal beliefs about the amount and type of punishment that offenders deserve to receive.

The most common and intractable opposition to placing emphasis on population reduction as the primary strategy for reducing overcrowding is predicated upon fear about potential public safety risks posed by alternative sentencing and early-release options. Critics who view crowding as mainly a problem of too little space rather than too many prisoners defend their convictions about the necessity of imprisonment by reference to what they view as the inconclusive and frequently inconsistent findings that characterize so much of the empirical research on the issue. From this perspective, in the face of widely acknowledged uncertainty and disagreement over the relative crime-reduction effects of prison versus community-based sanctions, the argument is that doubts should be resolved in favor of responding to overcrowding via prison and capacity expansion rather than more risky alternatives.

Finally, arguments against population reduction and for prison expansion approaches to controlling overcrowding are also made on purely financial cost-benefit terms. For example, if a broad policy of addressing overcrowding by releasing more offenders ultimately leads to higher rates of reoffending, any lower initial expense of alternative sanctions may be more than offset by victim costs and longer-term expenditures on subsequent rearrest, prosecution, and punishment. In addition, although clearly less tenable as an independent justification for preferring increasing capacity over population reduction strategies to reduce crowding, arguments in support of prison expansion often include reference to some of its more direct economic benefits. These range from job creation and other potential gains to the economies of rural communities where so many facilities are located, to the financial benefits to powerful political forces such as correctional unions and private corporations that play such a lucrative role in prison architecture, construction, and provision of necessary products and services essential to their operation.

The Road Ahead

Reconciling competing views on how to define and respond to prison overcrowding is one of the major issues in the field of corrections today. Much of the debate in the past transpired in the context of overcrowding litigation in state and federal courts. In the 1970s and 1980s, prisons in a majority of jurisdictions throughout the country were at one point or another operating under court orders or consent decrees related to inmate complaints of overcrowding and unconstitutionally deficient prison conditions. In the face of literally thousands of individual and class-action lawsuits by inmates and complaints from states about what they considered unwarranted federal intervention, however, Congress responded in 1995 by passing the Prison Litigation Reform Act. This imposed substantive and procedural limitations on the ability of inmates to raise legal challenges to the conditions of their confinement and on the power of federal courts to mandate prison reform. As a result, the number of facilities under court order to limit population size or otherwise remedy specific prison problems has declined substantially in recent years. Except in situations involving particularly egregious constitutional violations, therefore, efforts to make further progress are currently being pursued much more visibly in legislative and policy reform settings.

Judgments and decisions about the appropriateness of population levels and specific conditions of confinement vary from one jurisdiction to another, depending, for example, on the extent to which local policymakers consider inmate suffering a correctional philosophy or problem, and their relative emphasis on the retributive, deterrent, incapacitative, and rehabilitative goals of imprisonment. Ultimately, such judgments and decisions can only be made responsibly through a clear specification of the full range of goals and values that prisons are intended to pursue, and by rigorous theoretical and empirical assessment of the extent to which actual practices reasonably reflect those aims. Otherwise, regardless of which side prevails in debates over overcrowding, and even if gains are made by both camps, the danger remains that such successes may be achieved at the price of diverting attention and resources away from addressing underlying prison problems related to inferior or indifferent administration, sub-standard health and safety conditions, and inadequate or ineffective services and inmate programs.

❖

See Also: 4. Due-Process Rights of Prisoners; 5. Early Release; 7. Furlough and Work-Release Programs; 8. Gangs and Violence in Prison; 16. Prison Privatization and Contract Facilities.

Further Readings

Austin, James, et al. *Unlocking America: Why and How to Reduce America's Prison Population.* Washington, DC: JFA Institute, November 2007.

Bleich, Jeff. "The Politics of Prison Crowding." *California Law Review,* v.77 (October 1989).

California Department of Corrections and Rehabilitation. "Corrections: Moving Forward, 2009." http://www.cdcr.ca.gov/news/2009_Press _Releases/Oct_01.html (Accesed October 2010).

Haney, Craig. *Reforming Punishment: Psychological Limits to the Pains of Imprisonment.* Washington, DC: American Psychological Association, 2006.

Lawrence, Sarah, and Jeremy Travis. *The New Landscape of Imprisonment: Mapping America's Prison Expansion.* Washington, DC: Urban Institute, April 2004.

Pew Center on the States. *One in 31: The Long Reach of American Corrections.* Washington, DC: Pew Charitable Trusts, March 2009.

Pew Center on the States. *Prison Count 2010: State Population Declines for the First Time in 38 Years.* Washington, DC: Pew Charitable Trusts, March 2010.

Sabol, William, Heather West, and Matthew Cooper. *Prisoners in 2008.* Washington, DC: U.S. Department of Justice, Office of Justice Programs, Bureau of Justice Statistics, December 2009.

Stephan, James. *National Prisoner Statistics Program: Census of State and Federal Correctional Facilities.* Washington, DC: U.S. Department of Justice, Office of Justice Programs, Bureau of Justice Statistics, October 2008.

16

Prison Privatization and Contract Facilities

Antje Deckert
University of Auckland

William R. Wood
University of Auckland

In 1984, the newly formed Corrections Corporation of America (CCA) opened the first adult detention facility to be fully managed and run by a private corporation in the United States in over a century. This facility, the Houston Processing Center, was opened under a contract with the U.S. Immigration and Naturalization Services (INS) for the purpose of detaining immigrants facing deportation and administrative hearings. That same year, CCA took over management of the Tall Trees Juvenile Facility in Tennessee, followed in 1985 with the Silverdale Detention Facility in Hamilton County, Tennessee. Since the end of the 1980s, the number of correctional and detainment facilities operated by for-profit corporations in the United States has grown from about 70 to over 400, according to the most recent census by the Department of Justice (DOJ) in 2005.

This growth in private prisons parallels the growth of prison populations, with the number of people in prisons, jails, and other correctional facilities increasing from around 500,000 in 1980 to approximately 2.3 million in

2009. The growth of prison populations has been accompanied by a political and public embrace of the economic fruits of corrections. Communities throughout the United States that once rallied against the building of prisons in their backyards now routinely lobby for prisons to be built in their neighborhoods. Today, not only are correctional expenditures consistently justified as a necessary cost of crime reduction, but they are also touted as a net economic asset and vital employment sector throughout many regions in the United States.

The growth of private prisons within the last three decades thus represents only a part of the emergence of what critics routinely refer to as the prison industrial complex, a term used to denote not only the growth of private prisons, but also the increasing synergy of governmental, political, and corporate interests that have profited from the locking up of millions of Americans. While critics see private prisons as perhaps the most nefarious embodiment of a corrections-for-profit logic, supporters of private prisons argue that the administration of such facilities by private companies actually saves taxpayers money; works to a degree that is at least as effective, if not more so, than public prisons in terms of providing services and programs to inmates; and allows for more flexibility than public facilities in the ability to implement safer and more effective correctional innovations and technologies.

The historical development of both public and private prisons in America has its roots in the 18th and 19th centuries; of particular interest is the history between prisons and profit within the United States. The debate on the use and growth of private prisons in the latter 20th and early 21st centuries has given rise to several advantages (pros) and disadvantages (cons) of the use of private prisons and detention facilities today.

What Are Private Prisons?

The term *private prison* refers either to the process of transferring the operation of an existing public prison to a for-profit organization (usually referred to as an asset sale), or to the process of contracting a for-profit organization to design, build, and operate a new facility. Thus, private prisons are correctional and detention facilities that are built and/or administered by a for-profit organization for the purpose of incarcerating people for a net profit.

In the establishment of private correctional and detention facilities, governmental agencies and for-profit organizations generally enter into contracts that outline the primary physical, administrative, and performance standards to be followed by the contracting organization. As with publicly administered prisons and detention facilities in the United States, privately run facilities are also required to adhere to federal, local, and state laws and requirements pertaining to the rights and welfare of inmates and detainees, as well as other health and safety standards. In exchange for adhering to these standards, the private contractor is afforded a daily (or monthly) fee for each incarcerated prisoner. The paid fee is typically lower than the expenditure per inmate in a public prison or detention facility; hence the incentive for public agencies to enter into such contracts insofar as this reduces correctional expenditures.

History of Private Prisons and Detention Facilities

Profit has been a defining feature and motive for the use of incarceration for centuries, if not earlier. Early modern prisons in the 18th and 19th centuries in the United States were either privately operated prisons (private proprietary), or state-owned prisons designed to be run profitably by the state (public proprietary). In both cases, the link between prisons and profit was an assumed one, and prisoners would regularly be required to work for the cost of their incarceration. Larger prisons such as New York's Auburn and Sing Sing prisons, established in 1816 and 1925, respectively, both returned profits to the state, and Auburn was in turn a model for several other prisons in the north.

Yet, the most decisive link between punishment and profit in the United States emerged not in the north, but rather in the development of the convict-lease system following the Civil War in the American south. This system represented for all purposes a continuation of the plantation system that had existed under slavery, except that instead of owning slaves, plantation owners and other capitalists were able to "lease" convicted criminals from the state for use in hard labor. The emergence of the convict-lease system was facilitated by the passing of Black Codes and Jim Crow laws, to such horrifying ends that one historian of this era called it a system "worse than slavery." Plantation owners and other "lessees" had little incentive not to work black convicts to death, and in many southern states, 10 years was considered a death sentence. By the late 1880s, most southern states were in the business of using convict labor for their own work farms, with the Parchman farm in Mississippi in 1901 as the most well known. Oshinsky notes that as early as 1905, Parchman was able to return a profit to the state of at least $185,000.

Only in the late 19th and early 20th centuries did prisons gradually become public institutions explicitly barred from profit seeking. Between

1929 and 1940, a series of state and federal prison labor laws—most notably, the Hawes-Cooper Bill (1929) and the Ashurst-Sumners Act (1935)—effectively ended the sale of prison-made goods for private profit. These bills were popular with big business and labor unions, which both viewed prison labor as an "unfair business practice;" with the general public, particularly during the Great Depression, when jobs for able-bodied men were scarce; and with prison reformers, who were increasingly supportive of rehabilitation in lieu of hard labor. Between 1945 and the 1970s, prison populations remained largely stable throughout the United States as a result of the postwar boom and the establishment of moderate social welfare programs and benefits, including both the Great Society programs and the G.I. Bill. As late as the 1970s, the total prison population in the United States was less than 200,000.

Three Factors Influencing Privatization

Beginning in the 1970s, however, three factors emerged that set the stage for the return to private prisons: increased incarceration rates, the Reagan administration's support for privatization, and the Prison Industry Enhancement Certification program (PIE-Program).

First, policymakers and legislatures increasingly adopted "tough on crime" laws that increased the length of prison sentences and criminalized drug use in a way that radically grew the number of nonviolent offenders (in particular minority offenders) in prisons and jails. This was primarily a reaction to growing crime rates, recessions, state fiscal crises, and the loss of public support for correctional rehabilitation programs. The deinstitutionalization of mental health facilities in the 1970s and 1980s also contributed to the growth of prison populations. Prisons that had maintained fairly stable inmate populations for decades were suddenly overcrowded, conditions deteriorated, and state legislatures in particular were faced with the need to build more facilities within the reality of decreasing revenues.

Second, beginning in 1981, the Reagan administration embraced and promoted privatization within sectors that had for decades been largely fulfilled by public or quasi-public organizations. Education, healthcare, social services, and infrastructure in particular were all framed as "part of the problem" of ineffective and intrusive government that could be more efficiently provided by the private sector.

Finally, the passing by Congress of the PIE-Program in 1979 allowed individual states to sell goods produced by prisoners to other states for a profit, opening the door for individual states to make decisions regarding the contracting of prisoners and prisons to the private sector.

In the early 1980s, the argument for privatization was thus an attractive one for governments facing overcrowding and other correctional problems, particularly where it was argued that privatization could be done in a way to achieve a net savings for taxpayers. Private companies were already providing goods and services within prisons and detention facilities, as well as managing numerous juvenile and mental health facilities. In 1979, the Immigration and Naturalization Service (INS) began contracting with private firms to detain illegal immigrants, and in 1983, it awarded the first contract to CCA to fully manage and oversee the Houston Processing Center. By 1984, Texas, Florida, and Tennessee had passed laws allowing for private companies to administer correction and detention facilities, and a decade later, more than 30 states had passed similar laws.

By the late 1990s, the growth of private facilities in the United States had started to level off, but in 1998, the Federal Bureau of Prisons (BOP) began to contract with private companies to house federal inmates. The federal government was already using private companies for other detention facilities such as immigration, but prior to this time, only states and local municipalities had contracted for jails and prisons. The 1996 Immigration Reform Act, which increased penalties for illegal immigrants convicted of crimes, was a major driver in this decision, as was the continued use of private contractors for the housing of illegal immigrants facing review or deportation hearings, and the use of private facilities by the U.S. Marshals Service for the custody of federal detainees.

Between 1998 and 2005, the number of private correctional and detention facilities within the United States almost doubled, and the most recent national census by the DOJ in 2005 put the number of private prisons, jails, juvenile facilities, and detention facilities at 415. By 2009, about nine percent of the total U.S. prison population was incarcerated in private facilities. Beyond the United States, privately operated prisons have also emerged in countries such as Britain and New Zealand, and have grown the fastest in Australia, where the first private prison was opened in 1990, and today houses 17 percent of Australia's prisoners.

Pro: Advantages of Prison Privatization

Support of private prisons include financial or cost-savings arguments, performance arguments, and transparency and accountability arguments. In practice, these arguments are often presented together and frequently over-lap, but conceptually they involve three distinct positions, namely that (1) private prisons can be profitably managed at a "net savings" to governments and taxpayers, (2) this net savings can be achieved while providing equal or better quality of service to inmates than public prisons, and (3) the mechanisms of contractual agreements and accountability for meeting these agreements provide increased transparency over public prisons.

The ability of corporations to profitably run prisons at a net savings for taxpayers is the most central argument for pursuing privatization. The contracting of many prison services and the outsourcing of prison labor was already occurring by the 1980s, and the same logic of competition and cost savings applies to the argument that private companies can run prisons more efficiently than public agencies. As with other sectors such as education, healthcare, social services, and infrastructure that were also targeted in the 1980s, the argument is that profitability drives innovation, efficiency, and fiduciary responsibility—all of which affect the bottom line for taxpayers.

The three primary ways that innovation and increased efficiency have been applied specifically to reduce costs in private prisons has been in the areas of labor costs, construction costs, the application of newer technologies in prison design, and procurement of prison services and goods.

Cost Savings in Labor

Cost savings in terms of labor involves staffing as well as wages and/or benefits. Research on labor costs of public prisons has found that labor may account for up to two-thirds of overall operating costs. On average, private prison guards and staff generally make less in wages and benefits than their public counterparts, which results in cost savings to corporations. Supporters of privatization argue that much of this difference, however, is a result of union practices that routinely understaff public prisons, leave vacancies unfilled, and use other tactics in order to justify the common use of overtime. For example, in 2001, while the base pay for prison guards in California averaged $57,000 per year, some 2,400 guards made over $100,000 as a result of overtime. While most staff at public prisons are unionized, staff at private prisons generally are not, and managers of private facilities argue that this allows them flexibility in terms of reducing overtime pay, providing incentives and promotions that are based on performance instead of seniority, and affords more latitude for dismissing ineffective staff.

Cost Savings in Construction

Another way that private prisons are able to both cut costs to taxpayers and be more efficient is through the shouldering of prison construction costs and in the design of new facilities. Usually, the cost of building prisons and jails is financed by the public; however, many prisons built by CCA, GEO Group, and other corporations have been built using private financing, saving taxpayers either initial construction costs or, more frequently, bypassing the need for municipalities to raise funds through bonds or other measures. In the building of facilities, moreover, private companies are able to effectively utilize newer prison design and technologies that in turn reduce labor costs (particularly in the case of the need for fewer guards), and provide for increased monitoring and safety for both staff and inmates.

Cost Savings in Goods and Services

A third argument in the case of efficiency centers on the ability of private prisons to further subcontract for competitive provision of prison services and goods such as healthcare, education, clothing, textiles, and food. As with public prisons, some of these services may be performed by inmates themselves, and others may be contracted out to private companies, but private prison managers have argued that they have greater flexibility in the purchasing of such goods and services insofar as they are not beholden to more inflexible and expensive governmental procurement systems.

Evidence of Cost Savings

Supporters point to a substantial body of academic and government research that has found substantial cost savings over publicly run prisons. Individual studies in support of this argument are numerous, but perhaps more convincing have been several meta-studies that have compared individual studies, and which have concluded that on the whole, private prisons save money. Research by Geoffrey Segal and Adrian Moore, for example, examined 28 individual studies of privatization and found that 22 demonstrated savings without any significant impact on the performance or quality of those facilities. Several individual or meta-studies have found that operational costs of private prisons average 10 to 20 percent less than those of public prisons. More broadly, several studies (including Segal and Moore's) have found that the growth of private prisons has indirectly lowered the costs of corrections on the whole by creating a "spillover" effect that has fostered competition between public and private facilities, and forced public prisons to operate more efficiently. Finally, beyond the immediate arguments presented in terms of the cost savings to taxpayers, there are other secondary financial arguments that have been put forth. The CCA, for example, has noted that their private prisons, unlike public facilities, pay both income and property taxes. Proponents also argue that there are costs savings attached to the delivery of improved services and programs to inmates that are less easily quantified, but nevertheless substantial.

Performance Standards and Accountability

Agreements between the public and private sector require both parties to identify and specify objectives and key performance indicators. While private prisons are administered and run by private contractors, they are nevertheless reviewed and/or audited by public agencies or their representatives in order to ensure compliance of these agreements. Further, private prison contractors are often also required to adhere to performance standards that exceed those in public facilities. For example, contracts regularly include maximum occupancy caps to avoid overcrowding. Proponents see this as an advantage over public prisons where overcrowding is not inhibited by any specific means, and today it is in fact the norm in states such as California and New York. To the extent that overcrowding has been linked in academic research to increases in inmate violence and riots, inmate depression and other mental health problems, and physical health problems, the argument is that inmate occupancy restrictions not only bring prisons in line with state and federal requirements, but also save taxpayers and companies money through reduced costs associated with overcrowding. Several research studies have found evidence for these claims.

Beyond contractual compliance agreements, proponents point to the record of private prison accreditation under the American Correctional Association (ACA) guidelines. ACA accreditation requires facilities to meet a minimum quality standard in the delivery of goods and services to inmates, including food, clothing, physical conditions of confinement, healthcare, and rehabilitative programs. Accredited facilities must also meet health and safety requirements, including limits of inmate violence toward other inmates or staff, as well as limits on other types of disturbances such as riots or escapes. Research in 2005 on rates of ACA accreditation found that 44 percent of private facilities had been accredited, while only 10 percent of public facilities had met these standards. Today, ACA accreditation is standard for contracts between private prison operators and public agencies.

Con: Disadvantages of Prison Privatization

In response to arguments in defense of privatization, opponents counter that private prisons are not more cost-effective than public prisons, do not on the whole perform better than their public counterparts, and are actually less transparent and accountable. Beyond these counter-arguments, opponents also take positions that the linking of punishment and profit is ethically and perhaps even legally unsound, and that the use of private prisons maintains, if not exacerbates, racial inequalities in ways that mirror earlier forms of racial segregation in the United States.

Lack of Cost-Savings Evidence

Opponents point to a substantial body of research, including several studies conducted by federal and state agencies, that have found little evidence in support of the cost-effectiveness of private prisons. Some of these include studies from the U.S. Government Accounting Office (GAO) in 1996, the National Institute of Corrections (NIC) in 1998, the Bureau of Justice Assistance (BJA) in 2001, the Arizona Department of Corrections in 2010, and the state of Florida in 2010. These studies, critics argue, carry far more weight than the majority of studies conducted either by correctional corporations or affiliated organizations that have purported to find cost savings. To this last point, opponents argue that many of the studies supported by corrections corporations have been less than rigorous or have contained serious methodological flaws. A 2001 report from the DOJ that reviewed comparative research on cost-effectiveness supports this position. This report found that few of the studies on cost savings were reliable enough to make definitive conclusions on this point, and those that were reliable provided little evidence of cost savings over public facilities. This report further noted that costs for private facilities were likely to rise as the growing private sector would increasingly face similar problems encountered in the public sector, particularly in terms of recruiting and retaining competent staff.

In this vein, opponents have also noted that in their initial foray into privatization, companies were able to more readily "cherry-pick" newer and less problematic facilities (in particular, medium- or low-security prisons and detention facilities). They note that over time, however, private contractors have been forced into either building new facilities or taking over older and more problematic facilities—increasingly encountering the same problems as administrators at public facilities, and forcing the cutting of costs from other areas such as services and programs for inmates. One other primary consequence of this shift, argue critics, has been that private companies are increasingly targeting poorer and less financially sophisticated communities that, often faced with high unemployment and poverty, are willing to secure or guarantee bonds or other forms of financing from companies that specialize in derivatives and other high-risk investments.

Beyond the immediate question of comparative cost savings, opponents also argue that private prisons frequently entail a host of hidden costs. For example, the costs of proposals, negotiating contracts, and auditing performance standards compliance are borne by public agencies, although they are rarely figured into comparative studies. Costs of tax reductions and economic incentives (particularly in rural and poorer areas) are also frequently overlooked. In addition, some private facilities are authorized to transfer "problem" inmates to public facilities, which critics see as another form of cherry-picking.

Performance Arguments

Opponents of private prisons concede that public prisons have set the bar abysmally low in terms of their performance standards—particularly in terms of healthcare, rehabilitation programs, and the safety of staff and inmates. They also concede that, particularly in states with severe overcrowding problems, some private prisons have been able to perform on par with public facilities. As the private prison industry has grown, however, and as more data has become available, opponents argue that private prisons have not performed better on the whole than their public counterparts, and moreover, in several ways they have underperformed when compared to public facilities.

In particular, opponents have focused on research in the areas of safety and security, healthcare, and programming for inmates that suggests private prisons underperform when compared to public facilities. They point to research on the health of inmates, which has found that healthcare is often subpar to that of public facilities, particularly in the case of mental healthcare and care for diseases such as hepatitis and HIV/AIDS. In the case of safety, opponents also argue that private prisons may actually increase levels of inmate violence toward other inmates and prison staff, as well as prison guard brutality, an outcome they attribute to having fewer prison guards supervise more inmates, as well as to the fact that private guards receive less training on average than guards in public facilities. In the case of all three of these areas—safety and security, healthcare, and programming—every five years the Bureau of Justice Statistics conducts a national census of state and federal correction facilities, including private facilities. The most recent census, in 2005, revealed that on the whole, private prison facilities provided less of the following programs than public facilities: educational and treatment programs (basic adult education, secondary education, special education, occupational training), work assignments, psychological treatment, HIV/AIDS programs, and sex-offender treatment programs.

Critics thus argue that such data is not only problematic in terms of the immediate effects on inmates and prison staff, but also results in increased externalized costs to taxpayers. The concept of externalized costs in the case of private prisons refers to the idea that financial savings for corporations are borne by other sectors of society—in healthcare costs for released inmates, in compensation and costs for injured staff and inmates, and in terms of increased recidivism for inmates released from private facilities. Critics contend that to date, few studies have shown any reduction in recidivism from private facilities. Further, studies conducted on private facilities in Florida that purported to find a decrease have been questioned by the state itself. Moreover, argue opponents, there are several studies that suggest either no net decrease, or slight increases in recidivism, which they see as leading to further external costs in the form of increased victimization, policing and court costs, and further correctional costs.

Transparency

Opponents argue that contracts between governments and private companies that leverage the use of fines or other sanctions for noncompliance result in less transparency in the reporting of performance standards and other problems. Broadly, they argue that the profit incentive for meeting contractual agreements discourages accurate accounting of contractual performance indicators, particularly in the case of inmate and/or guard violence. In support of their argument, they point to numerous cases where problems with both inmates and/or guards went unreported, only to resurface later in the form of lawsuits. These include particularly egregious examples involving the repeated rape of a 14-year-old juvenile by a guard employed by Wackenhut (now GEO) at a private youth facility in Texas, and the prison-for-profit scheme of two juvenile court judges in Pennsylvania convicted in 2009 for their roles in closing down a public facility and subsequently opening a private facility, which one of the judges then stocked with youth offenders.

Critics also argue that compliance agreements between public and private agencies are frequently not enforced. New Mexico, which has one of the highest rates of inmates housed in private prisons, has repeatedly found contract violations by both CCA and GEO related to understaffing, but as of 2010 had not collected any fines. In the case of ACA accreditation, critics have noted several flaws with the accreditation process, including the fact that accreditation requires only minimal inspection of physical premises and inmates; audits do not use spot-checks, but are rather scheduled in advance, and the ACA is actually dependent upon prisons themselves for most of its funding.

Legal and Ethical Arguments

Legal arguments against the use of private prisons have to date been more theoretical than realized. No binding legal decision in any U.S. court in the last 30 years has seriously challenged the right of local, state, or federal governments to enter into contracts that allow private companies to manage and run correctional or detention facilities. This is unlikely to change in the near future, particularly in light of the *Turner v. Safely* (1986) Supreme Court decision (often referred to as the return of the "hands-off doctrine") that substantially limited the ability of judges to regulate the actions of prison administrators.

Critics argue, however, that there are unaddressed legal problems with the use of private prisons. For example, while U.S. laws prohibit the import of goods and services produced by convicts in other countries, government agencies are able to purchase low-cost goods and services produced by inmates in the United States. The argument here parallels court decisions in the early 20th century that found that the use of prison labor compromises free-market competition. Another argument raised by critics involves the use of administrative disciplinary procedures for inmates accused of violations and crimes, particularly where these decisions may result in increased sentences or more severe punishments. Opponents argue that these practices routinely conflate the function of sentencing with that of corrections, in effect ceding carceral authority to private corporations.

Ethical arguments against the use of private prisons are myriad, and involve a host of moral, religious, and social-justice platforms. One of the most frequent points made by critics is that the linking of prisons to profit shifts the focus on crime reduction away from proven, less-profitable strategies such as early childcare programs, prenatal healthcare for poor women, job training, and various other research-driven interventions that do not involve corrections. Further, critics point to the fact that corporations such as CCA and the GEO Group have donated large sums of money to political organizations such as the American Legislative Exchange Council that have in turn lobbied in support of tough-on-crime legislation.

Racial Disparities

Finally, opponents of private prisons argue that the overrepresentation of minority offenders in such facilities bears striking resemblance to earlier forms of racially segregated punishment in the United States. While only 13 percent of the total population, blacks in the United States currently constitute over 40 percent of the total U.S. prison population. Opponents of private prisons do not generally blame private prisons for this overrepresentation per se. Rather, they see private prisons as a larger part of the growth of prison populations over the last 30 years that has targeted black and minority populations—largely within an economic and ideological shift that has resulted in the creation of what William J. Wilson has called a class of the "truly disadvantaged." Within the United States, the combined effects of the War on Drugs, the severe curtailing of social welfare programs, reductions in education spending, and the loss of well-paying jobs for working-class Americans have returned prison populations to racial compositions not seen since the late 19th and early 20th centuries. As late as 1970, approximately 60 percent of federal and state inmates in the United States were white. By 2000, this number had decreased to around 30 percent, and in the mid-1990s, the DOJ reported that about one out of every four black men in the United States would spend time in prison at some point in his life.

To this end, critics argue that there are striking similarities between the mass incarceration of recently freed slaves shortly after the Civil War, and the mass incarceration of mostly African Americans after the introduction in the 1980s of the War on Drugs policies. Michael Hallet in particular has argued that (1) both time periods evidenced substantial economic and social changes that led to increased imprisonment rates and subsequent fiscal strain on governments; (2) during both periods, the majority of crimes for which offenders were convicted were nonviolent petty crimes with a seriousness that was recently elevated by changes in law or crime policy; (3) the majority of convicts were impoverished blacks; (4) in both time periods, politically influential entrepreneurs profited from the low-cost labor force or other profits the corrections system provided; and (5) both the convict-lease system and private prisons have a system in place to rank inmates according to their economic value.

See Also: 14. Prison Labor; 15. Prison Overcrowding; 17. Punishment Versus Rehabilitation.

Further Readings

Austin, James, and Garry Coventry. *Emerging Issues on Privatized Prisons.* U.S. Department of Justice, 2001.

Department of Justice. "Census Of State And Federal Correctional Facilities, 2005." http://bjs.ojp.usdoj.gov/index.cfm?ty=pbdetail&iid =530 (Accessed October 2010).

Hallett, Michael A. *Private Prisons in America: A Critical Race Perspective.* Chicago: University of Illinois Press, 2006.

Harding, Richard. *Private Prisons and Public Accountability.* New Brunswick, NJ: Transaction Publishers, 1997.

Lundahl, Brad W., et al. "Prison Privatization: A Meta-Analysis of Cost and Quality of Confinement Indicators." *Research on Social Work Practice,* v.19/4 (July 2009).

Oshinsky, David M. *Worse Than Slavery: Parchman Farm and the Ordeal of Jim Crow Justice.* New York: Free Press, 1997.

Segal, Geoffrey F., and Adrian T. Moore. *Weighing the Watchmen: Evaluating the Costs and Benefits of Outsourcing Correctional Services, Part II: Reviewing the Literature on Cost and Quality Comparisons.* Los Angeles: Reason Public Policy Institute, 2002.

Thomas, Charles W. "Correctional Privatization in America: An Assessment of its Historical Origins, Present Status, and Future Prospects." In *Changing the Guard: Private Prisons and the Control of Crime,* edited by A. Tabarrok. Oakland, CA: The Independent Institute, 2003.

Wacquant, Loïc. "From Slavery to Mass Incarceration: Rethinking the 'Race Question' in the U.S." *New Left Review,* v.13 (January–February 2002).

17

Punishment Versus Rehabilitation

Faye S. Taxman
Danielle S. Rudes
George Mason University

The criminal justice system is responsible for managing society's wrongdoers, under the notion that when someone commits a criminal act, they should receive a sanction that will punish or treat their behavior in a way that prevents future incidents, thus keeping society safe. A key player in this process is the sentencing judge. Though constrained by the structural features of plea bargaining, legislatively driven mandatory minimums (i.e., minimum periods of incarceration), and sentencing guidelines, the sentencing judge is responsible for determining the goals of sentencing. Generally, these goals are deterrence, incapacitation, retribution, and rehabilitation. Deterrence is designed to notify others of the consequences of criminal conduct and/or to respond to the behavior of specific individuals. Incapacitation is restriction of the liberties of the individual through confinement in a closed setting (prison, jail, or special facility) and is designed to physically prevent criminal conduct. Retribution is the dosing of punishment commensurate to the behavior of the individual, including his criminal history. Finally, rehabilitation is the goal of helping the individual alter his behavior to become more pro-social.

While the purpose of the sentence is in the hands of the sentencing judge, correctional agencies have the responsibility for executing the sentence and managing the offender during the period of correctional control. In the hands of correctional agencies, the tools that are used for punishment are often the same as rehabilitation, and therefore the debate is one of punishment versus rehabilitation, or the comingling of the two. Punishment and rehabilitation often comingle, with implications for achieving specific goals.

Methods of Punishment and Rehabilitation

There are four primary methods used to punish and/or rehabilitate offenders in the United States: incarceration, sanctions and controls, community programs and services, and treatment.

Incarceration

The United States is known for its use of incarceration as a primary punishment tool. In 2007, the Pew Foundation reported there were over 2.2 million adults (about one per 100) in prisons and jails each day. The per-capita rate of U.S. incarceration is among the highest in the Western world, surpassing all European countries, South Africa, Russia, and China. Removal from society inflicts punishment on the wrongdoer by limiting civil liberties and by restricting the individual's ability to make independent decisions. Incarceration also provides a symbol to others in the community that such behaviors warrant punitive action, which is considered general deterrence. Incarceration has a demonstrative effect on individuals, as detention provides state control over their total being. Prisons focus as a total institution and exact punishment over individuals by controlling their daily lives, including their physical movement as well as their opportunities and choices.

While incarceration represents the most severe liberty restriction, sanctions and community controls also employ mechanisms for limiting offender mobility. As part of official probation and parole practices, these are termed *conditions of release*. These conditions create a "prison without walls" where individual behavior is controlled and subjected to a number of checks and balances. The conditions range in severity based on individual limitations and the degree to which the person is held accountable. These controls augment traditional supervision, which includes face-to-face contacts with an assigned officer. The purpose of direct contact is to monitor adherence to release conditions.

Day Programming, House Arrest, and Curfews

The notion behind day programming is that the individual reports to a center or office where they will be confined for the day, or set hours during the day. The purpose is to limit the person's interactions in the community while providing education or clinical treatment services at the center to assist the person in becoming more pro-social. The day-programming model provides a framework for limiting the activities of the individual while allowing them to reside in the community during the period of correctional control.

The house-arrest scenario confines the individual to their place of residence during the period of supervision. Some are offered the ability to work in the community, but must be confined at home during nonworking hours. Some house arrest initiatives require the person to be on an electronic monitor or use random phone calls to verify the person is at home.

Curfews and place limitations are predefined as either a time of the day the person must be at their residence, or certain places where the individual is forbidden to go. These restrictions are designed to limit the behavior of the individual to either temporal or spatial factors that contribute to his criminal behavior.

Technology: Electronic Monitoring, GPS Systems, and Kiosks

Technology can assist with limiting and monitoring the movement and activities of offenders. Electronic monitoring devices (ankle bracelets) are worn by the individual. The device needs to be near equipment that illustrates the person is within the confined area. Some of these devices also include a breathalyzer to ensure that the person is not consuming alcohol, or mechanisms to ensure that the correct individual is being monitored, such as voice verifiers and fingerprint scanners. A more sophisticated version of the electronic monitoring system utilizes the Global Positioning System (GPS), where the individual's movements can be traced. These devices are used to restrict the individual's activities and ensure that he or she does not go into unauthorized areas. They provide the most comprehensive tools to ensure that individuals are abiding by the conditions of release, since their daily movements can be tracked.

Many systems have developed kiosk machines to allow individuals to check in with their supervision officer and, in some cases, to provide a breathalyzer test. The kiosk replaces the more traditional administrative supervision where the individual mailed in a card periodically to indicate that they were crime-free, employed, and overall doing well. The kiosk provides a technological tool to increase supervision contacts without overburdening supervision staff.

Drug Testing, Breathalyzers, and DNA Samples

Many supervision agencies use biological testing to determine the substance use of the individual under supervision. These processes require the individual to provide a urine sample and have that sample tested to detect a myriad of substances. Individuals on medications such as methadone, buprenorphine, naltroxene, or any pain medication must provide medical verification of the prescribed medication. Positive drug tests can lead to technical violations. The same is true with breathalyzers, which are used to detect alcohol use in quantities that are above the legal limit or in violation of the conditions of release.

Many states are now requiring that offenders provide a DNA sample for inclusion in a database of law violators. The databases are useful for law enforcement and other officials to monitor the whereabouts of known offenders. They can also potentially be used in crime prevention.

Face-to-Face Contacts

The purpose of this punishment and supervision tool is to increase the contacts between the individual and the probation or parole officer in order to provide oversight and to ensure that the individual is aware of his conditions of release.

Programs, Services, and Treatment

While custody and liberty restrictions represent two types of punishment, a third type comes in the form of programs or services offered by community correctional or judicial interventions. Conditions set by courts or parole boards specify whether individuals are required to participate in treatment programs—approximately 50 percent of those in supervised release have such requirements. An increasing trend is to include conditions addressing mental health, substance abuse (including alcohol), and other social problems. Specialized court programs exist for homelessness, veterans' services, domestic violence, and other issues. This trend suggests a movement in the punishment system toward encouraging offenders to change their behavior as part of a strategy to reduce recidivism.

Treatment is a fourth form of restriction that typically serves the goal of rehabilitation. Offender treatment generally focuses on behavior, attitudes, and values. Being in treatment alters the daily lives of individuals through requirements and by requesting that the individual alter his behavior. Behavioral change requires a commitment to a new lifestyle and maintenance of new behavior.

Treatment itself involves several processes that affect liberties: (1) awareness, where an individual learns about the antisocial, criminal, and other unhealthy aspects of his cognition and behavior; (2) action, where the individual participates in a myriad of activities that assist in learning new skills to manage behavior and attitudes, and (3) maintenance, where the individual participates in activities to support the changes in attitudes, behaviors, and values. The treatment process involves individuals addressing a variety of issues affecting their engagement in criminal behavior. These issues include reconsidering the people with whom they associate, who either participate in or condone criminal behavior; their daily activities, including places of employment, residence, and recreational or leisure activities; and paying psychological attention to people, places, and things that affect impulsive behaviors, mood swings, or unmet needs.

Treatment is designed to affect all aspects of their lives; through the treatment process, individuals are expected to learn about societal expectations, conventional norms and behaviors, and requirements of being a prosocial individual. Treatment, like other forms of liberty restrictions, places demands on the individual by requiring attendance and participation in a myriad of activities. These are akin to liberty restrictions in that the person is held accountable and required to attend programming. The amount of programming varies from several hours a day to several hours a month.

Pro: Benefits of Pairing Punishment and Rehabilitation

The debate about punishment versus rehabilitation has generally occurred at the sentencing stage. While the sentence typically specifies a primary goal, correctional agencies are required to manage behaviors with similar tools, regardless of the stated goals. The public is interested in reducing offending behavior, and believes that this is likely to occur when the goals of sentencing are comingled. The three punishment goals of sentencing—deterrence, incapacitation, and retribution—are built on the assumption that individuals will alter their behavior if the response from the criminal justice is punitive. Rehabilitation also aims to adjust individual behavior, but the focus is on tools that are directly tied to trying to change the behavior. Often, the tools used to either punish or rehabilitate are similar.

Liberty restriction tools require attention to the quantity and quality of daily activities available to inmates. GPS and electronic monitoring theoretically limit individuals' physical movements while helping individuals understand movements or patterns that may be problematic. The same is true of required meetings for services (or treatment), where individual liberties are constricted based on treatment requirements, either educational or vocational. Face-to-face contact is another sanctioning tool that require offenders to visit with supervisory officers frequently. During these interactions, probation or correctional officers can communicate with offenders using change language (pro-social or therapeutically driven) or motivational enhancement therapies combined with surveillance and monitoring. In fact, it is possible through these contacts to use brief interventions that can be designed to change the offender. Correctional agencies make substantive choices about using these tools for the purposes of punishment and/or rehabilitation.

Offenders are more likely to change their behavior in response to the actions of the correctional agency than merely through the stated sentencing goals. Even though the stated purpose of a sentence may be punishment, correctional agencies often determine the way in which the individual is managed. This is accomplished through various supervision-related requirements. Offenders who perceive that they are being handled fairly during these processes are more likely to be responsive to the goals of sentencing. This is not the case when offenders perceive their treatment or situation as unfair. The use of similar tools for punishment and rehabilitation makes the ultimate goal transparent to the offender. This also speaks to the push for correctional agencies to use tools that reduce recidivism. Given that most systematic reviews focus on the use of treatment over punishment, correctional agencies are encouraged to use tools that will make the offender more responsive.

Finally, in many ways, the public is less interested in the concept of goals than they are interested in the outcomes or products from the system. While judges are seldom required to document their outcomes, correctional agencies are often required to do so as a way of demonstrating the impact of various programs and services. For example, in their infamous reviews of the impact of correctional programming, the Washington State Institute of Public Policy focused on three select outcomes: recidivism, costs, and benefits to society. Their report does not differentiate between punishment or rehabilitation programs, but rather illustrates the differences among programs on their outcomes and the cost versus benefits. The concept of "what works" is used by scholars and practitioners to focus on changing offender behavior, but it gives little attention to program orientation (rehabilitation versus punishment). Instead, "what works" or "best practices" projects are guided by the programs and services that improve outcomes where the benefits outweigh the costs. Studies of this type note that work and vocational education in prison is more effective than cognitive behavioral therapy, but community programming that includes treatment is most effective, which is consistent with other reviews. In the end, it is not the sentencing goals that matter, but rather offender outcomes.

Con: Drawbacks of Pairing Punishment and Rehabilitation

For many, the punishment versus rehabilitation debate centers on competing goals or complementary tools, and the fallout of mixing different correctional goals, such as sentencing goals versus managing the offender population. Concerns also center on the issues of fairness and equity as compared to system efficiencies.

From a therapeutic perspective, treatment should not be considered punishment. If treatment becomes part of punishment, then concerns are raised that the goals of treatment are undermined by the punishment demands and by the coercion into care. A major concern is that treatment cannot be ethically delivered when the client is not volunteering for care. Clinicians raise issues about the appropriateness of treatment when the client is not ready or willing to be involved in treatment services. The coerced nature of treatment is controversial in that the concept of free will suggests individuals should determine their own values, attitudes, and behaviors. However, when treatment is part of a criminal sanction, individuals must change their ways or violate their sentencing decision. The line between punishment and voluntary treatment decisions is therefore blurred under the coerced treatment model. The empirical literature suggests that those with legal mandates to treatment have equal or slightly better treatment outcomes than voluntary subjects. Research firmly supports the importance of treatment or rehabilitation-type programs in correctional settings to improve outcomes, despite clinical issues regarding the provision of treatment.

Efficiencies Versus Integrity

A long-lasting tension in the justice system focuses on efforts to improve efficiencies. Due process or procedural justice often falls by the wayside under pressures to be efficient. In 1992, Malcolm Feeley argued that criminal court processes often impose punishment through processing outside traditional sentencing. Feeley's analysis sets forth the notion that punishment is "doled out" by and from the criminal justice process. In his analysis of lower courts, informality, swiftness, and access to justice can contribute to the punishment process. Individual defendants are often swallowed up by the justice process when efficiency is prioritized over concerns about integrity or fairness. In the end, the way in which decisions are made undermines the focus that brought the individual to the attention of the court (arrest). Rather, attention is centered on the "deal" worked out through the advocacy system of justice. This results in efficiencies that may appear to be beneficial to the operations of the justice apparatus, but affect the integrity of the procedures. Individuals are left wondering whether their constitutional rights were protected or whether justice exists.

Several studies illustrate how the criminal justice process may be yielding punishment through the process itself. At the front end of the system, jurisdictions vary in terms of the use and availability of pretrial release supervision. Pretrial supervision is designed to limit the use of pretrial incarceration for those without means. Many jurisdictions favor the private bond system, but this process has inherent biases in that an independent party (for profit) determines who they will provide with collateral funding. This means that indigent people do not always have equal access to justice during the adjudication process. In fact, many people with misdemeanor offenses find themselves detained in jail during the pretrial period. To compensate for this, many criminal justice systems give credit for time served pretrial, thereby reducing overall sentence length for those individuals who are convicted. However, this compensation overlooks those who are not convicted or for whom the charges are *nolle prosequi*, or wrongfully punished. Practices such as this reinforce the concept of criminal process becoming punishment.

Substance Abuse Treatment Shortfalls

In about half of all orders for probation and/or parole services, offenders are mandated to obtain substance abuse treatment services. Most misdemeanor and many felony sentencing decisions are no longer informed by presentence investigations; this varies considerably across jurisdictions. This means that sentencing decisions are affected by the negotiated plea (i.e., the nature of the offense) and the state or federal sentencing guidelines (based on conviction offense and criminal history). If a case goes to trial, which is rare, the conviction offense will drive the sentence. Few systems have substance abuse counselors in place to thoroughly assess of the severity of the disorder or to consider how the abuse of substances affects criminal behavior. About one-third of males and half of females in the criminal justice system have a substance use disorder warranting treatment, and over half of judicial orders require substance abuse treatment.

This is complicated by the fact that few probation and/or parole agencies directly offer substance abuse treatment. Instead, it is up to the convicted individual, based on the conditions of release, to obtain treatment. To comply with treatment conditions, these individuals must find services and, if needed, must pay for the services themselves. Current estimates suggest that on any given day, the public health treatment system handles less than 10 percent of the offenders who need care; most public health treatment systems have long waiting lists, indicating the lack of available services. Also, recent literature on effective substance abuse treatment services indicates that few available treatment services are of sufficient clinical quality to address the substance abuse treatment needs of offenders. Continued drug use while on supervised release is one of the largest reasons for technical violations during probation or parole. This is affected by two factors: the failure of the individual to obtain required services, and the failure of the treatment system to deliver treatment services that are of sufficient quality to assist individuals in the recovery process.

Backend Sentencing

Finally, backend sentencing often is a byproduct of mixing different correctional goals. When correctional agencies use rehabilitation tools to manage offenders, they open the door to new infractions for the violation of conditions of release. Revocations for parole and probation make up nearly 40 percent of new prison admissions. In this way, individuals are punished for failure to comply with the conditions of release through reinstatement of incarceration conditions. Commonly, offenders are churned through the criminal justice processes through sentencing, supervision, incarceration, and technical violation hearings. Moreover, the standards for provision of legal counsel in revocation hearings are not as stringent as for formal trials, which results in more decisions rendered against offenders. In the pursuit of administrative managing of volumes of cases, safeguards are not in place to protect the rights of individuals. Throughout the justice and correctional processes, the tools of punishment are intertwined with the purpose of the procedure and the methods by which people are handled. When individuals are recycled through the criminal justice system with relaxed procedural standards, it can seriously undermine the purpose of punishment as well as the goals of sentencing.

Conclusion

While ongoing research exalts the promise from rehabilitation-type programs, treatment-type programs have larger effects than punishment-only programs in reducing recidivism. Adding rehabilitation-focused programs (treatment) improves the likelihood that individuals will change their behaviors. Coerced treatment is effective even if the individual is not willing and interested in changing his behavior. The real question is whether recidivism should be the outcome measure in the punishment versus rehabilitation debate. If the goal is recidivism reduction, then correctional agencies that comingle both punishment and treatment are more likely to yield better outcomes than those that employ merely punishment. Yet, there are compromises to offering rehabilitation programs in this manner. For example, rehabilitation programs are more likely to result in better offender outcomes, but they can also increase technical violations and back-end (revocation) sentencing.

Over the last several decades, scholars and practitioners have pursued the punishment versus rehabilitation debate as an either/or problem. However, effective treatment (and therefore behavior change) can be facilitated within a coerced treatment model (punishment). Further, effective treatment has another advantage in that it adds to the legitimacy of the criminal justice system. Research has shown that many people will be involved in the criminal justice system during their lives—one in three black males, one in seven Hispanic males, and one in 14 white males—and the expanding net of the justice system has led to a consideration that the system is illegitimate, unfair, and unrelenting. Punishment-oriented programs that focus on liberty restrictions either in closed settings or within the community contribute to this perception because they increase the likelihood of further violations. The psychological literature affirms that negative reinforcers (punishments) seldom result in sustained change. This suggests that efforts to use external controls suffer from the assumption that individuals know how to change their behavior, attitudes, and values, and have incentives to change. Quality treatment programs, on the other hand, provide tools that give individuals the necessary skills to change and the incentives to improve their lives. Rehabilitation, if delivered with integrity, offers individuals an opportunity to become productive citizens. It also demonstrates to the individual that the criminal justice system is less interested in churning (recycling) practices and more interested in ensuring that wrongdoers correct their behaviors. In the end, the larger societal goals of punishment can also be achieved by pursuing rehabilitation (quality treatment) policies. Given that the tools of punishment and rehabilitation can be similar, the debate should not be about punishment versus rehabilitation, but rather how to deliver quality programs that result in reduced recidivism.

See Also: 7. Furlough and Work-Release Programs; 13. Preventive Detention; 14. Prison Labor.

Further Readings

Argersinger v. Hamlin, 407 U.S. 25 (1972).

Feeley, M. M. *The Process Is the Punishment: Handling Cases in a Lower Criminal Court.* New York: Russell Sage Foundation, 1992.

Friedmann, P. D., F. S. Taxman, and C. Henderson. "Evidence-Based Treatment Practices for Drug-Involved Adults in the Criminal Justice System." *Journal of Substance Abuse Treatment*, v.32/3 (2007).

Goffman, Erving. *Asylums: Essays on the Social Situation of Mental Patients and Other Inmates.* New York: Random House, 1961.

Killias, M., and P. Villetaz. "The Effects of Custodial Versus Non-Custodial Sanctions on Reoffending: Lessons From a Systematic Review." *Psicothema*, v.20/1 (2008).

Taxman, F. S., J. M. Byrne, and A. Pattavina. "Racial Disparity and the Legitimacy of the Criminal Justice System: Exploring Impacts on Deterrence." *Journal of Health Care for the Poor and Underserved*, v.16/4, Supp. B (2005).

Taxman, F. S., M. Perdoni, and L. Harrison. "Treatment for Adult Offenders: A Review of the State of the State." *Journal of Substance Abuse Treatment*, v.32/3 (2007).

18

Religious Rights

Kamesha Spates
Colorado State University-Pueblo

Michael D. Royster
Prairie View A&M University

Key issues that pertain to the constitutional rights of incarcerated individuals have emerged over the last few decades. Recent attention to prisoners' constitutional rights has incited interesting debates, with religious rights at the forefront of these discussions.

The First Amendment of the U.S. Constitution stipulates legal protection of religion and religious exercise to all U.S. citizens. Accordingly, the First Amendment prohibits Congress from adopting laws that will inhibit freedom of religious exercises and practices. However, until the mid-20th century, there was very little constitutional protection of religious rights for the incarcerated. Traditionally, only limited religious rights were extended, and only the mainstream Christian doctrines, Catholics and Protestants, were accommodated. Now, religious rights within the penal system parallel those typically practiced in the outside world.

During incarceration, inmates commonly experience religious conversions. A religious conversion often likens the experiencing of a religious epiphany or spiritual rebirth. When this occurs, the individuals consciously seek to redefine their current and past selves in an attempt to establish social control over their lives. Approximately 30 percent of the prison population participates in some form of religious service or program. Present-day prisons house offenders from an array of religious backgrounds. Increasingly diverse prison populations show the need to accommodate a variety of religious expressions.

Prison overcrowding and undesirable prison conditions sparked concern about the civil rights of those incarcerated during the 1960s and 1970s. Interests in the role of governmental restriction on inmates' religious rights were at the forefront of these discussions. Prior to these times, very little attention was given to the rights of the incarcerated. Courts set precedence for these issues based on the notion of "substantial burden." This premise implies that the government may only "substantially burden a person's religious practices if they prove that their actions are in the best interests of the state." This is a difficult task. Both the Religious Freedom Restoration Act of 1993 and the Religious Land Use and Institutionalized Persons Act of 2000 were attempts to protect, at least to some degree, prisoners' religious rights. In the case of *Employment Division, Department of Human Resources of Oregon v. Smith* in 1990, the court ruled that as long as the law does not exhibit favoritism toward a particular religion, inconveniencing one's religious freedoms is of no consequence.

Significant growth in the U.S. prison population—and in some cases, major overcrowding—often interferes with daily prison operations, and the added tensions between religious freedom and social control prove a daunting task for prison administrators. Contemporary moral and legal disputes question whether or not the incarcerated deserve religious rights. What is the value of allotting convicts religious rights? And if these rights are granted, just how much should prison administrators curtail an inmate's religious practices? These issues are central in arguments of supporters and critics alike.

The History of Religious Rights

Religion has been an intricate part of the U.S. penal system since its beginning. Religious rights are protected under the First and Fourteenth Amendments. The First Amendment protects U.S. citizens' rights to limited expression of their religious beliefs, while the Fourteenth Amendment provides U.S. citizens with equal protection under the law. However, inmates' constitutional rights are not as clear-cut. Prisoners' civil rights became a primary concern during the mid-20th century, and petitions for major prison reform emerged during the 1960s and 1970s. Widespread prison overcrowding, violence, and inhumane conditions were brought to the forefront of these discussions. Consequently, the courts also began to examine the difficult matter of the exercise of religious rights in a confined setting.

The complexity of such issues has led many to express an opposition to unrestricted freedom of religious expression for inmates. In the 1940 case *Cantwell v. Connecticut*, courts defended the liberty for citizens to hold religious beliefs; however, one's actions in implementing these rights are based on regulation for the protection of society. Similarly, such rights are regulated among inmates in order to ensure safety and harmony among prison populations. *Turner v. Safety*, in 1987, set the precedence for religious rights in correctional settings. The case held that prisoner rights can be limited by regulations with a reasonable cause, if doing so is in the best interest of the institution. Prior to the 1960s, the courts were reluctant to examine inmate rights claims due to complexities involving the separation of church and state. Before this case, courts would rarely intervene in these cases involving inmates' religious expression. In the last 40 years, a variety of court decisions have validated the premise that prisoners should retain constitutional protections, within reason, while incarcerated.

Three Levels of Scrutiny

Religious rights cases are determined on the basis of examining appropriate levels of judicial scrutiny in relation to individual prisoner's religious rights. There are three levels of scrutiny that the courts are permitted to utilize in reviewing laws that obstruct constitutional rights: strict, intermediate, and minimal, and the criterion used to pass constitutional muster is virtually the same at all levels. In these cases, the courts seek to examine and uphold the government's interest and the goal of the law, and to evaluate the case under the proper level of scrutiny. The higher the level of scrutiny employed in the case, the more rigid the review process. Freedom of religion is protected by way of strict judicial scrutiny from governmental invasion. However, it has been difficult to find a suitable balance between an inmate's religious rights and those of government and penological interests. Presiding judges face difficult decisions, which at times could compromise the safety of the penal institution. Even the slightest alterations in prison policy could breed resentment and possibly even danger.

Attempts at balancing offenders' constitutional rights with government and penological interests has proven challenging. Prior to the 1960s, convicted offenders were thought to have forfeited all constitutional rights in place of those granted by state or federal correctional facilities. Recent gains have resulted in the passing of a number of substantive rights. Such rights guarantee inmates' protection of constitutional rights as well as the right to challenge any failures to receive procedural protection. Although legitimate penological interests still remain a priority among prison officials, offenders are now expected to receive the same constitutional rights as nonoffenders.

Providing reasonable yet permissible accommodations to inmates has proven a daunting task for prison administrators. Inmates classified as Protestants, Catholics, or Jews have fared much better in terms of accessibility to worship services and other religious resources. Inmates who choose to adhere to unconventional religious practices are seen by prison administrators as an inconvenience. For instance, Buddhists and followers of traditional Native American spiritual practices have historically undergone a great deal of difficulty in prisons. Issues such as inadequate access to religious materials, ceremonies, and spiritual leaders remain an intricate matter for contemporary inmates.

Access to Religious Services and Expression

Inmates frequently attend religious services. During a typical week, religious services are held Friday, Saturday, and Sunday evenings. Some inmates also have the option to attend informal prayer sessions led by religious leaders within their units. Some inmates also attend informal, inmate-directed prayer sessions conducted in their respective units. Prayer sessions are typically held once or twice per week. In total, inmates could attend religious services as many as four to five times in a given week. Prison chaplains play multifaceted roles within the corrections system. They often serve as counselors, administrators, educators, and overseers of religious services and community organizations. As a result, prison chaplains serve as an essential liaison between inmates and their higher power.

Despite the fact that prisoners are legally protected under the First and Fourteenth Amendments, they still face challenges in adhering to their religion, and many of the challenges are beyond their control. Widespread issues range from inadequate prison security or hostility toward minority religions to lack of readily available, religion-specific materials and chaplains, according to the U.S. Commission on Civil Rights. Convincing prison administrators that inmates' desires to participate in religious activities are genuine has also been a stumbling block. Rights of some religious groups have been inhibited by officials presuming that religion was being used as a decoy to convey radical political agendas or illegal drug and gang activity. Prison security must assure that inmates refrain from using religious expression to smuggle contraband items, violate established rules, or interfere with the process of justice administration. Therefore, in some cases, few efforts have been taken to ensure protection of an inmate's civil rights behind bars.

Obstacles to Rights

An additional dilemma surrounds bureaucratic obstacles for reporting infringements to inmates' rights. The courts face a difficult challenge in providing a safe haven to report complaints or violations. There have been complaints of prison administrators ridiculing inmate complaints and in some cases throwing them in the trash.

Advocates for inmates' religious rights face challenges due to the multitudes of religions, both established and new, and whether or not political and judicial powers recognize the legitimacy of the religion in question. The challenge deepens over the dispute of whether or not the First, Eighth, or Fourteenth Amendments grant absolute protection of the freedom of religious expression, relative protection, or no protection. By absolute protection, inmates have unrestricted ability to worship their religion. The Eighth Amendment, which prohibits "cruel and unusual punishment," including excessive deprivation, has the potential for providing inmates with further latitude for religious expression. However, the criterion for evaluating the legitimacy of a religion is questionable. The religion of mainline Christianity and "American civil religion" tend to function as the measuring stick for evaluating the favorability of other forms of religious expression.

Although the First Amendment theoretically grants inmates protected rights to practice their religion without governmental regulation, the nature of such institutionalization creates several logistical impossibilities. An example of prison guidelines and religious requirements that lack full compatibility with freedom of religious expression include the consumption of unaltered solids and liquids that come from outside the institution, such as partaking of communion wine in Christianity, or hallucinogenic *peyote* in Native American religions. Incompatible practices include animal and human sacrifices.

Interpreting the constitutional amendments as granting absolute protection such that few, if any, restrictions are placed on an inmate's freedom of religion would entail security breaches leading to a breakdown of the correctional institution. Examples of such conflicting interests would be if facilities were to allow inmates a leave of absence during Hajj season to uphold the fifth pillar of Islam requiring a pilgrimage in Mecca, or if prisons allowed the sacrifice of animals for practitioners of Santeria.

Religions that have received the least amount of recognition include cults. In this context, the term *cult* means new religions, which emerge at a faster rate than public officials and correctional facilities can determine their religious aims and objectives. In addition, many indigenous groups have their own religions, yet they face challenges due to their relatively small size and distance from more mainstream religions despite their religion's years of existence.

Religious plurality impacts the dynamics of prison culture. Religious rights also affect the dynamics of prison culture by creating additional accommodations for inmates, and providing clear definitions of both religious provision and restrictions placed on inmates within the context of maintaining security.

Prison employees play a significant role in religious practices among inmates because they control the movements of the entire population from dorms and cells to chapels. They also monitor their possessions, such as books, papers, and sacred objects, such that maintenance of law and order presides over religious rights. The order of a lockdown due to a security threat or a widespread medical outbreak such as a stomach or flu virus would lead to an indefinite suspension of corporate religious expression.

Determining the Parameters

Determining the parameters of inmates' religious rights depends on the type of prison and the jurisdiction of the prison, be it a federal or state prison or a public or private prison; and the prisoner's level of security, such as minimum, medium, maximum, death row, or protective custody. Additional underlying issues include the interpretation of laws by the various lower courts and enforcement within the facilities with respect to a complex organizational structure that includes majors, assistant wardens, wardens, and boards of directors, and may extend to the state lieutenant governor and governor.

Prisons have become islands unto themselves where discussions of the Constitution are concerned. Prior to the 1960s, there was widespread approval that offenders were not entitled to the same constitutional protections that they benefited from prior to their conviction. This hands-off approach governed the minds of courts, prison officials, and society alike. Pervasive support for these tactics curbed discussions of constitutional violations among inmate populations.

Accordingly, inmates suffered both intentional and unintentional civil right infringements at the hands of state and federal prison facilities. Intentional violations included hostility toward nontraditional religious groups to outright denial of religious practices, in addition to instances in which prison officials disposed of prisoner civil right complaints. Unintentional violations of offender's civil rights consisted of prison officials seeking to maintain strict power, control, and safety over their environment, with limited resources available to support all denominations equally.

Legality of Religious Rights

Under normal circumstances, religious rights are mandated under strict constitutional scrutiny. However, courts have been unable to establish clear measures for the proper extent of scrutiny for prisoner's religious rights cases. Thus, rulings on these cases remain both difficult and ambiguous. Essentially, the courts require plaintiffs to demonstrate that the government placed a considerable burden on their religious practices.

Claims of religious and racial discrimination generated a series of claims filed by African American Islamic prisoners during the 1960s and 1970s. In 1961, these claims led to the *Sewell v. Pegelow* case. Prison officials at the U.S. Reformatory in Lorton, Virginia, were accused of isolating Muslim prisoners and denying them proper medical treatment for three months. Unlike their religious counterparts, Muslims were denied privileges to meet with religious advisors, wear religious symbols of faith, and adhere to religious diets.

Cruz v. Beto (1972), the first case filed by an inmate to reach the Supreme Court, asserted that the inmate's civil rights had been violated. The inmate argued that the prison administrators violated his rights by failing to provide him with necessary accommodations to practice his Buddhist faith. The Court decided that prisoners who adhere to faith-based principles other than traditional belief systems cannot be denied opportunities to practice their religion.

In 1987, in the areas of personal appearance and clothing, the courts decided in *Turner v. Safley* and *O'Lone v. Estate of Shabazz* that disregarded prisoners' requests. For instance, male Orthodox Jews are required to wear a long beard. Native American religions require men to wear their hair long. There are many sacred items, such as marijuana, *peyote*, communion, beads, and candles that have traditionally been deemed as contraband. Marijuana use and possession is prohibited unanimously in all prisons in the United States, such that a prisoner cannot claim it as a sacrament. Alcohol is normally banned from prison, including attempts to ferment fruit, corn, and juices from behind bars. However, in 2005, the Wisconsin governor signed Senate Bill 174, which gives provision to clergy to administer a maximum of two ounces of holy communion wine to inmates under supervision. In the *Dettmer v. Landon* case, a Virginia district court granted Dettmer, an inmate, access to candles as part of religious practice in the Church of Wicca, despite the fact that candle possession poses a severe security threat. However, prison officials have the authority to determine adequate storage for the sake of security.

Inmates' requests for religious dietary restrictions have also prompted an assortment of lawsuits. In the 1975 case of *Kahane v. Carlson*, the courts ruled that prison officials must not unreasonably restrict an inmate's diet. However, the courts also ruled that ways in which accommodations are permitted would be at the discretion of prison officials.

In terms of dietary restrictions, Islamic and Jewish beliefs must be considered. In the case of Islam, it is required that meats be *halal* if they are going to be used for consumption. *Halal* standards include more than just the absence of pork; foods must also be free of pork byproducts, as must the machinery at the processing and packaging plant. Additional requirements include slaughtering according to specific religious regulations. In the case of Judaism, kosher requirements vary, with Orthodox Jews having the most restrictive standards. Kosher requirements in some communities include all of the standards, just as *halal* in Islam; however, the person processing the meats must be regarded as kosher. Kosher designation extends to nonmeat products, including soaps, breads, and various prepackaged foods.

The challenge of religious plurality arises because there are variations in both Judaism and Islam. Second, the prisons and states have parameters set by a complex budget, such that adhering to legally sanctioned dietary request by inmates may not be economically feasible. If economic feasibility has been resolved and the kosher or *halal* products have been shipped to the prison units, then an additional problem can arise if the products are not prepared in a separate kitchen.

Muslim and "Mainstream" Religious Accommodations

The phenomenon of high rates of African Americans converting to Islam while incarcerated produces evidence of the existence of a causal relationship between long-term sentencing and taking the *shahada*, the initial act of becoming a Muslim through profession of faith. Prison-proselytized African American Muslims primarily fall into one of two categories: temporary "jailhouse religion" adherents, and long-term, committed believers. The desire for a new identity and the hope to lead a new productive life serves as a common ground for both groups. The concrete, disciplined structure of Islam, compared to the fluidity of other popular religions; the external identity renewal; additional means for coping with the boredom and harsh reality of incarceration; and implications of "model inmate" status collectively add to the appeal of the faith.

Added concerns for Muslim inmates include uninterrupted *salat*, which refers to the five mandatory prayers, the right to grow facial hair, and Islamic attire. The state of New York leads the nation for having the most inclusive stance for advocating religious rights on behalf of Muslims, with approximately 40 Muslim chaplains.

Believers belonging to dominant religious groups can exercise more of their religious rights than their nonmainstream counterparts. Inmates of Protestant, Jewish, or Catholic religions often fare better in comparison to those of other minority religions. They often receive special accommodations and greater access to religious resources. Inmates who adhere to mainstream religions receive passes to attend faith-based services and other special privileges. On the other hand, those adhering to unconventional religious principles have been, at times, denied these same privileges.

When an inmate is denied such religious accommodation, he or she can argue that his or her First, Eighth, and Fourteenth Amendment rights have been violated. Budgetary limitations are insufficient defense. For example, prison administrators can defend their position based on the fact that they provide a choice of foods, including fresh-picked produce from the perimeter of the facility. However, based on a unanimous Supreme Court decision made on July 23, 2009, in the *Sisney v. Reisch* case, "prepackaged kosher meals" must be provided if requested, rather than the prison's interpretation of what the administrative staff regards as kosher.

Prison administrators have been assigned the complex task of ensuring appropriate separation between church and state. Tension arises when prison officials attempt to maintain balance between legitimate penological interests and an offender's civil right to adhere to his religious principles behind bars. Realizing the importance of this, the Religious Freedom Restoration Act (RFRA) and the Religious Land Use Institutionalized Persons Act fought to extend the notion of religious choice to U.S. prisons. As a result, contemporary U.S. prisons seek to promote an environment where inmates are free to choose their religious preferences rather than to promote religious participation.

Pro: Arguments Supporting Prisoners' Religious Rights

According to the U.S. Bureau of Justice Statistics in 1993, approximately 32 percent of prisoners participate in religious activities, and supporters state that religion positively influences the lives of adult offenders. Religion also acts as a buffer to minimize the initial shock of serving prison time. Inmates who participate in religious activities tend to have lower rates of disciplinary confinement and depression, and higher rates of self-esteem. Researchers have also found significant correlations between religiosity and prison adjustment.

Often, the most prominent reasons that inmates join religious affiliations are safety and companionship. Religious affiliates are more likely to exhibit pro-social behavior and therefore are less likely to be confrontational. When confrontation does arise, group affiliation will most certainly provide an inmate with physical protection.

Furthermore, religious social networks can play a significant role in an inmate's perception of self-worth. Adult offenders report that spending time with other "saints" helps keep them out of trouble. Similarly, religiosity decreases trivial, yet negative behavior. For example, bouts of arguing are reduced by as much as 70 percent. This is significant, since arguing is usually a precursor to physical disputes. Involvement in religious activity not only decreases incidents of arguing, it also reduces antisocial behavior. Providing prisoners with a "new lease on life" is an important part of inmate rehabilitation. Therefore, faith-based programs are inexpensive alternatives to education or vocational programs. Letting inmates participate in religious activities makes prisons more manageable and safer.

In addition, inmates joining religious organizations while incarcerated have advantages that outlast their prison sentence. Reentry into society is a critical time in an offender's life, yet some researchers posit that involvement in faith-based programming while serving time reduces recidivism rates after inmates are released. Preliminary evidence suggests that religious commitment and involvement decreases the likelihood of subsequent minor and serious criminal behavior.

Religious affiliations merit a variety of privileges. Although factors vary by institutions, collective motivations range from social to material aspects. Inmates may benefit from interacting with offenders from other units, and they are frequently permitted to receive civilian visitors, who serve as a focal connection to the outside world. They may also receive extra snacks during weekly or biweekly bible study sessions. Sessions often translate into having a longer period out of their cell or dormitory to do the things they enjoy. Inmates are typically delighted to receive additional privileges. They fear losing their established benefits and therefore rarely jeopardize them.

The greatest argument of those who favor granting inmates religious rights focuses on the Eighth Amendment and the belief that religion is necessary for an inmate to adequately bear the punitive element of the incarcerated life; such denial would be inhumane and just shy of prison abuse. Deprivation of religious expression could potentially equate to deprivation of food and water as a basic need.

The Religious Freedom Restoration Act of 1993 (RFRA) gained bipartisan support, but still faced major hurdles in the Senate. There was concern of a potential abundance of frivolous lawsuits and a fear that prison administrators might receive impractical demands for religious accommodations. In response to the RFRA, many states took a proactive approach. To circumvent these issues, some state departments of corrections opted for permanent withdrawal from directly providing religious services to inmates. As a result, many volunteers have intervened to ensure that prisons are able to offer a variety of religious services to inmates.

Supporting organizations have played a critical role in advocating for the religious rights of prisoners. Prisons have embraced the influx of nonprofit and volunteer aides. With growing prison populations and increasingly tighter budgets, prisons have increasingly come to depend on these organizations to coordinate religious services. According to Guidestar. org, there are approximately 444 nonprofit organizations serving in a prison ministry capacity; this number is based on those that file IRS tax returns. A variety of organizations have surfaced during the 20th century. Prison Fellowship Ministries (PFM) is one of the few organizations to achieve worldwide recognition. The organization was founded in 1976 by Charles W. Colson, a former prisoner incarcerated on Watergate-related charges in the 1970s. PFM is the largest prison outreach and criminal justice reform organization in the world. This Christian-based organization serves inmates in all 50 U.S. states and approximately 110 countries worldwide. Most outreach ministries represent Protestant Christianity, and are a central part of the prison system.

Con: Arguments Opposing Prisoners' Religious Rights

In the United States, the boundaries between constitutional rights and prison rights are ambiguous. In addition, the political philosophical variations affect legal interpretation, enforcement, and legislation enactment. Prison officials fear that prisoners will use religion politically or as a shield for gang activity. Also, they argue that inmates can easily elude prison regulations by evoking a religious principle.

Those arguing against religious rights in U.S. prisons often question the sincerity of the inmates' commitment. Feeding this uncertainty is the notion of "jailhouse religion." Critics argue that inmates embrace religion in response to the considerable stress experienced upon their arrival, only to indubitably return to criminal patterns upon their release. Furthermore, some prison officials assume that inmates participate in religious activities because they believe doing so might increase their chance of early parole. Some inmates do practice religion in order to be seen as righteous by prison staff and administrators.

Also, many argue that inmates' desires to join religious affiliations are primarily to ensure that their individual needs are met. Along those lines, some inmates have communicated insincere purposes for joining religious groups in prison. Some use religion toward gaining material wealth, which often accumulates in the form of music or musical instruments, religious materials, and even additional phone and visitation privileges, For others, special food privileges generate interest.

Prison officials face many challenges in trying to ensure inmates' religious rights. For instance, ensuring that all religions are treated equally is a significant challenge. Economic and budget restrictions only complicate this matter. Given the rapid rate of the emergence of new religions, establishing specific criteria for determining a given religion's legitimacy is an additional challenge.

Prison administrators have the authority to set parameters for inmate's physical grooming, including appropriate hair lengths. However, many Rastafarians wear their hair in dreadlocks as a form of religious expression. Despite laws that protect inmates' rights toward practicing their religion, Congress had previously ruled that just cause for administrative interference would include cases where the practice poses a security threat. According to the Virginia Department of Corrections Operating Procedure No 864.1, made effective on December 15, 1999, inmates became subject to living in administrative segregation for failing to comply to the policy regarding maximum hair length and facial hair. Arguments used to justify that dreadlocks pose a security threat include the ability to hide weapons in the hair, or the ability to drastically change their appearance in the case of an escape.

Kendall Gibson served over 10 years of his 47-year sentence at the Greensville Correctional Center, due to his refusal to cut his hair and shave his beard in adherence to his religious-based beliefs and values. Ivan Sparks lived in segregation for the same activity in Buckingham Correctional Center. Rastafarian Kevin Smith was unsuccessful in his lawsuit against several South Carolina correctional staff who shaved his head against his will, as ruled by the decision made by the U.S. Court of Appeals Fourth Circuit on July 31, 2009.

A number of critics claim that granting religious rights to inmates can compromise the safety of an institution. For instance, providing inmates with an abundance of freedom runs the risk of mitigating prison authority. Also, unequal treatment among inmates could instigate hostility between religious groups. Others are concerned that religion can be used as a disguise for illegal activities. Further, the religious diversity in the United States poses a challenge in terms of what or how many accommodations must be made while maintaining adequate security measures.

Correctional institutions face the challenge of making compromises between adhering to the legal requirements they must uphold from various judicial levels and taking necessary measures to maintain a prison's order and security. Often, these goals are incompatible. When such dilemmas occur, the administrators must decide which of the two violations would be the lesser of two evils in any given context.

Making accommodations for inmates can present measurable security risks. A minimal risk might be accommodating Muslim inmates during the month of Ramadan, in which no solids or liquids are to be consumed during the daylight hours. Kitchen staff and security might ease up on strict meal schedules or on the restriction of inmates' movements and offer a separate meal time for Muslims after sunset.

Opponents to offering religious rights to inmates often argue that the continuous tension and struggle between inmates and prison staff might lead to granting an excess of rights to the point that correction institutions would be unable to function. In other words, those who argue to curtail inmates' religious rights might achieve a better result by granting limited rights and adding privileges, such as increased freedom of religious expression, and using their discretion to suspend such privileges as needed. However, doing so could subject the institution to additional lawsuits, which could further hurt their budget.

See Also: 3. Cruel and Unusual Punishment; 4. Due Process Rights of Prisoners; 6. Free Speech Rights of Prisoners; 10. Legal Assistance for Prisoners.

Further Readings

Alternative Religions Educational Network. (2003). "The Legal Basis for Wicca." www.aren.org/documents/purplebook.pdf (Accessed January 2010).

Anderson, Cheryl B. *Ancient Laws and Contemporary Controversies: The Need for Inclusive Biblical Interpretation.* New York: Oxford University Press, 2009.

Bellah, Robert. "Civil Religion in America." *Journal of the American Academy of Arts and Sciences,* v.96 (Winter 1967).

Clear, Todd R., Patricia L. Hardyman, Bruce Stout, Karol Lucken, and Harry R. Dammer. "The Value of Religion in Prison." *Journal of Contemporary Criminal Justice,* v.16 (February 2000).

Clear, Todd, Bruce Stout, Harry Dammer, Patricia Hardyman, and Carol Shapiro. *Prisoners, Prisons and Religion: Final Report.* Newark, NJ: Rutgers University, 1992.

Clear, Todd R., and Melvina T. Sumter. "Prisoners, Prison, and Religion: Religion and Adjustment to Prison." In *Religion, the Community, and the Rehabilitation of Criminal Offenders,* edited by Thomas P. O'Connor and Nathaniel J Pallone. New York: The Haworth Press, 2002.

"Coercive Religion in America's Prisons: Unfair Sentence." *Church and State,* v.14 (March 1, 2003).

Daggett, Dawn M., Scott D. Camp, Okyun Kwon, Sean P. Rosenmerkel, and Jody Klein Saffran. "Faith-Based Correctional Programming in Federal Prisons: Factors Affecting Program Completion." *Criminal Justice and Behavior,* v.35 (July 2008).

Davidson, Steed V. "Leave Babylon: The Troupe of Babylon in Rastafarian Discourse." *Black Theology: An International Journal,* v.6/1 (2008).

Denny, Frederick Matthewson. *An Introduction to Islam, Third Edition.* Upper Saddle River, NJ: Prentice Hall, 2006.

Guidestar Nonprofit Organization. *Analyze Nonprofit Report*. (2010). http://www2.guidestar.org (Accessed January 2010).

Johnson, Byron R. "The Faith Factor and Prisoner Reentry." *Interdisciplinary Journal of Research on Religion,* v.4 (2008).

Johnson, Byron R. "Religiosity and Institutional Deviance: The Impact of Religious Variables Upon Inmate Adjustment." *Criminal Justice Review,* v.1 (1987).

Kerley, Kent R., and Heith Copes. "Keepin' My Mind Right: Identity Maintenance and Religious Social Support in the Prison Context." *International Journal of Offender Therapy and Comparative Criminology,* v.53 (April 2009).

Kerley, Kent R., Todd Matthews, and Troy C. Blanchard. "Religiosity, Religious Participation, and Negative Prison Behaviors." *Journal for the Scientific Study of Religion,* v.44 (2005).

Kinney, Nancy T. "The Implication for Inmate Rights of the Voluntary Provision of Religious Services." *Criminal Justice Policy Review,* v.17 (June 2006).

Miyashita, Mayu. "*City of Boerne v. Flores* and Its Impact on Prisoners' Religious Freedom." *New England Journal on Criminal and Civil Confinement,* v.25 (1999).

Potter, Dena. "Rasta Inmates Spend Decade in Isolation for Dreadlock Hair." *USA Today* (2010). http://www.usatoday.com/news/religion/2010-05-08-rastafarian-dreadlocks_N.htm (Accessed September 2010).

Russell, Steve. "American Indian Religion in the Iron House: Searching for Some Accommodation." *Contemporary Justice Review,* v.11 (September 2008).

Solove, Daniel. "Faith Profaned: The Religious Freedom Restoration Act and Religion in the Prisons." *The Yale Law Journal,* v.106 (November 1996).

State of Wisconsin Legislature. *Senate Bill 174.* (2006).

Sundt, Jody T., and Francis T. Cullen. "The Correctional Ideology of Prison Chaplains: A National Survey." *Journal of Criminal Justice,* v.30 (2002).

Sundt, Jody L., and Francis T. Cullen. "Doing God's Work Behind Bars: Chaplains' Reactions to Employment in Prison." In *Religion, the Community, and the Rehabilitation of Criminal Offenders,* edited by Thomas P. O'Connor and Nathaniel J. Pallone. New York: The Haworth Press, 2002.

Sundt, Jody L., and Frances T. Cullen. "The Role of the Contemporary Prison Chaplain." *The Prison Journal,* v.78 (September 1998).

Thomas, Jim, and Barbara H. Zaitzow. "Conning or Conversion? The Role of Religion in Prison Coping." *The Prison Journal,* v.86 (June 2006).

United States Court of Appeals Fourth Circuit. *Smith v. Ozmint.* http://pacer.ca4.uscourts.gov/opinion.pdf/076558.P.pdf (Accessed September 2010).

Vessola, Mark A. "Harmony Behind Bars." *The Prison Journal,* v.87 (June 2007).

19

Sex Offender Treatment

Chrysanthi S. Leon
University of Delaware

Sex offenders have accounted for an increasing share of the incarcerated population in the United States since the 1970s. Worldwide, research investigating effective methods of treating people convicted of sex crimes has increased dramatically. Although treatment is infrequently available in prison, many people convicted of sex offenses, as well as others without criminal convictions who suffer from sexual addictions, do include treatment in their paths to desistance.

Treatment can prove a challenge to define and apply to sex offenders in prison, but can include surgical intervention, pharmacological intervention, or counseling in the form of talk therapy. Surgical intervention typically involves castration, in the form of the removal of the offender's testes. Pharmacological intervention can include estrogen or antiandrogen therapy (chemical castration), but may also include medication to treat underlying disorders such as depression. Counseling may be in groups, one-on-one, or through supported reentry initiatives such as the Containment Model or Communities of Concern.

Controlled-outcome studies are generally unavailable, but research shows measured success and reason for limited enthusiasm, especially from the Canadian correctional example. Ethical and practical problems suggest the need for careful attention to how sex offender treatment is implemented.

History of Sex Offender Treatment

In the early through mid-20th century, criminal sexual deviants were favored objects of study by the emerging disciplines of criminology, psychiatry, and psychology. Leading scholars in these fields believed that the scientific study of such individuals would yield methods for early identification, intervention, and possibly the prevention of future sexual offending. As with other criminal populations, actual research related to treatment methods and evaluation was severely limited in practice. But several important clinical and correctional studies took place, creating a foundation for knowledge about sexual violence. By the end of the 20th century, the study of sexual offenders in the United States was no longer central to criminology or the psychological sciences, but was located in more practice-based knowledge, often affiliated with state departments of correction. The practice of sex offender treatment had emerged by the early 21st century as a significant cottage industry, with some standardization and credentialing achieved through professional associations and the involvement of the federal government.

In the 1930s and 1940s, governmental and public energy surrounding the problem of sexual deviance was funneled primarily into the passage and refinement of laws to civilly commit certain offenders, often with rehabilitation underneath more incapacitative intentions. A decade later, rehabilitation was the dominant correctional ideology, for sexual criminality as well as all other offenses. By far the most important debate in corrections between 1950 and 1980 involved the potential for and proper role of the rehabilitation of criminals. There was widespread support for psychiatry as the solution to the problem of crime. Many scholars have written about the importance of the medicalization of social control in the mid to late 20th century, and in particular the importance of psychiatry and its related treatment professions in shaping conceptions of the normal and the abnormal. Sex offenders turned out to be a crucial proving ground for psychiatric expertise at a time when its status and credibly were hotly debated.

From the vantage point of the postwar period, criminal sexual deviance was one component of the larger study of sexuality. For example, the Kinsey report, *Sexual Behavior in the Human Male*, published in 1948, received international attention, and remains a touchstone for the study of sex. From the extreme of the abnormal sexual psychopath to the worrisome possibility that sexual deviance was actually normal, sex was a major center of debate during this period. The Kinsey researchers included homosexuality and a variety of other behaviors classified as criminal, such as exhibitionism, in their inquiries.

In the 1970s, Quaker prison reformer Fay Honey Knopp became concerned by the lack of specialized treatment services available for sexual
abusers. In 1976, her organization, the Safer Society Foundation, began
tracking the development of specialized sex offender treatment programs.
Safer Society has periodically conducted national surveys, which are the
single best source of information about current practice in the United States.
In addition, abusers, their families, professionals, and others can contact the
foundation for referrals as well as publications tailored to educate practitioners and the public.

In the mid-1990s, as states and the federal government passed increasing
numbers of new sex offender laws, a federal clearinghouse for information, the
Center for Sex Offender Management, solicited input for new strategies. The
experts who responded rated "knowledge development" as a high priority.
Unfortunately, little federal leadership has since materialized. In some states,
professional groups have been able to institutionalize their own standards,
such as those of the national Association for the Treatment Abusers, which
provides the best dissemination of current research and practice through its
annual training conferences and through its journal, *Sexual Abuse.*

Research Findings on Treatment Efficacy

The Kinsey research remains, to date, the largest and most detailed study of
sexual behavior of a sample of the general population. More recent research,
much of which has included treatment efficacy as a variable, has instead
sampled from people in treatment at a particular location (clinical samples)
or from those arrested, convicted, or incarcerated for sexual offenses (criminal justice or correctional samples). These provide useful information, but
are severely limited in their ability to generalize. As a result, what is known
about who sexually offends, and what works to stop their future offending,
is limited to the groups who have already entered treatment or the justice
system. Since the vast majority of sexual offending is not detected by either
of these systems, solid claims cannot be made about what would work with
most offenders.

Nonetheless, several important studies point in useful directions. New
Jersey and California are among several states that have had continuous
institutional dedication to the assessment and treatment of sex offenders.
For example, California legislators invested in a state-of-the-art research
and treatment facility for sex offenders in the early 1950s in response to a
series of publicized sex crimes; in the 1960s and 1970s, California's Men-

tally Disordered Sex Offender Program was the standard-bearer for sex offender treatment practitioners across the country; and most recently, the Sex Offender Treatment and Evaluation Project helped pioneer the relapse-prevention approach to sexual offending.

In California, early use of sexual psychopath laws to civilly commit certain sexual offenders allowed clinical studies that showed small successes for treatment. A clinical sample at Norwalk State Hospital claimed a 2–4 percent recidivism rate for those who completed treatment, as contrasted with an 8–15 percent rate for those who failed treatment. Later research at California's Atascadero State Hospital, published in 1969, found similar results.

But nationally, very few followup studies were conducted. More commonly, offenders undergoing treatment would have their prior records investigated for a retrospective measure: Were these offenders repeaters? This is not a true measure of recidivism, but was often conducted as a substitute, and continues to be used today. For example, in Baltimore, Manfred Guttmacher found that a very small correctional sample of sex offenders referred for therapy between 1939 and 1949 had a recidivism rate of five percent.

Research began to increase in the 1980s. In 1996, the U.S. General Accounting Office published an examination of the research literature that found 22 published articles on the effectiveness of sexual offending treatment programs. Methodological limitations prevented any determinations of the impact of treatment on recidivism, although most authors believed it was promising.

An important strand of sex offender treatment has developed as a modification of Alcoholics Anonymous, with its focus on accountability and on sexual deviation as a compulsion or addiction to be managed. Relapse prevention, the subclass of cognitive behavioral treatment pioneered in California, remains prevalent nationwide despite a rigorous followup study released in 2005 that found no treatment effect. A randomized clinical study of California's relapse prevention program compared the reoffense rates of offenders treated in an inpatient program with the rates of offenders in two untreated prison control groups. As highlighted in a 2005 article in *Sexual Abuse: A Journal of Research and Treatment* by J. K. Marques and colleagues, no significant differences were found among the three groups in their rates of sexual or violent reoffending over an eight-year followup period.

Meta-analytic reviews of multiple sex offender treatment studies attempt to control for the various design and other methodological problems that have plagued evaluation research. In 2002, R. K. Hanson examined 43 studies on psychological sex offender treatment, finding an average sexual offense recidivism rate of 12.3 percent for treatment groups and 16.8 percent for comparison groups. Most recently, the Campbell Collaboration Group on Crime and Justice has begun a systematic review in this area. Their first publication included a meta-analysis of studies by F. Lösel and M. Schmucker in 2005. This review found 69 studies with adequate information for review, including both published and unpublished research in English, German, French, Dutch, or Swedish, as well as a wide range of treatment interventions. The meta-analysis found a sexual recidivism of 11.1 percent for the treated group and 17.5 percent for the comparison group over an average followup period of five years. As the authors point out, this seems like a modest effect, but given the low base rate of sexual recidivism, treatment creates a reduction of nearly 37 percent. However, more research most be conducted to determine which treatments are most successful, and to isolate how and why they succeed. But the current state of research does provide modest support for adult sex offender treatment, and particularly for cognitive behavioral modes.

Sex Offender Therapy: Current Principles and Practices

Surgical and Chemical Castration

Surgical castration is infrequently used today. The 2005 meta-analysis found a large treatment effect for it, but cautioned against drawing conclusions. None of the castration studies met criteria for adequate research design, since castrated offenders could not be compared with similar controls. In most jurisdictions, convicted sex offenders volunteer for surgical castration in exchange for early release from prison, to lessen parole restrictions, or to avoid the numerous serious side effects associated with chemical castration. Thus, as Lösel points out in the 2005 meta-analysis, research suggesting it is effective is unsubstantiated, as people who volunteer to be castrated are an unusual group who will be different in many crucial ways from the majority of sex offenders.

Chemical castration is typically used in tandem with other treatment modalities. Offenders in the community under supervision can have chemical castration as one of a number of conditions of their release, but it may be more symbolic than practical. Most people who commit sex crimes do so because of a variety of influences on their behavior, including the desire to express anger through violence. The hormones that cause and sustain sex drives may not play any role at all in an individual's urge to commit a sex crime. Thus, it may be a preferable alternative to surgical castration from the offender's perspective, and it may appeal as "just deserts" to a concerned public, but there is little reason to rely upon it as a true cure, and no reason to make it a mandatory requirement for any offender.

Psychiatric Diagnoses and Clinical Treatments

Contemporary treatment approaches may include diagnoses of paraphilia (repeated, intense sexual arousal to social deviant stimuli) as well as non-sex-specific diagnoses, including antisocial personality disorder. The American Psychiatric Association's Diagnostic and Statistical Manual (DSM) has fine-tuned its diagnoses for sexual offending behaviors from sexual deviation to paraphilia since its first publication; but these diagnoses have always been within the general category of personality disorder. According to this official view, pedophilia, voyeurism, sexual sadism, transvestism, and homosexuality have all been understood as behaviors that resulted from inappropriate objects of sexual fantasy and gratification. People with these disorders belong in a psychiatrist's office because their behaviors and compulsions are abnormal and cause the individual distress. In general, the DSM has been contested and controversial, and perhaps better suited to bureaucratic purposes such as insurance billing than to rehabilitation. But the distance between the DSM's formal categories and the practitioner in the field may be even more pronounced in the area of sexual offending, in part because sex offender law is written to flexibly accommodate a wider variety of problematic individuals as mentally disordered.

Clinical approaches to sexual offending may be psychoanalytic or cognitive behavioral. Psychoanalytic approaches, grounded in Freudian analyses of early fixations, are most often employed in private practice for individuals seeking extensive talk therapy. But even in those contexts, therapy that focuses more on changing patterns of thought and conduct is becoming more common. In prison and other institutional settings, almost all therapy is cognitive behavioral, and typically conducted in group rather than individual counseling sessions.

Cognitive behavioral therapies, and particularly relapse prevention, focus on the offense cycles that give rise to criminal sexual conduct. Individuals learn to recognize their own particular patterns that lead to sexual offending. They are taught to focus on the earliest triggers that cause a physical arousal response, and to make choices that avoid or control those triggers.

Both psychoanalytic and cognitive behavioral approaches may focus on reducing deviant sexual arousal. In addition to cognitive behavioral techniques that address conscious thought processes, some treatment may also include aversion or satiation therapy. These approaches can discourage sexual fantasies that include inappropriate objects (such as children) or can focus on encouraging sexual fantasies that seem more likely to lead to pro-social behavior. In verbal or masturbatory satiation, an individual is led through inappropriate fantasies through visual or verbal cues and encouraged to fantasize or masturbate past the point of completion or orgasm. Conditioning therapies can also include the use of an olfactory cue such as ammonia—after a course of operant conditioning, an offender who is in the early stages of arousal to an inappropriate object can break open an ammonia capsule in order to break the arousal cycle. These approaches have been included in the treatments examined through meta-analyses, but their efficacy independent of other treatment has not been rigorously established.

The Containment Model

Although individuals can seek out treatment on their own, sex offender therapy is often part of correctional supervision. The containment model is a synthesis of best practices selected from a survey of parole and probation officers who manage sex offenders and is promoted by the American Parole and Probation Association and the Center for Sex Offender Management. No state has fully implemented it, though most have adopted some of its principles, especially in sex offender treatment programs in state hospitals and prisons. The original containment model from 1996 contain five, mutually reinforcing components:

1. A philosophy that values public safety, victim protection, and reparation for victims as the prime objectives of sex offender management
2. Implementation strategies that rely on agency coordination, multidisciplinary partnerships, and job specialization
3. A containment approach that seeks to hold sex offenders accountable through the combined use of both the offenders' internal controls and external criminal justice measures, and the use of the polygraph to monitor internal controls and compliance with external controls
4. Development and implementation of informed public policies to create and support consistent practices
5. Quality control mechanisms, including program monitoring and evaluation, that ensure prescribed policies and procedures are delivered as planned

The third component is most unique to sexual offending, as it mandates surveillance methods such as polygraph monitoring to measure deviant arousal and compliance with offense-avoidance plans.

The containment model succeeds in institutionalizing jurisdiction-sharing between correctional officers and treatment practitioners. In an era in which treatment for criminal offenders is generally denigrated, sex offender treatment maintains a limited stronghold through its collaboration with and subjugation to corrections. Sex offender assessment and therapy lack a licensing program, professional examinations, university-based professional education, or an ethics code—all traditional markers of professions. Although clinical sessions with offenders may be conducted by psychologists or psychiatrists, most assessment and treatment programs in the justice system use lower-status personnel such as social workers, marriage and family therapists, and polygraph administrators. Sex offender specialization is a growing field because states that authorize the containment model and its variants also contract for assessment services.

This collaboration, in turn, creates ethical and implementation problems. Outside of the correctional context, participation in therapy is premised upon voluntariness, as well as a confidential and close relationship between therapists and patients; however, treatment may be mandated for some convicted sex offenders. In other cases, participants may elect treatment in order to earn good time or otherwise benefit their case for a reduced sentence or for less burdensome supervision conditions. In most states, participants must sign a waiver allowing their therapists to communicate freely with correctional officers or others in the justice system, including information about past crimes that may result in new prosecutions. These constraints on voluntariness and confidentiality may have a chilling effect on the therapeutic relationship, which in turn may prevent successful program completion. Even in the best of circumstances, it may be impossible to determine whether treatment has caused internal change as well as external compliance. But in the correctional context, offenders may have much more incentive to comply with therapy regardless of their personal motivation.

Indefinite Incarceration

At the most extreme end of the spectrum, sex offender therapy may be the premise for indefinite civil commitment. Twenty-one states and the federal government now have sexually violent predator laws that authorize the hospitalization of certain sex offenders after the completion of their sentences. The U.S. Supreme Court has held that this is properly considered treatment, and not punishment, despite evidence that only a fraction of the thousands of sex offenders civilly committed nationwide actually participate in treatment while confined. Additional debate centers on the definition of the illness for which treatment through civil commitment is mandated. No state laws require a finding of paraphilia, instead allowing other diagnoses that contribute to a finding of some level of compulsivity and related likelihood of reoffense. As a result, the population of committed individuals are a heterogeneous group and often do not conform well to contemporary treatment modes, all of which require admissions of guilt as an early stage of therapy.

In *U.S. v. Comstock* (2010), the Supreme Court recently held that sex offenders may be civilly committed indefinitely by the federal government. The Court ruled that the U.S. Constitution's necessary and proper clause allows for this, despite concerns regarding the autonomy of states, as expressed in the dissent by Justice Thomas, which Scalia joined in part. Part of the Comstock ruling relied on the fact that the federal statute in question focused on individuals who were "sexually dangerous" because of a "mental illness" and bore a strong relationship to a 1949 law allowing the federal detention of mentally ill, dangerous prisoners. The Comstock decision did not address the issue of clinical treatment of sex offenders, nor did it resolve other potential challenges to federal civil commitment, including those related to equal protection and due process. Future appeals can be expected to continue to test the usage of mental illness as the premise for indefinite commitment, although not on the grounds decided in Comstock regarding federal authority.

The Future of Sex Offender Therapy

Recently, clinicians have argued for a move from relapse prevention to something more like a self-regulation model of sex offender treatment. This builds upon the research of Dr. Karl Hanson, a Canadian correctional clinician and researcher who has both pioneered assessment and treatment approaches and has produced meta-analyses of recidivism studies. The self-regulation model moves from reliance on static risk factors (aspects of an offender's record or identity that cannot change and therefore cannot be affected by treatment), to dynamic risk factors for re-offense, such as social support and stressors such as substance abuse or mental illness. Consistent with Hanson's 2007 report on the Dynamic Supervision Project, which included all of Canada as well as Alaska and Iowa, research has shown that risk assessments using these kinds of factors can reliably sort offenders into risk categories. A correctional sample in Maryland, which uses this approach in a state that provides no assistance for offender treatment, where clients pay out of pocket and treatment is provided on a sliding scale, has shown promising results. Future research will thoroughly examine the effects of this approach to treatment and recidivism.

Some communities are adapting the containment model to provide community support and accountability to released sex offenders. Circles of Concern (also called Communities of Concern or Accountability) have been pioneered by religious communities in order to provide links to housing, employment, and other supports crucial to re-entry. The Circles adapt the surveillance and therapeutic principles of containment and combine them with the principles of restorative justice. Most require that participants have either successfully completed a prison therapy program, or are currently engaged in therapy. Participants meet frequently with a small group of community members, which may include representatives of victim advocacy organizations, law enforcement, and other interested parties. The meetings are used to provide a pro-social environment as well as informal social control. Participants discuss their experiences, thoughts, and feelings, with special attention to high-risk situations and triggers. Members of the circle listen and provide advice when asked, and communicate with treatment or correctional professionals when appropriate. Anecdotal research indicates success, but no rigorous outcome research has been published.

Pro: Arguments in Support of Sex Offender Treatment

Both research and practice in the area of sexual offending have improved dramatically over the previous decades. Especially when therapy follows the cognitive behavioral model, outcomes are positive, but there is little to no empirical support for surgical or pharmacological interventions on their own. Sex offender therapy appears to be, on balance, cost effective. Providing evidence-based treatment to individuals on probation and parole appears to play a role in reduced recidivism. Sex offender treatment in prison may allow for earlier releases as well as reduced likelihood of re-offense, both of which save correctional dollars. Increased public safety and the efficient use of correctional resources both justify the provision of sex offender treatment.

Moral considerations may also call for correctional treatment. If sexual offending is viewed as a problem of impulse control or of some other disease-related causation, then justice would require making it possible for offenders to improve their conditions rather than simply warehousing them for long periods.

Con: Arguments Opposing Sex Offender Treatment

There may not be enough evidence as to how sex offender therapies work, and for whom, to justify the costs. Robust research is needed to establish causalities and identify the most appropriate subjects for treatment. Standardization through licensing or a nationally approved credentialing process is not comparable to that required of other specialties. As a result, the practice of sex offender treatment is largely unregulated. Until research and professionalization increase, the generally low rate of recidivism for untreated sex offenders may not justify additional treatment interventions.

Most sex offender treatment is not offense-specific, and most treatment groups are heterogeneous mixes of different kinds of offenders, especially in institutional settings like prisons. Available research has not established treatment efficacy for particular offense types; therefore, it may be unwise to require statutory rapists, for example, to undergo the same kinds of therapeutic interventions required of child molesters and stranger rapists.

Children and adolescents who have sexually offended may also be too young to benefit from specialized sex offender treatment. Although a recent 20-year followup of adolescents found treatment effects, the treatment program in that research is unusual rather than representative of most programs for adolescent sex offenders. Few programs are able to provide treatment that sufficiently distinguishes among offense types. Few view adolescent sexual offending in the context of larger family issues; in contrast, many approach them as younger versions of adult sex offenders. Particularly with young people, who are less likely to have fixed sexual preferences than adults, intervening in their development without rigorously tested treatment modes may cause more harm than benefit. The stigmas and other problems associated with being singled out as sexually deviant may outweigh the largely unproven benefits. Further, research shows that most adolescents who offend sexually will age out of their offending—few are charged for subsequent sexual crimes past their early 20s. Special sex offender treatment may not be justified.

In addition to limitations about what we know sex offender treatment can accomplish, there are reasons to worry that well-intentioned efforts can have counterproductive effects. In particular, while treatment may attempt to build empathy in offenders, the concept is vaguely defined, and its achievement in a penal environment may be impossible.

See Also: 8. Gangs and Violence in Prisons; 12. Mentally Ill and Mentally Challenged Inmates; 17. Punishment Versus Rehabilitation.

Further Readings

Alexander, M. A. "Sex Offender Treatment Efficacy Revised." *Sexual Abuse: A Journal of Research and Treatment,* v.11 (1999).

Aos, S., P. Phipps, R. Barnoski, and R. Lieb. "The Comparative Costs and Benefits of Programs to Reduce Crime." Olympia, WA: Washington State Institute for Public Policy, 2001.

Association for the Treatment of Sexual Abusers. *Practice Standards and Guidelines for Members.* Beaverton, OR: ATSA, 2001.

Beech, T., and A. S. Fordham. "Therapeutic Climate of Sexual Offender Treatment Programs." *Sexual Abuse: A Journal of Research and Treatment,* v.9 (1997).

Blanchard, G. T. *The Difficult Connection: The Therapeutic Relationship in Sex Offender Treatment.* Brandon, VT: Safer Society, 1998.

Blasingame, G. *Developmentally Disabled Persons With Sexual Behavior Problems: Treatment, Management, and Supervision.* Oklahoma City: Wood 'N' Barnes, 2001.

Bonner, B., C. E. Walker, and F. Berliner. *Children With Sexual Behavior Problems: Assessment and Treatment.* Washington, DC: HHS, 1999.

Center for Sex Offender Management. *The Collaborative Approach to Sex Offender Management.* Silver Spring, MD: Center for Sex Offender Management, 2000.

Correctional Service of Canada. *Standards for the Provision of Assessment and Treatment Services to Sex Offenders.* Ottawa: Correctional Service of Canada, 2000.

English, K., S. Pullen, and L. Jones. *Managing Adult Sex Offenders: A Containment Model.* Lexington, KY: American Probation and Parole Association, 1996.

Fass, Paula S. *Kidnapped: Child Abduction in America*. New York: Oxford University Press, 1997.

Frisbie, Louise V. *Another Look at Sex Offenders in California*. Sacramento: California Department of Mental Hygiene, 1969.

Furby, L., M. Weinrott, and L. Blackshaw. "Sex Offender Recidivism: A Review." *Psychological Bulletin*, v.105 (1989).

General Accounting Office and United States House of Representatives Committee on the Judiciary and Subcommittee on Crime. *Sex Offender Treatment: Research Results Inconclusive About What Works to Reduce Recidivism*. Washington, DC: 1996.

Guttmacher, M.S. *Sex Offenses: The Problem, Causes and Prevention*. New York: Norton, 1951.

Hanson, R. K., A. Gordon, A. Harris, J. Marques, W. Murphy, V. Quinsey, and M. Seto. "The Effectiveness of Treatment for Sexual Offenders." *Sexual Abuse: A Journal of Research and Treatment*, v.14 (2002).

Kafka, M. "Psychopharmacological Treatments for Nonparphilic Compulsive Sexual Behaviors." *International Journal of Neuropsychiatric Medicine*, v.5/1 (2000).

Knopp, F. H. *Retraining Adult Sex Offenders: Methods and Models*. Brandon, VT: Safer Society, 1984.

Laws, D. R. "Olfactory Aversion: Notes on Procedure, With Speculations on Its Mechanism of Effect." *Sexual Abuse: A Journal of Research and Treatment*, v.13 (2001).

Leon, Chrysanthi. *Sex Fiends, Perverts and Pedophiles: Understanding Sex Crime Policy in America*. New York University Press, in press.

Lösel, F., and M. Schmucker. "The Effectiveness of Treatment for Sexual Offenders: A Comprehensive Meta-Analysis." *Journal of Experimental Criminology*, v.1/1 (2005).

Lundstrom, F. *The Development of a New Multi-Disciplinary Sex Offender Rehabilitation Programme for the Irish Prison Service*. Dublin, Ireland: Irish Prison Service, 2002.

Lynch, M. "Pedophiles and Cyber-Predators as Contaminating Forces: The Language of Disgust, Pollution, and Boundary Invasions in Federal Debates on Sex Offender Legislation." *Law and Social Inquiry*, v.27 (2002).

Marshall, W. L., and L. E. Marshall. "The Utility of Random Controlled Trial for Evaluating Sexual Offender Treatment: The Gold Standard or an Inappropriate Strategy?" *Sexual Abuse: A Journal of Research and Treatment*, v.19 (2007).

McGrath, R. J., and G. F. Cumming, et al. *Current Practices and Trends in Sexual Abuser Management. Safer Society 2002 Nationwide Survey.* Brandon, VT: Safer Society Press, 2003.

Miner, M. H. "How Can We Conduct Treatment Outcome Research?" *Sexual Abuse: A Journal of Research and Treatment,* v.9 (1997).

Nicholaichuk, T. "Sex Offender Treatment Priority: An Illustration of the Risk/Need Principle." *Forum on Corrections Research,* v.8/2 (1996).

Polizzi, D. M., D. L. MacKenzie, and L. J. Hickman. "What Works in Adult Sex Offender Treatment? A Review of Prison and Non-Prison-Based Treatment Programs." *International Journal of Offender Therapy and Comparative Criminology,* v.43 (1999).

Prentky, R. A. "A 15-Year Retrospective on Sexual Coercion: Advances and Projections." *Annals of the New York Academy of Sciences* v.989 (2003).

Prescott, David, ed. *Knowledge and Practice: Challenges in the Treatment and Supervision of Sexual Abusers.* Oklahoma City: Wood and Barnes Publishing, 2007.

Price, Stephen. "Understanding Sexual Offending Behavior." Sex Abuse Treatment Alliance. (2009). http://www.satasort.org (Accessed November 2010).

Reumann, M. G. *American Sexual Character: Sex, Gender, and National Identity In the Kinsey Reports.* Berkeley: University of California Press, 2005.

Righthand, S., and W. Carlann. *Juveniles Who Have Sexually Offended: A Review of the Professional Literature.* Washington, DC: Office of Juvenile Justice and Delinquency Prevention, 2001.

Rose, Nikolas S. *Inventing Ourselves: Psychology, Power, and Personhood.* New York: Cambridge University Press, 1996.

United States v. Comstock, No. 08–1224 (May 17, 2010).

West, M., C. S. Hromas, and P. Wegner. *State Sex Offender Treatment Programs: 50-State Survey.* Colorado Springs: Colorado Department of Corrections, 2000.

Worling, J. R., and A. Litteljohn, et al. "20-Year Prospective Follow-Up Study of Specialized Treatment for Adolescents Who Offended Sexually." *Behavioral Sciences and the Law* (2009). http://www.interscience.wiley.com (Accessed November 2010).

Zimring, F. E., A. R. Piquero, and W. G. Jennings. "Sexual Delinquency in Racine: Does Early Sex Offending Predict Later Sex Offending in Youth and Young Adulthood?" *Criminology and Public Policy,* v.6 (2007).

20

Shaming Penalties

Leonard A. Steverson
South Georgia College

S haming has long been associated with methods of social control
throughout the world's history. All three of the major components of
the criminal justice system—policing, the courts, and corrections—
have played a part in this social process, particularly the correctional system
and the courts, from which many of the shaming methods were promul-
gated. The earliest human shaming elements were much less formal and
often involved society's citizens policing themselves in this manner.

Early shaming punishments, which involved public humiliation and
degradation, provided physical as well as emotional pain to offenders, and
were highly popular in the American colonial period. The punishments,
which consisted of public denouncement, banishment, restraint and display
in public places, whipping, mutilation, the wearing of signs, and dunking
practices were designed to inflict devastating humiliation. By the mid-1800s,
as Western nations experienced increased urbanization and the lessening
of the social controls inherent in small communal life, these practices were
discarded for sentences using incarceration.

In the United States in the 1970s, shaming measures again became popular as tougher penal sentences began to be perceived by the courts and
citizens as ineffective. Judges across the country doled out sentences that
incorporated shaming in the punishments; though they were less severe and
incorporated less physical pain, they still relied on emotional pain. Wearing

signs or clothing that reveal past criminal activity, affixing bumper stickers that disclose a drunk driving charge, advertising crimes in newspapers, and other measures have become the new shaming penalties.

Many people advocate shaming sentences as they are viewed as an effective way of deterring crime, especially if used along with apologies and informal means of restitution within the larger context of a system of justice that focuses on reintegration of offenders as well as victim's rights. Others feel that shaming methods are overly punitive, debasing, and are basically holdovers from the days when public displays of shaming punishments simply created a label that offenders were unable to live down. The debate over shaming as an effective means of punishment continues in the United States and globally.

Punishment as a Means of Social Control

Punishment has existed in some form throughout human existence. Different forms of redress have been utilized to punish those who violate the social norms, primarily those that prohibit harm to others. Many early codes of conduct, for example those found in the Code of Hammurabi and the Old Testament, declared that some type of debt must be paid to someone who was wronged by another person (the debt to be paid by the offender). The concept of *lex talionis* required a punishment in kind ("an eye for an eye") and during the Middle Ages in Germany, the practice of *wergeld* required the offender to financially compensate the victim. Much later, the systematic, forced exile of offenders, called *transportation,* would be implemented, and still later, the institution of incarceration appeared in the criminal justice system.

There are several different justifications for punishment: retribution, deterrence, incapacitation, rehabilitation, and expiation. Retribution has long been a fundamental component of punishment and refers to the idea that offenders should be punished as a matter of justice—it encompasses a "just deserts" ideology in which the offender deserves to be punished for the harm done to others (as in *lex talionis*). Another key justification is deterrence, which relies on the threat of punishment to stop people from committing crimes. Incapacitation, or restraint, promotes the idea that offenders are unable to inflict further harm or damage due to the fact that they are incarcerated, banished, or under strict supervision designed to thwart other criminal behavior; in this manner, citizens are protected from offenders. The justification of rehabilitation, also called *offender reformation*, is a newer explanation for punishment and is a progressive ideal that focuses on changing the behavior of offenders and returning them to society as useful citizens. Finally, expiation refers to the idea that punishment should include some degree of suffering on the part of the offender; this justification normally requires shaming and embarrassment in its application.

The Emotion of Shame and the Punishment Process

From a psychological perspective, shame is considered a secondary emotion, along with guilt, embarrassment, and regret, as these are more social in origin than the primary emotions of anger, fear, sadness, and happiness, which are more biological and are closely related to emotions in animals as well as humans. Because of this distinction, the former have traditionally been labeled social emotions or, more recently, self-conscious emotions. Social or self-conscious emotions have specific characteristics: They require a level of self-awareness, require a maturation process (and therefore surface in late childhood), are needed in order to develop complex social goals, do not correspond with distinct facial expressions (except for the physiological response of blushing, which appears with shame or embarrassment), and can have both positive and negative features. The emotion of shame possesses the characteristics of the social emotions. The word *shame* comes from the German *skew*, which means to cover, a reference to the uncomfortable feeling of being exposed and a desire to cover oneself to avoid the pain of social stigma. The closely related emotion of embarrassment refers to a condition in which a person reacts to an uncontrollable and unpredictable offense. The response typically results in an unsettling feeling of awkwardness and discomfort. The emotion of embarrassment typically is unintentional and self-inflicted; however, a type of embarrassment called *strategic embarrassment* refers to a type that is used to debase and harm the reputation of someone. This is the type of embarrassment that is also called *shaming*, which has been used to compel people to conform to social norms.

When coupled with strategies intended to punish someone for a rule infraction, whether an informal punishment by members of a community or a formal punishment by a judicial body, the terms *shaming penalty* or *shaming punishment* are often used. The often-stated purpose of this type of punishment is to bring the offender in line with community standards of behavior and create a more orderly and peaceful society. Opponents of shaming penalties, however, maintain that other motives may be present, and doubt the penalty's ability to do any real good. In fact, shaming penalties are sometimes seen as contributing to the problem of criminal behavior on a social level and problems with self-respect on a personal level.

A Brief History of Shaming as Punishment

Informal methods of banishment are some of the world's oldest shaming penalties, and were used in many societies throughout history. These were forms of punishment in which someone found committing a deviant act was expelled from the community and forced to find a new residence in another village. Prior to industrializing and urbanization, when close-knit communities were the normal arrangement and where much value was placed on belonging and a shared history, people who were exiled from their communities were viewed with great suspicion by people in the receiving village. The similar practice of shunning currently exists in some religious communities in the United States, where the rulebreaker is not physically banished, but is simply ignored by others in the society; often, the shunned person leaves the group out of sheer embarrassment and shame.

England's Legendary Shaming Tools

England has a long and well-recorded history of shaming punishments. The open exhibition of offenders was common in the medieval period, and the devices known as the stocks and pillory were often employed. These shaming instruments were a common sight in communities throughout Europe and later in the American colonies. The stocks were a wooden contraption adopted by the English from the Romans and were used to punish people for drunkenness or other minor offenses. The device was comprised of two lateral pieces of wood with holes for the offender's legs when they were locked together; some also had beams that locked around the wrists. The sentences in the stocks usually lasted from a couple of hours up to a whole day. Often located in a prominent area of the community such as the market square or village, the contraption restrained the seated offender while the citizens would gaze at the wrongdoer and often throw stones, sticks, mud, rotting food, and other undesirable items at him. The offender was often placed in the stocks on market day so more citizens would be on hand to humiliate him.

Closely related to the stocks was the pillory, an apparatus normally used for more severe offenses, such as those involving some form of dishonesty. Instead of having the offender seated, the pillory forced the offender to stand. This vertical device allowed the offender's hands and head to stick out of the device's holes, and sometimes the deviant's ears were nailed to the contraption. As with the stocks, citizens would gawk at the violator and throw things. While trapped in these instruments of torture, the offender would often try to avoid the pelting and would tear his ears to avoid the items being hurled; even if his ears remained intact during the period of punishment, upon removing him from the pillory, the authorities sometimes pulled the offender away without removing the nails first. In addition, the offender's nose was often split or other cuts were made in the face, or branding was carried out, leaving a permanent mark that followed the offender for life. Merchants who cheated citizens had rotten food or drinks poured on them or burned at their feet while restrained in the device. Shaming sentences served at both the stocks and pillory sometimes resulted in more than just humiliation; offenders often died from the physical punishment received on the instruments.

Public whipping, also called flogging, was also a means of humiliating offenders of various crimes. Whipping posts for vagrants, thieves, insubordinate servants, and a host of other offenders were used to publicly display the punishment for all to observe. The subjects were often stripped of clothing in order to further injure and disgrace them. Whipping also occurred as the criminals were led down streets tied to the back of a cart, in an activity called "riding the cart's tail."

Women and Shaming

Another method of shaming required the offender to wear some type of shaming insignia that announced to the other citizens the nature of the offending behavior. A famous example of shaming in literature can be found in Nathaniel Hawthorne's *The Scarlet Letter*, in which the main character, Hester Prynne, a young woman in Puritan New England in the 17th century, is forced to wear the letter "A" (for the sin of adultery) on bright red cloth stitched to her clothing. Factual examples are often found in the history of this era: "drunkards" were often required to wear a placard with the letter "D," thieves were required to wear a "T," forgers had to wear an "F," and disreputable women were required to wear a "B," for bawd. Sometimes, the visual representation did not require a sign, as when liars were forced to wear a whetstone (a heavy stone used to sharpen blades) around their necks. In a similar vein, there are also accounts of the use of the "drunkard's cloak," in which local alcoholics were required to wear a wooden barrel around town.

The ducking stool was another invention created to torment and humiliate those who engaged in unacceptable behavior; often, the people subjected to this punishment were women. The device consisted of a wooden or metal chair or stool attached to a board that was used to submerge people in ponds or rivers. The ducking stool was used to degrade and shame people for the offenses of prostitution, slander, fighting, and cheating. Women who gossiped or nagged (referred to as *scolds* during this period) were often punished in this manner.

Women also primarily bore the brunt of a very harsh instrument called the *brank*, also called the scold's bridle or the gossip's bridle. The device was essentially a metal cage that fit around the offender's head. It contained a plate of iron affixed with spikes that fit into the person's mouth, and was sometimes tied to a pillory or other stationary object or connected to a chain used to lead the scold down the streets to a jeering mob. The brank had the additional effect of causing pain and bleeding if the person attempted to speak or move her tongue. There are several reasons for using methods that create wounds not visible to an audience, seemingly contrary to public shaming, which is supposed to make wounds highly noticeable for the desired effect. Borrowing from the literature on torture (an activity often used in shaming), those carrying out the shaming methods might receive some type of sadistic pleasure from the abuse or simply enjoy the excitement of the activity. They also might rationalize the behavior as leading to specific deterrence by making the violator a better citizen, possibly seeking revenge from the person for some earlier incident, or simply justifying the infliction of nonvisible wounds as a collateral feature of carrying out orders meant to shame offenders visibly.

Other methods of shaming were quite innovative. "Riding the stang," for example, was punishment for offenders of domestic violence in which the abusers were hoisted onto a platform and paraded through the streets in a noisy procession of citizens who sang, played instruments, and generally joined in on embarrassing the offender. A related practice, termed *rough music*, occurred in Europe prior to 1800; this punishment involved neighbors banging on pots and pans, blowing horns, yelling, and making other irritating sounds to draw negative attention to an offender of a minor community-rule infraction.

Opposition Emerges

At the end of the Victorian era in England, which some have considered the heyday of retributive shaming, some key figures and opposition groups began to actively oppose the practice of humiliation and shame to control citizen behavior. For example, Sigmund Freud, the creator of psychoanalysis, believed that shame helped maintain patterns of psychopathology that unless removed, would worsen with time, and manifest itself in unusual ways. Feminist groups also began to examine how a focus on shaming penalties had disproportionately affected women throughout history—branks and ducking stools were often used to keep disobedient "scolds and gossips" in their place and silence any behavior deemed disrespectful to men. Also, some scholars in the budding field of criminology in the 20th century came to believe that labeling someone as a deviant created a situation that perpetuated the offending behavior, and that shaming simply aided this process, to the detriment of society.

Many of these shaming methods made their way from Britain to the American colonies. All of them were used to maintain order by public humiliation and to act as a deterrent to further criminal acts by the punished offender or to serve as a warning to onlookers who might want to test the waters by violating community norms.

Sometimes, there was a fine line between humiliation as punishment and torture, and sometimes the public punishment ended in death. Hangings and other types of execution were also intended to humiliate with the added corollary of the offender being unable to live down the shame. The offenders' families were left with the stigma of having a loved one publicly humiliated to death in a gruesome fashion and, according to the place and time period, displayed for the entertainment of a cheering crowd.

The Current Context of Shaming

Shaming as it currently exists can be found in many forms. Stigmatizing publicity is the most common type, and refers to the publishing of offender information to a wide audience through some medium (such as in newspapers, on billboards, and on local television stations). Literal stigmatization occurs when offenders are court-ordered to have some type of signage that reflects their criminal activity (such as on clothing, bracelets, bumper stickers, and lawn signs); this is a modern adaptation of the scarlet letter. Self-debasement involves the offender being required to wear a sign announcing the offense in a public place such as a local courthouse. Contrition is a component of the new model of offender reintegration, and requires the violator to make amends through an apology to the victims or community; often, the apology requires the offender to humble him or herself to the offended party or parties.

While most forms of shaming use an audience in a public forum to reinforce the effects of humiliation, shame can also be created in private settings. The torture of offenders, for example, often takes place in this private context. Shaming techniques that involve torture can be illustrated in the treatment of prisoners in the Abu Ghraib prison in Iraq by American soldiers. The events that came to light in 2004 involved acts of humiliation in which military correctional officers forced detainees to strip naked and walk in front of female correctional staff, pose in embarrassing poses, participate in sexual acts, be treated like animals (i.e., being led around on a leash and forced to bark), be exposed to religious and other cultural denigration, and be placed in terrifying situations. People who are tortured, such as the Abu Ghraib inmates, are made to feel helpless and totally under the control of their captors, leading to dehumanization that creates profound feelings of shame and inferiority that often last long after the direct torture has ended.

Reintegrative shaming is a prominent model that stresses that the shaming should express community disapproval, but allow the violator to return to the community without the lingering stigma and labeling of having committed a criminal offense. Closely related to reintegrative shaming is the broader philosophy of punishment known as restorative justice. In opposition to retributive justice, which is based on punishment for its own sake, restorative justice seeks to make the offender accountable for deviant behavior, but still able to reintegrate back into society after the punishment has been given. The concept of restorative justice has four components: the use of restitution the offender must make to the victim, the use of psychological compensation to the offended, the social process of punishing the offender, and the action of shaming the offender. Shaming is required for the offender to fully understand the nature of the offending behavior, to compensate the victim personally (not through a third party such as an insurance company or taxpayer), and to be eventually reintegrated into society. A successful reintegration requires society to have a reintegration ceremony in addition to the previously occurring shaming ceremony. Shaming, in this model, is used to restore the offender, victim, and society rather than simply humiliate the offender or to entertain others.

Pro: Arguments in Support of Shaming Penalties

Advocates report certain factors that make shaming an effective alternative to the traditional means of punishment. The use of shaming as a specific as well as general deterrent is a potential benefit; the idea that it will deter future offending behavior and even send a message to others is appealing to many. Offenders, given a choice between traditional punishment and shaming methods, often choose the former to avoid the stigma of wearing a sign or doing a demeaning activity. In addition, others who view this shaming penalty often decide not to act in a way that would result in this fate.

Benefits for Citizens and Society

Penalties for offenders that use shame can be attractive to citizens, as they can be more economically feasible than prison sentences or other expensive and overly long sentences. The costs of signs, advertisements, bumper stickers, or custom-made T-shirts pales in comparison to prison-related costs. In addition, community service involving undesirable tasks performed publicly in order to humiliate actually makes the offender a benefit to the community through free labor and, as a by product, could increase that person's sense of self-worth though the accomplishment of a necessary, albeit degrading, task.

Shaming also has some major benefits for society in that it creates cohesion in communities where it is practiced. When there is a visible sign of the consequences of behavior that is deemed harmful, the messages of right and wrong are clearly differentiated and enforced through laws and punishments. Shaming fosters shared cultural expectation of its citizens, thereby creating unity and order. It also exhibits fairness in the judicial process.

In recent decades, there has been a national, even international, move to a style of policing called *community policing* or *community-based policing,* which involves a greater involvement by the community in dealing with its specific, localized problems. This has been seen as a positive departure from a more traditional model of policing that leaves all social control responsibilities to the police, which creates a chasm between the police and community. Restoring some power to the people to control their community has shown positive consequences. The emphasis on community as a resource that is beneficial in community policing can be extended to the judicial and correctional systems as well. A renewed focus on community life could create an environment favorable to shaming as a beneficial social control agent, a means to strengthen community life, and a way to control crime.

Although it has been claimed by some opponents that shaming is debasing and disrespectful, the opposite outcome is often found in family life. Shaming punishments often occur in families with the intention to socialize children appropriately and for their own welfare, as well as that of others. Often, the punishments are provided to youngsters in a highly respect-ful manner that instills the basic conceptualization of right and wrong; the same respect can be shown to offenders in a broader system of justice. While early models of shaming in history were based on devaluation and ridicule of the person, the restorative justice model promotes a respectful manner of shaming.

Alternative to Prison and Lowered Crime Rates

Shaming also has a part to play in avoiding some of the deleterious side effects of incarceration. Prisons often become a training ground for devi-ance, and inmates often learn new skills from other inmates, creating a more dangerous society than before they were incarcerated. In addition, prisons are breeding grounds for violent behavior, and inmates are often needlessly harmed by other inmates. To protect themselves, prisoners often join gangs, particularly organized along racial lines, and these gang affiliations continue upon release. Also, due to the labeling of offenders, reentry becomes very difficult for ex-convicts. Shaming sentences can be therefore safer for both the offender and society.

Critics of shaming often create a dichotomy between shaming practices and incarceration sentences, claiming that as an alternative to prison, sham-ing uses self-degrading embarrassment for offenders; this implies that prison sentences do not. Shaming is inherent in prison punishments as well—of-fenders receive a degradation ceremony when they enter prison, have their hair shorn, are given standard uniforms and a number, are subjected to full-body cavity searches, and must perform bodily functions and shower in the presence of corrections officials and other inmates. In addition, the fact that they are imprisoned creates a stigma for not only the inmate, but also the inmate's family and friends. Therefore, shaming practices are inherent in both forms of punishment.

Shaming can be a highly effective form of lowering crime rates. Many Western nations, including the United States, have high crime rates com-pared to other countries. Japan, for example, has both a relatively low crime rate and a high incidence of shaming practices. Many scholars conclude that the reason is the cultural value on honor and the consequences of dishonor prevalent in Japan and some other Asian countries.

In shaming offenders, an emphasis is also placed on the victim, some-thing often lacking in the criminal justice system. Public shaming gives a very visual reminder that a person has committed a crime against another person and that they were the wronged party. A greater focus on the victim is important in controlling crime by showing that they are important and not simply ignored.

Con: Arguments Against Shaming Penalties

Arguments against shaming penalties often start with the claim that the punishments are debasing and degrading. When these penalties are used, a message is sent to society that the correct response to unacceptable behavior is to dehumanize people who violate social norms, and that the government has tight control of citizen behavior. This idea runs counter to those of a democratic society.

Opponents also point to the philosophy of retribution in shaming sentences. If people use punishment solely due to a retributive rationale, the focus is on punishing the offender simply to make society feel satisfied. A look into the past reveals the inhumanity in how hangings, lynching, and other forms of torture were used as entertainment at the offender's expense. If the philosophy is the same, shaming cannot be moral.

The effectiveness of shaming as punishment is another argument used against it. Little empirical evident exists to show the efficacy of shaming as opposed to traditional methods of punishment. Critics argue that although the punishment might have been effective in early times in very close-knit communities, they are ineffective in our modern industrialized society. Unless people really care about what others think of them, deterrence will rarely occur.

Ineffective and Counterproductive

Another major argument is that not only are shaming punishments ineffective, they can actually be counterproductive. Opponents point to the labeling effect that prohibits ex-offenders from being successfully reintegrated into society due to the stigma of being labeled a criminal. Sometimes, the label creates a self-fulfilling prophecy, which means that someone given the label of criminal will begin accept the label to the point that they will simply act according to the dictates of the label. There are also those convicted of offenses who are actually innocent of the charges, but due to labeling, become deviants. The issue of labeling should be a consideration for those jurisdictions where newspapers publish the names and pictures of people who have been arrested for various offenses but who have yet to be convicted.

The same is true of other forms of media such as television, the Internet, and radio news, although radio does not have the additional stigmatizing effect of pictures. The ideas of the presumption of innocence and the right to due process have little meaning if a person is found guilty in the news media. Being publicly humiliated among one's peers prior to conviction by one's peers can create a label that can lead to the self-fulfilling prophecy and create a pathway to future criminal activity.

It is possible that judges who use nontraditional means of sentencing can use punishments that vary widely from one offender to the next. Traditional sentences have guidelines and follow certain prescribed formulas. The idiosyncratic method of sentencing used in shaming creates less consistency in punishments. In addition, many sentences handed out by judges are reversed, suggesting to opponents that the traditional forms of sentencing are more appropriate.

If shaming penalties are employed on a large-scale basis, it is possible that a "culture of shame" could be created and become the norm in the sentencing of offenders. Many people feel that such a philosophy is archaic and unproductive. Although judges primarily mete out shaming penalties, it can (and has been) spread to other agents of the criminal justice system, including the police and correction authorities. Although having jail inmates dress in chain gang–era stripes or requiring male inmates to dress in pink uniforms might create good press, the likelihood of rehabilitation is low. Abuses of power are a potential byproduct of a culture of shame.

Proponents of reintegrative shaming argue that shaming methods, when appropriately applied, will reintegrate the offender into society in part due to a ceremony returning them to the community. In financially strapped areas and periods of economic depression, this component can simply be removed, and the offender only receives the degradation ceremony in which humiliation and shame are applied. In this case, the person has no opportunity to lose the label of deviant, and could forever carry a stigmatizing mark.

It is unlikely that all offenders who receive a shaming penalty will receive the benefits of the punishment, even if the penalty is beneficial. Offenders with developmental disabilities, mental disorders, or certain physical conditions could be unsuitable candidates. Sociopaths, without the requisite ability to experience compassion or empathy for others, would likewise be totally unsuitable candidates for shaming punishments.

Certain groups lacking power have suffered the brunt of shaming punishments throughout history. Those without financial resources such as vagrants, slaves, servants, and the lower classes generally, as well as others without political power and social status, such as women (in particular cultures) and people of minority racial or ethnic status, have suffered the brunt of humiliating practices; meanwhile, those of higher status were often able to avoid such indignities of public derision. There is no control in place to ensure that everyone will be treated equally in regards to shaming penalties; the inequities of the past can easily return. In the many courts around the country with judges of various stripes, equality under the law cannot be guaranteed.

In modern urban life, many people do not experience the close bonds of the communities in which they live; often, they occupy residences or live in a different town in which they work. Transience is also common today, and people move to new areas without developing close ties to their new communities. Without the controlling influence of what others in the community think of one's behavior, a person is less like to feel the need to conform. In addition, communities have different norms, and if a new transplant does not agree with those norms, he or she will be less likely to "buy in" to the new normative structure. Thus, adherence to the customs of the host culture will be less important to the newcomer, and shaming will be less effective than it would for a person raised in the area that has incorporated those norms.

Cruel and Unusual Punishment

Another major argument of opponents of shaming is that the U.S. Constitution requires that "cruel and unusual punishment" shall not be inflicted upon citizens. Although the phrase "cruel and unusual punishment" first appeared in the English Bill of Rights in 1689, the words were later incorporated into the American Bill of Rights as the Eighth Amendment. Normally, the point of contention with this amendment is what actually constitutes cruel or unusual punishment. Many legal scholars contend that "cruel" refers to the infliction of psychological as well as physical pain. "Unusual" refers to the vast array of strange punishments that have been endorsed—from the early stocks, pillory, and ducking stool to the more recent bumper stickers, notices in newspapers, and shirts that announce a person's criminal actions.

See Also: 3. Cruel and Unusual Punishment; 4. Due Process Rights of Prisoners; 8. Gangs and Violence in Prisons; 12. Mentally Ill and Mentally Challenged Inmates; 17. Punishment Versus Rehabilitation; 19. Sex Offender Treatment.

Further Readings

Alkadry, Mohamad G., and Matthew T. Witt. "Abu Ghraib and the Normalization of Torture and Hate." *Public Integrity*, v.11/2 (2009).

Andrews, William. *Old-Time Punishments*. Detroit: Singing Tree Press, 1970.

Barnes, Harry Elmer. *The Story of Punishment: A Record of Man's Inhumanity to Man*. Montclair, NJ: Patterson Smith Publishing Corporation, 1930.

Bazemore, Gordon, and Mara Schiff. *Restorative Community Justice: Repairing Harm and Transforming Communities*. Cincinnati, OH: Anderson Publishing Co., 2001.

Book, Aaron S. "Shame on You: An Analysis of Modern Shame Punishment as an Alternative to Incarceration." *William and Mary Law Review*, v.653 (1999).

Braithwaite, John. *Crime, Shame, and Integration*. Cambridge: Cambridge University Press, 1989.

Cos, Stephen. *The Big House: Image and Reality of the American Prison*. New Haven, CT: Yale University Press, 2009.

Dayan, Colin. *The Story of Cruel and Unusual*. Cambridge, MA: The MIT Press.

Earle, Alice Morse. *Curious Punishments of Bygone Days*. Detroit: Singing Tree Press, 1968.

Etzioni, Amitai. "Back to the Pillory?" *The American Scholar*, v.68/4 (1999).

Friedman, Lawrence M. *Crime and Punishment in American History*. New York: Basic Books, 1993.

Hibbert, Christopher. *The Roots of Evil: A Social History of Crime and Punishment*. Phoenix Mill, UK: Sutton Publishing Limited, 2003.

Johnstone, Gerry. *Restorative Justice: Ideas, Values, and Debate*. Portland, OR: Willan Publishing, 2002.

Katchadourian, Herant. *Guilt: The Bite of Conscience*. Stanford, CA: Stanford University Press, 2010.

Markel, Dan. "Are Shaming Punishments Beautifully Retributive? Retributivism and the Implications for the Alternative Sanctions Debate." *Vanderbilt Law Review*, v.54/6 (2001).

Nussbaum, Martha C. *Hiding From Humanity: Disgust, Shame, and the Law*. Princeton, NJ: Princeton University Press, 2004.

Reckless, Walter C. *The Crime Problem*. Englewood Cliffs, NJ: Prentice-Hall, 1973.

Vorbruggen, Meike, and Hans U. Baer. "Humiliation: The Lasting Effect of Torture." *Military Medicine*, v.172/Suppl. 1 (2007).

Index

Index note: Chapter titles and their page numbers are in **boldface**.

About the General Editor

William J. Chambliss is professor of sociology at The George Washington University. He has written and edited more than 25 books and numerous articles for professional journals in sociology, criminology, and law. His work integrating the study of crime with the creation and implementation of criminal law has been a central theme in his writings and research. His articles on the historical development of vagrancy laws, the legal process as it affects different social classes and racial groups, and his attempt to introduce the study of state-organized crimes into the mainstream of social science research have punctuated his career.

He is the recipient of numerous awards and honors including a Doctorate of Laws Honoris Causa, University of Guelph, Guelph, Ontario, Canada, 1999; the 2009 Lifetime Achievement Award, Sociology of Law, American Sociological Association; the 2009 Lifetime Achievement Award, Law and Society, Society for the Study of Social Problems; the 2001 Edwin H. Sutherland Award, American Society of Criminology; the 1995 Major Achievement Award, American Society of Criminology; the 1986. Distinguished Leadership in Criminal Justice, Bruce Smith, Sr. Award, Academy of Criminal Justice Sciences; and the 1985 Lifetime Achievement Award, Criminology, American Sociological Association.

Professor Chambliss is a past president of the American Society of Criminology and past president of the Society for the Study of Social Problems. His current research covers a range of lifetime interests in international drug-control policy, class, race, gender and criminal justice and the history of piracy on the high seas.